Educational Qualitative Research in Latin America

Studies in Education and Culture
(Vol. 11)
Garland Reference Library of the Humanities
(Vol. 1751)

Studies in Education and Culture

David M. Fetterman, Series Editor

Educational Qualitative Research in Latin America

The Struggle for a New Paradigm

Edited by
Gary L. Anderson
Martha Montero-Sieburth

GARLAND PUBLISHING, INC.
A MEMBER OF THE TAYLOR & FRANCIS GROUP
New York & London
1998

Library of Congress Cataloging-in-Publication Data

Educational qualitative research in Latin America : the struggle for a new paradigm /
    edited by Gary L. Anderson, Martha Montero-Sieburth.
                p.   cm. — (Garland reference library of social science ;
    vol. 1751. Studies in education and culture ; vol. 11)
        Includes bibliographical references and index.
        ISBN 0-8153-1353-5 (alk. paper)
        1. Education—Research—Latin America.   2. Education—Research—
    Latin America—Methodology.   I. Anderson, Gary L., 1948–
    II. Montero-Sieburth, Martha.   III. Series: Garland reference library of social
    science ; v. 1751.   IV. Series: Garland reference library of social science.
    Studies in education and culture ; vol. 11.
        LB1028.25.L29E38   1998
        370'.7'098—dc21   97–22805
                                                                            CIP

Printed on acid-free, 250-year-life paper
Manufactured in the United States of America

To Paulo Freire
    —G.A.

To the memory of Lucy Therina Briggs, whose lifetime commitment in making the Aymara language available beyond South America was a clear expression of her love for indigenous peoples; and to the memory of Gilman J. Hebert and his joy, love, and life. He lived, understood, and expressed bilingual education and biculturalism at their best.

                                        —M.M.-S.

Contents

Series Editor's Preface

This series of scholarly texts, monographs, and reference works is designed to illuminate and expand our understanding of education. The educational activity each volume examines may be formal or informal. It may function in an exotic and distant culture or right here in our own backyard. In each book, education is at once a reflection and a creator of culture.

One of the most important motifs sounding through the series is the authors' efforts to shed light on educational systems from the insider's viewpoint. The various works are typically grounded in a phenomenological conceptual framework. However, they will vary in their manifestation of this common bond. Some authors explicitly adopt anthropological methods and a cultural interpretation of events and circumstances observed in the field. Others adopt a more generic qualitative approach—mixing methods and methodologies. A few adhere to a traditional phenomenological philosophical orientation.

These books are windows into other lives and other cultures. As we view another culture, we see ourselves more clearly. As we view ourselves, we make the familiar strange and see our own distorted images all the more clearly. We hope this immersion and self-reflection will enhance compassion and understanding at home and abroad. An expression of a common human spirit, this series celebrates our diversity.

David M. Fetterman

Stanford University and
Sierra Nevada College

Introduction

This book emerged, in part, out of frustration the editors felt at the lack of availability in English of Latin American research in education, particularly accounts of qualitative studies. We found that our North American colleagues were largely unaware of the remarkable work that Latin American qualitative researchers had done over the last two decades. Several years ago, partly in response to this problem, the Center for Educational Research and Services (CISE) of the National Autonomous University of Mexico (UNAM) and the College of Education of the University of New Mexico began a series of small conferences to bring together Latin American and North American qualitative researchers to share their work.[1] These yearly conferences have resulted in the publication of three edited books that bring together the papers that were presented (Rueda Beltrán, Delgado Ballesteros, and Campos, 1991; Rueda Beltrán and Campos, 1992; and Rueda Beltrán, Delgado Ballesteros, and Jacobo, 1994). Since these books were not translated into English, the need for a vehicle to bring Latin American qualitative research to a North American audience remained unmet; thus, the need for this book.

Some work is available in English. Several North American ethnographers have published from their own fieldwork on schooling in Latin America (e.g., Hornberger, 1987, 1989; Paradise, 1994a, 1994b), and several Latin Americans who are currently at North American universities have published qualitative research done in North America (Suárez-Orozco, 1987; Montero-Sieburth and Pérez, 1987; Montero-Sieburth, 1993, 1994). Macías (1990, 1992), a Chicano scholar, has done research in Mexico with the goal of helping North American teachers more effectively teach Mexican immigrant children. Little is known, however, about Latin American researchers engaging in qualitative educational research in Latin America.[2] To further complicate matters, some of the work done in Latin America exists only as research monographs, master's theses, and unpublished documents. At the end of the book, we have provided a list of addresses of research centers and institutes where many of these documents can be found.

We hope that this book lays a foundation for continued dialogue between North American and Latin American qualitative researchers as well as for the formulation of new paradigms. We also hope it leads to a cross-fertilization of findings, methods, and epistemological debates among educational researchers throughout the hemisphere.

The Struggle for a New Paradigm

Like their North American counterparts, Latin American educators have undergone an important shift in educational research and practice. The discourses of positivism and quantity are being complemented by new discourses of ethnography and quality. Despite heavy criticism by ethnographers, positivism in Latin America has thrived under different philosophical strands.[3]

In the last two decades a number of attempts have been made to delineate characteristics of an educational research paradigm more relevant to the Latin American social reality (García Huidobro and Gutiérrez, 1984; Latapí, 1980, 1988, 1990; Tedesco, 1985, 1987, 1992).

For example, Tedesco (1987) has proposed a new research paradigm that reflects the following Latin American social realities:

1. An educational system in which the failure to incorporate marginalized sectors at basic levels coexists with an impressive expansion of the system at higher levels. This polarization means that traditional problems of provision of basic educational services exist side-by-side with modern problems of educational technology and the improvement of the quality of curriculum and instruction.

2. The need to legitimate "popular knowledge" as a form of knowledge equal to scientific/technical knowledge. Because of the unequal generation and distribution of scientific/technical knowledge, many Latin American researchers of the last three decades have attempted to use popular knowledge as a basis for solving problems of housing, education, and health.

3. A movement away from the influence of economic and social reproduction models and toward a more process-oriented, localized approach capable of analyzing a complex field of social forces and the role of social actors in the construction of their reality.

4. Increased attention to research at the classroom level and to the dif-
    ference between the cultural capital of students and that required for
    success in school.

As Tedesco (1987) indicated a decade ago, this emerging new paradigm would move educational research in Latin America toward more
qualitative research studies.

According to García Huidobro and Gutiérrez (1984), Latin American research has suffered from dependency on North American and European paradigms (and funding agencies) and a lack of systematic communication among Latin American researchers. These authors argue that
previous paradigms (even social reproductivist ones drawn from a Marx-
ian analysis) have been transferred from center to periphery with little
adjustment for the unique characteristics of Latin American educational
and social reality. In fact, some have expressed the opinion that there is
some danger that as free trade agreements flourish and more Latin Americans receive advanced degrees in U.S. and European educational institutions, educational ethnography will become "the latest intellectual import"
(García Huidobro and Gutiérrez, 1984, p. 14).

However, North Americans should not make the mistake of thinking
that Latin American qualitative research in education is merely a pale reflection of work done in Europe and North America. Although Latin
American qualitative researchers have received influences from abroad, the
evolution of their work responds to internal forces and can be traced back
at least to the late 1960s.

Qualitative research in Latin America has flowed from two primary
sources: the work of cultural anthropologists, primarily the group that
formed at Mexico City's Polytechnic University under the leadership of
Elsie Rockwell (author of Chapter One, this volume) and a long tradition
of participatory research inspired by Paulo Freire and driven by a profound respect for popular knowledge (" *el saber popular* ") as a necessary
base from which to promote educational and social change.[4] This respect
for local, cultural contexts is also, of course, a trademark of educational
ethnography.

As Batallán (author of Chapter Two, this volume) indicates, many Latin
American researchers who embraced ethnographic methods had previous
experience with popular education movements that utilized participatory
approaches to educational research. During the 1960s, while North American qualitative academic researchers in education were producing their

first studies (Henry, 1963; Jackson, 1968; Smith and Geoffrey, (1968), Latin Americans, through the influence of Paulo Freire, were pioneering forms of participatory action research through the identification of "generative themes" in poor communities. (See Magendzo, 1990 and Vaccaro, 1990, for accounts in English of a "second generation" of participatory research in Chile.) Thus, the "ethnography movement" in education in the U.S. and the "popular education movement" in Latin America date to the same general period.[5] Due to a lack of availability of work in translation and, perhaps, a chronic lack of interest among North American academics in knowledge produced in "third world" countries, there has been little cross-fertilization between Latin and North America, and North Americans have yet to appreciate the rigor and diversity of Latin American qualitative research.

By the 1970s, a diverse group of Latin American social and cultural anthropologists were taking educational issues as the focus of their work. Unlike the work of popular educators, who tended to focus on non-formal sectors of education, these ethnographers of education began to study classrooms and schools in the formal educational system. Some of the first studies were comparative, focusing on country-specific case studies of schooling. Of particular interest were cases about the failure of schools, obstacles to students' learning, and the codes of control of teachers (Avalos, 1985, 1989).

As Rockwell points out in Chapter One, researchers early on focused on non-formal alternatives to the state school systems, in part because of critiques of public schooling by Paulo Freire, Ivan Illich, and Social Reproduction theorists. The existence of military dictatorships during the 1960s and 1970s in many Latin American countries also kept the public schools off-limits to some qualitative researchers. The documentation of specific non-formal education projects produced by the Latin American popular education movement has been followed closely by some North American researchers, particularly those in the area of adult education. Nelly Stromquist's (Chapter Four in this volume) study of the popular education project led by Freire from 1990 to 1992 in São Paulo demonstrates that this interest remains strong. In addition, Anita Barabtarlo y Zedansky and Margarita Theesz Poschner (Chapter Eight in this volume) describe their own indebtedness to the popular education movement in their chapter on participatory research and teacher professional development. Elvira Souza Lima, in her brief overview of Brazilian qualitative research in Chapter Seven, documents the parallel development of ethnographic and participatory action research in that country.

On the other hand, Bertely and Corenstein (Chapter Three in this volume), while acknowledging the existence of both traditions in Latin America, perceive little cross-fertilization between popular educators and educational ethnographers. While acknowledging the importance of the popular education movement, they find their substantive and methodological issues distinct from those of educational ethnographers, who see social change as more evolutionary. Bertely and Corenstein argue:

Ethnographic studies raise the veil from small fragments of reality so that the actions and voices of repressed subjects that have been overpowered by the imposition of stereotypes constructed by hegemonic groups can be distinguished. Ethnographers can present their collaborators with an interpretation of the data collected. They can also contribute to the social interpretation of subjects and to the gradual modification of the content or implementation of educational policies. (Chapter Three, " An Overview of Ethnographic Research in Mexico," this volume)

While there may be disagreement among the authors in this volume about the extent of influence among qualitative research traditions, at least the following four influences can be identified:

1. A network of anthropologists and qualitative sociologists throughout Latin America, many inspired by the work of researchers at the DIE in Mexico, whose objective is the creation of knowledge about schooling, with an emphasis on addressing issues of school failure (see Batallán, Bertely and Corenstein, Rockwell, Souza Lima, and Zorrilla, this volume).

2. A body of research that documents education in nonformal sectors inspired by participatory projects of adult popular education (see Schmukler and Stromquist, this volume).

3. Qualitative researchers with an interest in the ways participatory models of qualitative research can be applied to the pre-service training and ongoing development of teachers (see Brenes, et al. and Barabtarlo y Zedansky and Theesz Poschner, this volume).

4. Training programs, workshops or courses carried out by individuals and/or institutions attempting to introduce qualitative research into the quantitatively driven research mainstream. This latter tradition is illustrated by the Workshops for Democratic Education in Chile (Vera

and Argumendo, 1976; Magendzo, 1990); the workshops designed
by Barabtarlo y Zedansky and Theesz Poschner (this volume) in
Mexico; and those sponsored by the Organization of American States
under the Multinational Center for Educational Research and the
Ministry of Education in Costa Rica, as well as the introduction of
qualitative research courses by Montero-Sieburth at the University of
Costa Rica and the National University of Heredia (Morales and
Ugalde, 1985) and subsequent development by Brenes, et al. (this
volume) into teacher training in Costa Rica.

In spite of the impressive work that was being done, qualitative research in Latin America did not meet with immediate and full acceptance.
In some contexts its introduction was gradual, often tested by Ministries
of Education through forums and workshop offerings, and later as bona
fide research courses. Yet suspicion about its nature probably has more to
do with its being associated with local popular education initiatives and
grass-roots efforts that are deemed politically "to the left." Thus the role of
ethnographers in these situations is queried in terms of the political stances
being taken. In other cases qualitative research has become an option that
research institutions within Latin America want to explore in order not to
be behind their neighbors to the north, but also as a means to find answers
to their research queries that go beyond the explanations provided by quantitatively driven national studies.

Since most of the teachers throughout Latin America are women, it is
not surprising to find clusters of female teachers and researchers being
interested in qualitative research both as an incentive to conduct research
and, more importantly, as a means to impact their communities. Such
interest has shown that qualitative research is gradually becoming one of
the research domains in which women have gained their own "voice" and
where their critiques in gender studies, issues of inequality, language, and
oppression are creating openings and academic spaces (Delgado Ballesteros,
1992; Zavella, 1993).

Through the presentation of each of these chapters we have attempted
to demonstrate the variability and intensity with which qualitative research
has taken hold in Latin America. We have not offered qualitative studies
about bilingual education because most of the current analyses in highland Peru, Ecuador, and Bolivia have tended to be sociolinguistic studies
and not ethnographic or qualitative studies. However, it is likely that ethnographic research has already worked itself into these linguistic arenas,

and we expect to see qualitative studies of first and second language acquisition, indigenous groups' cultural ways, and political issues about bilingual education being published in the near future. Overviews in English of this sociolinguistic work are available from Bolivia (Albó and d'Emilio, 1990); Ecuador (Moya, 1990); Nicaragua (Gurdián and Salamanca, 1990); and Peru (López, 1990).

In summary, our role has been to identify some of the general trends, issues, concerns, and foci of qualitative research in Latin America and to build some bridges between Latin American and North American qualitative researchers. We also have attempted to capture the types of approaches which have emerged and will continue to do so as qualitative research gains its place within academic and non-formal educational settings. Our attempt has been to draw attention to the discourse surrounding qualitative research in Latin America and to challenge researchers in North America to discover the thinking of their neighbors to the south. We believe we have a great deal to learn from each other's research and commitment to the field. This is the beginning of many future conversations.

Notes

1. The first three sessions of this annual conference, called "Interamerican Symposium on Ethnographic Research in Education" were held in Mexico, New Mexico, and Costa Rica. Participants have included researchers from Argentina, Brazil, Canada, Costa Rica, Mexico, and United States.

2. In recent years it has become more difficult to define the scholarly boundaries between Latin America and what we call North America—the United States and Canada. Individual researchers, in light of the fact that they often cross borders for education or jobs, are similarly hard to assign to one country.

3. Regina Gibaja (1988), calls for greater attention to the various ways positivism manifests itself:

   There are no distinctions nor criteria which define positivism within current research trends nor within quantitative or qualitative research. Therefore it is necessary to identify the type of positivism which is being discussed, whether it is Comte's positivism of the XIX century or the positivism of behaviorism (Gibaja, 1988, p. 85) (translated by Martha Montero-Sieburth).

4. The history of participatory research can be traced to methodologies used by social science researchers and militants in the Soviet Union after the Revolution of 1917, in China during the Cultural Revolution, in African countries such as Tanzania and Zimbabwe during the 1960s and 1970s, in Latin America during the agrarian reform in Chile during the 1960s, and throughout numerous adult education projects in Brazil, Mexico, Peru, Colombia, Central America, and the Caribbean during the decades of the 1970s and 1980s (Loera-Varela, 1986).

5. The application of ethnographic research derived from traditional anthropological methods to schooling mushroomed during the 1970s in North America. Micro-ethnography and macro-ethnography emerged as linguistic studies and social analysis in the work of Frederick Erickson and John Ogbu, respectively. The sociology of education and "new

sociology" provided ethnographic research in the 1980s and 1990s with the basis for developing "critical ethnography"—ethnography linked in practice to social, economic, and political explanations (Anderson, 1989).

References

Albó, X. and d'Emilio, L. (1990). Indigenous languages and intercultural bilingual education in Bolivia. *Prospects* 20(3), 321–330.

Anderson, G.L. (1989). Critical ethnography in education: Origins, current status, and new directions. *Review of Educational Research* 59(3), 249–270.

Avalos, B. (1985). Training for better teaching in the Third World: Lessons from research. *Teaching and Teacher Education*, 1(4), 289–299.

Avalos, B. (1989). *Enseñando a los Hijos de los Pobres: Un Estudio Etnográfico en América Latina*. Ottawa, Ontario, Canada: International Development Research Center.

Delgado Ballesteros, G. (1992). Las diferencias de género en los usos del lenguaje en el aula. In M. Rueda Beltrán and M.A. Campos (Eds.), *Investigación etnográfica en educación*. México, D.F.: Universidad Nacional Autónoma de México.

García Huidobro, J.E. and Gutiérrez, G. (1984). *Perspectivas y orientaciones de la investigación educacional en América Latina*. Santiago, Chile: CIDE.

Gibaja, R.E. (1988). Acerca del debate metodológico en la investigación educacional. *La Educatión*, 103, 81–94.

Gurdián, G. and Salamanca, D. (1990). Bilingual education in Nicaragua. *Prospects*, 20(3), 357–364.

Henry, J. (1963). *Culture against man*. New York: Random House.

Hornberger, N. (1987). Schooltime, classtime, and academic learning time in rural highland Puno, Peru. *Anthropology and Education Quarterly*, 18(3), 207–221.

Hornberger, N. (1989). Can Peru's rural schools be agents for Quechua language maintenance? *Journal of Multilingual and Multicultural Development*, 10(2), 145–159.

Jackson, P. (1968). *Life in classrooms*. New York: Holt, Rinehart & Winston.

Latapí, P. (1980). *Elementos distintivamente latinoamericanos en la investigación educativa en la región*. Paper presented at Seminario '80: La investigación educacional en América Latina, Santiago, Chile.

Latapí, P. (1988). Participatory research: A new research paradigm? *The Alberta Journal of Educational Research*, 34(3), 305–312.

Latapí, P. (1990). Some challenges for educational research in Latin America. *Prospects*, 20, 51–57.

Loera-Varela, A. (1986). *Can participatory research give us an emancipatory insight on popular knowledge?* Unpublished paper for Noel McGinn's class, Reading on Research, Harvard Graduate School of Education.

López, L.E. (1990). Development of human resources in and for bilingual intercultural education in Latin America. *Prospects*, 20(3), 311–320.

Macías, J. (1990). Scholastic antecedents of immigrant students: Schooling in an immigrant-sending community. *Anthropology and Education Quarterly*, 21(4), 291–318.

Macías, J. (1992). The social nature of instruction in a Mexican school: Implications for U.S. classroom practice. *The Journal of Educational Issues of Language Minority Students*, 10, 13–25.

Magendzo, S. (1990). Popular education in nongovernmental organizations: Education for social mobilization? *Harvard Educational Review*, 60, 49–61.

Montero-Sieburth, M. (1993). Corrientes, enfoques e influencias de la investigación cualitativa para latinoamérica. *La Educación*, 116, 491–518.

Montero-Sieburth, M. (1994). The effects of schooling processes and practices on potential "at risk" Latino high school students. In S. Nieto and R. Rivera (Eds.), *The education of latino children in Massachusetts*. Amherst: University of Massachusetts Press.

Montero-Sieburth, M. and Perez, M. (1987). Echar pa'lante, moving onward: The dilemmas and strategies of a bilingual teacher. *Anthropology and Education Quarterly*, 18(3), 180–189.

Morales, J. and Ugalde, J. (1985). *Informe final del curso de capacitación en investigación cualitativa*. Organización de los Estados Americanos, Programa Regional de Desarrollo

Educativo, Centro Multinacional de Desarrollo Educativo y Ministerio de Educación Pública, San José, Costa Rica.

Moya, R. (1990). A decade of bilingual education and indigenous participation in Ecuador. *Prospects*, 20(3), 331–344.

Paradise, R. (1994a). Spontaneous cultural compatibility: Mazahua students and their teachers constructing trusting relations. *Peabody Journal of Education*, 69(2), 60–70.

Paradise, R. (1994b). Interactional style and nonverbal meaning: Mazahua children learning how to be separate-but-together. *Anthropology and Education Quarterly*, 25(2), 156–172.

Rueda Belrán, M. and Campos, M.A. (Eds.). (1992). *Investigación etnográfica en educación*. México, D.F.: Universidad Nacional Autónoma de México.

Rueda Beltrán, M., Delgado Ballesteros, G., and Campos, M.A. (Eds.). (1991). *El aula universitaria: Aproximaciones metodológicas*. México, D.F.: Universidad Nacional Autónoma de México.

Rueda Beltrán, M., Delgado Ballesteros, G., and Jacobo, Z. (Eds). (1994). *La etnografía en educación: Panorama, prácticas y problemas*. México, D.F.: Universidad Nacional Autónoma de México.

Smith, L. and Geoffrey, W. (1968). *The complexities of an urban classroom*. New York: Holt, Rinehart & Winston.

Suárez-Orozco, M. (1987). "Becoming somebody": Central American immigrants in U.S. inner-city schools. *Anthropology and Education Quarterly*, 18, 287–299.

Tedesco, J.C. (1985). Paradigmas de la investigación socioeducativa. *Revista Latinoamericana de Estudios Educativos*, 15(2), 11–41.

Tedesco, J.C. (1987). Paradigms of socioeducational research in Latin America. *Comparative Education Review*, 31(4), 509–532.

Tedesco, J.C. (1992). New strategies for educational change in Latin America. *Bulletin 28: The Major Project of Education in Latin America and the Caribbean*. Santiago, Chile: UNESCO-OREALC.

Vaccaro, L. (1990). Transference and appropriation in popular education interventions: A framework for analysis. *Harvard Educational Review*, 60, 62–78.

Vera, R. and Argumendo, M. (1976). *Los talleres de educadores como modalidad de perfeccionamiento operativo*. (Research monograph). Buenos Aires: Centro de Investigación Educativa (CIE).

Zavella, P. (1993). Gender and power: Reconstructing Latino ethnography. *Urban Anthropology and Studies of Cultural Systems and World Economic Development*, 22(3–4), 231–236.

Section I

An Overview of Qualitative Research in Latin America

The three chapters in the first section provide overviews of the origins, current status, and new directions of qualitative research in Latin America. We begin the book with a chapter by Elsie Rockwell, who provides an account of the evolution of research at the Department of Educational Research (DIE) of Mexico's Polytechnic University. It is perhaps appropriate to begin here since, as Graciela Batallán points out in Chapter Two, the DIE was influential in the early days of the development and legitimation of ethnographic methods in education. In 1980 the Latin American Network of Qualitative Research on Schools (RINCUARE) was formed, and the DIE hosted a month-long seminar that brought together for the first time a group of Latin American qualitative researchers interested in the study of schools. Two of this volume's authors, Graciela Batallán, from Argentina, and Nelly Stromquist, originally from Peru, were instrumental in the creation of this early network.

In Chapter Two Graciela Batallán describes the evolution of ethnographic research in Chile and Argentina. She describes the influence of Clifford Geertz's brand of interpretive anthropology on researchers in these countries and the simultaneous influence of the more critical works of Agnes Heller and Antonio Gramsci, largely through the influence of Chilean and Argentinean ethnographers like Veronica Edwards, Justo Ezpeleta, and Eduardo Remedi, who worked or studied at the DIE in Mexico. She provides an extensive review of qualitative research in the southern cone from studies that include teachers as researchers to ethnographic studies of school failure in public schools.

Chapter Three provides an overview of qualitative research in Mexico by two Mexican authors, María Bertely, a graduate of the DIE, and Martha

Corenstein, a qualitative sociologist. Bertely has done extensive ethnographic work in indigenous communities in Mexico; she reviews much of the recent literature on the contributions that ethnographic studies have made regarding the role of schools in Mexican indigenous communities. The two authors also provide an overview of qualitative research in Mexico, organizing their discussion under three dimensions: the institutional and political, the curricular, and the social.

Readers interested in the development of qualitative research in Brazil should consult Chapter Eight, in which Elvira Souza Lima provides an overview along with an account of her own action research on teacher development in a rural Brazilian community.

Chapter One
Ethnography and the Commitment to Public Schooling
A Review of Research at the DIE

Elsie Rockwell

Ethnography, as Geertz (1983) has reminded us, works by the light of
local knowledge. Researchers draw on common pools of ideas disseminated throughout the academic world, yet they interpret them through
local references, sharpen them in local debates, and use them to understand local realities. It is in this sense that I will trace the ethnographic
research done at the Department of Educational Research (DIE)[1] in Mexico,
recognizing commonalities and noting divergences. The intellectual and
political context for this research was marked by a growing commitment
to public schooling built up by progressive educators in Latin America. I
propose to show how this commitment underlies and explains much of
the conceptual orientation and thematic range of ethnography at the DIE.

Research is always indebted to academic traditions and constructed
within particular institutional settings. In Mexico a long history of anthropological contributions to education preceded our research. During
the present century distinguished ethnologists such as Manuel Gamio,
Moisés Sáenz, Julio de la Fuente, and Gonzalo Aguirre Beltrán helped
forge a tradition of rural and bilingual education responsive to national,
regional, and indigenous cultures, and they wrote accounts of their experience and research.[2] Nevertheless by the mid-1970s only a few researchers (Modiano, 1974; Schensul, 1976) had done in-depth studies of Mexican schools. The ethnographic study of formal education gained legitimacy
in Mexico toward the end of the decade primarily at two research institutes, the Center for Research and Advanced Studies in Social Anthropology (CIESAS),[3] and the Department of Educational Research (DIE), both
founded in the 1970s.

The DIE offered several conditions that allowed a tradition in ethnographic research to be built up over the years. The department's involvement in national educational reforms had led to increasing contact with
authorities and teachers and interest in what was occurring in schools. To

pursue this interest, the initial group of researchers at the DIE supported
alternative approaches, including intensive fieldwork and interpretive analysis. The DIE's interdisciplinary orientation nevertheless forced those of us
involved in ethnography to be explicit about the epistemological assumptions of our research and to engage in theoretical discussions across many
fields. A commitment to collective research projects reinforced this orientation. The interdisciplinary experience also influenced the master's program. This program was designed to incorporate students into ongoing
research projects, and thus allowed many of them to acquire practical training in ethnography.[4] The graduate seminars also became the locus for discussing critical sociological theory and educational policy. Continuous
exchange with other Latin American scholars centered the academic concerns on issues vital to the region. Throughout the years, many of the
practices and ideas adopted and generated by ethnographers at the DIE
were further disseminated through courses, workshops, conferences, and
publications,[5] and have been taken up by other researchers.

Work at the DIE has been diverse, and several methodological and theoretical orientations have been adopted. For this review I have adopted a
rather strict definition of *ethnography*, as research characterized by time in
the field, attention to the cultural dimension, and production of texts that
both include contextualized, interpretive descriptions and engage in theoretical dialogue.[6] I have not included the numerous educational development projects and diagnostic or evaluative studies done at the department
that incorporated qualitative methods at some stage. My particular view of a
collective, long-term experience perhaps distorts some of the intentions of
my colleagues, and it necessarily stresses consensus by using a partially ficti-
tious "we" that glosses over internal debate. Yet I hope that the review will
serve as an adequate introduction to ethnography at the DIE.

The first part of the text traces some of the educational issues in Latin
America that influenced the conceptual debates at the DIE. In the second
section I review those studies carried out at the department that have shed
some light on the everyday life of schools, and I attempt to make clear
their thematic coherence. In the final part I discuss the general orientation
of this work in relation to other traditions of ethnographic research.

From Deschooling to Reclaiming Public Schools: The Latin American Debate

In Latin America, as in much of the world, a strong current of criticism of
formal schooling was unleashed by the political movements of the 1960s.

The voices of Ivan Illich and Paulo Freire were initially the strongest in the region. Early critical publications from the United States and, later, the thrust of reproduction theory from Europe converged with the general dissatisfaction with the course of schooling in the region. As a consequence many Latin American educators joined in the search for non-formal alternatives to public schools, in what came to be known as the popular education movement. Yet over the past two decades—and strongly bound up with the ongoing struggle for a democratic society—a shift has taken place among progressive educators in Latin America toward revaluing public schools and reclaiming them for popular education.[7] This position has faced new challenges and has been forced to respond to neo-liberal policies, which have effected fundamental changes in educational systems in recent years. The discussions that accompanied these political confrontations have influenced educational research in the region and therefore merit closer examination.

The Freirian tradition was forged during the 1970s, particularly in countries (Brazil, Chile) dominated by military dictatorships, and was sustained largely by a wide network of church-backed popular education projects. Those involved in the movement tended to be highly critical of official schools. They advocated and established community-based, nongovernmental alternatives for educating the rural and marginal urban (primarily adult) population and in the process developed a substantial stock of innovative methods and materials. The movement was far from monolithic. In fact it led to a wide variety of experiences, which reflect the diversity of local groups and interests it engaged.

At the same time in other countries such as Peru and Mexico federal governments undertook radical educational reforms of public schools at the primary and secondary levels. In Mexico President Luis Echeverría (1972–1978), intent upon reversing the negative image resulting from the government's massacre of students at Tlatelolco in 1968, gave high priority to education. He convened scholars associated with the radical political movement of the 1960s to participate in the reform. Many educators, including some at the newly founded DIE, collaborated in writing national textbooks for elementary school, designing ways to introduce innovative teaching methods and promote critical thinking. The accent was on transforming public schools.

Toward the late 1970s, however, researchers of the region began to question whether the recent curricular reforms and the significant growth of school systems in Latin America were actually leading to a democratization of schooling. Quantitative evidence disclosed the extreme regional and class differences in access to schooling. At the DIE, our initial ethnographic research during these years also muted the enthusiasm generated by the reform. Fieldwork unearthed the complexities of the classroom interaction that surrounded the use of the new textbooks (Rockwell and Gálvez, 1982), and found an unforeseen "hidden curriculum" (Paradise, 1979), which seemed to subvert the explicit intentions of reformers. The practical difficulties of transforming schools became evident.

Both the criticism of formal schools by the popular education movement and the disillusionment of educators with the possibilities of transforming schools were fertile ground for the dissemination of reproduction theory, which entered Latin America through early translations of the works of Althusser, Bowles and Gintis, Baudelot and Establet, Bourdieu and Passeron, Broccoli and Foucault.[8] Several widely read Latin American authors of the 1970s (Labarca, 1977; Ponce, 1974; Vasconi, 1973) had developed similar theories. At that time educational researchers in the region began to attribute the social reproduction of class structures to differential schooling and analyzed teaching and textbooks largely in terms of the inculcation of dominant ideologies.

During the early 1980s, reproduction theory was questioned and reformulated in the English-speaking world on various grounds.[9] Proponents of symbolic interactionism, working in the ethnographic tradition, stressed human agency and cultural production as mediating processes for social reproduction. More significantly, the strength of the feminist and minority movements contested the primacy of class domination as an explanation within the reproductivist perspective, and added gender, race, and ethnicity to the agenda. The prevalence of countercultures among certain school-going youths in developed countries also posed a challenge, and resistance theory evolved to account for the apparent failure of the reproduction paradigm.[10] However, resistance theory, grounded in the cultural production of differences within schools, tended to reinforce reproduction theory. In the long run it strengthened one of the basic arguments: what happens in schools contributes more to building and preserving the divisions within society than it does to breaking down pre-existing barriers between classes, genders, and races. As Paul Willis has put it recently, "the crucially interesting thing about cultural reproduction is how (really and potentially) critical resistant or rebellious forces become contradictorily tied up in the further development and maintenance of the 'teeth-gritting,' harmony of capitalist formations" (1990, p. 102).

The surge of critical ethnography in education, particularly in the see p. 27 United States,[11] further elaborated the significant contributions of the theories of cultural reproduction and resistance. At the same time it has added a new dimension: the commitment to transforming educational practices and the belief that this is possible through participatory or emancipatory research projects. This particular current—critical pedagogy— has been strongly inspired by Freire's early work, which has recently enjoyed a significant revival in the United States. The tendency is to develop and document alternative, critical practices that counteract the assumed reproductivist character of ordinary schooling, yet this basic thesis is rarely questioned.[12]

During the same period reproduction theory was being challenged in Latin America on somewhat different grounds.[13] Scholars in the Marxist tradition in Latin America had long questioned the relevance of structuralist neo-Marxism for understanding Latin American history, and they were looking to the works of Gramsci and of the Peruvian Marxist, Mariategui, for new ways of analyzing issues of the state, democracy, and culture in the regional context.[14] Developments in Nicaragua, El Salvador, and Guatemala demanded new explanations. Though there were different positions in the debate, all insisted on taking into account the structural and cultural differences between the developed world and Latin America, where pre-Hispanic and colonial legacies are articulated with modernity in specific and complex ways. These discussions made their way into the educational sphere. It became clear that the presumably universal assertions of the theory of reproduction, which largely reflected the relatively stable French society and culture (Bourdieu and Passeron, 1977), did not correspond to Latin American societies (Tedesco, 1983).

Certain arguments pressed upon Latin American educators the urgency of rethinking the nature of public schools. While Althusserians had seen the school system as an "ideological state apparatus," essential for the control of the popular classes, critics of this theory pointed out that the most repressive regimes of the region had not extended schooling but rather had tended to eradicate or restrict access to the educational institutions which had been built up—largely in response to popular demand—during previous regimes. Moreover, a popular appropriation of schooling, rather than opposition to schooling, was actually occurring in different parts of Latin America. At times this process was rooted in the traditions that were most distant from the official culture represented, presumably, by the public schools, as is shown in Juan Ansión's (1990) study of indigenous communities in the Peruvian Andes. Finally, contrary to what was occurring in developed countries, in Latin America there was little correspondence between the expanding education system of the 1970s and a highly differentiated and dependent economic structure, which neither required nor supported what formal education had to offer (Tedesco, 1987).

Latin American societies were (and are) of course deeply divided—culturally, politically, and economically. Social inequality is reflected in low retention rates and unequal access to schooling. Yet formal public schooling, it was argued, had often provided an equalizing experience for those who survived within the system, attenuating, for a time at least, the strong gender, class, and ethnic distinctions reproduced through other social practices.[15] Furthermore, though generally managed and regulated by centralized governments, education systems—particularly public universities—had been centers of dissident political organization. Massive radical teacher movements in many countries added evidence of the contradictory position of teachers in relation to the state. On this basis some scholars concluded that public education in Latin America, as unequal and inadequate as it had been, had contributed more to producing a "critical rationality" than an "instrumental rationality" (Rama, 1984).

Some of the initial ethnographic work at the DIE was leading to similar conclusions, as researchers discarded the possibility of finding a simple economic rationality in the practices observed in Mexican primary schools. We used the concept of *appropriation*[16] to signal the possibility of students making their own, and in the process transforming, practices and contents offered by ordinary public schooling. As we phrased it at the time:

In spite of the subtle control of the posture, attention and actions of each child, in spite of the ideological incision implicit in many classroom practices, and in spite of the selective presentation of humanity's knowledge—with its exclusion of both popular culture and advanced science—, within schools there occur, simultaneously, processes of appropriation of knowledge which are meaningful to dominated classes. When state control restricts these processes of appropriation, children find ways of resisting. They find ways of regaining the meaning of the daily encounter with their peers which schooling itself has converted into an everyday reality (Ezpeleta and Rockwell, 1983, p. 77).

However, the situation was far from promising. Latin America was (and is) still far from achieving universal primary education. Dropout and illiteracy rates were high and rising and very few students had access to middle and higher education. A great social divide was being constructed through exclusion from school. For some time regional researchers had used Bourdieu's notion of "cultural capital" and Bernstein's of "restricted codes" to account for low achievement, yet it soon became clear that the unequal provision of teachers, class time, and books—rather than initial student differences— explained much of school failure.[17] The sheer magnitude of educational problems in the region convinced many educators that only a strong public education system, necessarily funded by the state, could begin to give the majority population access to the relevant knowledge and cultural patrimony traditionally reserved for the elites (Tedesco, 1987). However, the possibility of achieving even universal primary education faced new problems during the 1980s as financial crises and shifting political alliances redefined the parameters of public policy in the region.

Recent trends in Latin American education have contributed to rethinking the significance of public schools. The radical critique of state schooling, still strong in some sectors, converged with strong conservative currents of opinion, which have opposed federal intervention in education, attacked national curricula and textbooks, and advocated limiting access to higher education. As in other parts of the world, recent neoliberal economic policies have led to profound transformations of public education in Latin America. These policies have often entailed withdrawal of public funding from certain educational and cultural domains, decentralization, a search for cost-effective measures linked to strict evaluation, and increased participation of private sectors. In Mexico conservative groups have pushed for certain curricular and organizational changes in elementary education that would reverse some important gains of the 1970s. Moreover, economic restructuring and social polarization have affected both the relative quality and the exchange value of public education.

In response to these political trends, progressive educators in Latin America have maintained an ongoing regional debate. Their attention has turned increasingly to strengthening and improving public schooling rather than to promoting non-formal alternatives.[18] While acknowledging that current economic conditions restrict public funding, they are searching for new strategies to redress the severely unequal distribution of formal education. In this political arena it has become necessary to rethink curricular contents, explore the possibilities of local autonomy and control while guaranteeing federal funding, and comprehend the dynamics that connect government policies, educational bureaucracies, and everyday school life.[19]

In the process the Freirian notion of *conscientizaçao* through education has worn thin. On the one hand, the transition toward democracy required intense political and civic organization, and this social movement, rather than education, became the natural locus for promoting political consciousness. On the other hand, the vital task of socializing relevant school knowledge,[20] in the sense of assuring its equal social distribution, was recognized as an essential step toward a more democratic society. A key concern has thus been to recover pedagogical issues, including discussion of the ways of teaching and learning conventional school contents, which the sociological study of schooling during the late 1970s had "subsumed under categories such as ideology and symbolic violence" (Tedesco, 1987).

Theoretical Implications
This ongoing debate deeply influenced theoretical discussions, political positions, and research agendas at the DIE. One of the consequences was a rethinking of the relationship between schooling and the state. In Mexico the formation of the post-revolutionary (1910–1940) centralized state and the growth of a federally funded national school system were so strongly intertwined that it has been particularly tempting to attribute all educational action to the central government authorities.[21] However, as researchers at the DIE turned to the analysis of particular historical moments, regional configurations, and levels of governance, they distinguished the multiple social actors involved in the formulation of educational policy and its actual implementation in institutions, even within the highly centralized Mexican system.

Our initial fieldwork in a number of ordinary public primary schools offered convincing evidence that "the state" could not be thought of as the univocal, all-powerful agent that appeared in much educational discourse. It was clear that official policies, themselves contradictory, filtered down through multiple levels and were enacted, or contested, by numerous local governing and non-governing groups. Similarly, the tendency to consider teachers simply as "agents of the state" not only overlooked their status and interests as workers but also ignored their personal biographies and commitments. Finally, it became evident that both children and parents made demands and contributions that effectively, though unequally, marked the course of public education. Clearly these various actors possessed a significant negotiating leverage; in fact, we concluded, no school could possibly exist, despite all the panoptical control a state might deploy, without their knowledgeable concurrence.

Some of our initial reflections on the everyday realities of schooling (Rockwell, 1982b; Ezpeleta and Rockwell, 1983; Rockwell and Ezpeleta, 1985) attempted to open the conceptual space needed to observe processes that could not be attributed to the machinations of "the state." As occurred in other countries, the tradition of Marxist historiography provided us a strong antidote to the structuralist versions that had molded reproduction theory. The works of Antonio Gramsci, E.P. Thompson, and Raymond Williams, particularly, supplied some of the missing links: a notion of hegemony, as distinct from domination; a view of state formation interwoven with civil society; and a wide range of concepts dealing with the cultural sphere. These ideas helped us rethink the institution of schooling and understand social and cultural reproduction in different ways (Rockwell, 1986a, 1987b). Other European authors, such as Habermas, Foucault, and Lacan, became important references for some researchers.

The course of our reflections accorded with developments in educational theory in the English-speaking world in the early 1980s (e.g., Apple, 1983; Wexler et al., 1981; Willis, 1981; Connell, 1983; Giroux, 1983). Nevertheless, our perception of the Latin American context led to a particular emphasis in ethnographic research. DIE researchers tended to stress the tensions between different social groups involved in defining what actually constitutes the culture of ordinary schooling. This perspective differs from the focus on the production of cultural identities that come into conflict with dominant school patterns yet in the end tend to reinforce social differentiation, which has been a common theme of many ethnographies in the Anglo-American critical tradition (Willis, 1977; Everhart, 1983; Weis, 1984; Holland and Eisenhart, 1990; Foley, 1990). In the latter view, countercultures produced by students and teachers tend to operate against formal schooling; in the former, local knowledge used by students and teachers in ordinary schools tends to reshape the culture of schooling.[22] This distinction may not be purely conceptual; rather it may reflect fundamentally different cultural processes occurring through schooling in different contexts and periods. As educational ethnography widens its comparative and historical perspective, we may have to accept that almost anything can happen in the actual places commonly called "school." Rather than assuming that a single cultural process, such as that proposed in the classical version of reproduction theory (Bourdieu and Passeron, 1977), can explain the dynamics of formal education in any context, we should move toward articulating the multiple and complex cultural processes actually documented in everyday school life.

Certain conceptual tools have allowed DIE researchers to systematically relate ethnographic research with the larger political issues. First, studies often selected social processes such as negotiation, socialization, control, resistance, in which something vital was at stake, something that depended on the outcome of the play of forces involved in school life. These studies show how everyday processes can determine such aspects as access to free schooling, the definition of teachers' work, the appropriation of knowledge, or the interpretation of textbook lessons.

Second, DIE researchers sought a concept of everyday life that would recover human agency, in the phenomenological tradition (Schutz, 1970), but would not be divorced, through some macro-micro divide, from broader social processes of reproduction (Heller, 1977); structuration (Giddens, 1984); and state formation (Holloway, 1980). They have also drawn on the work of authors such as G.H. Mead, Geertz, and Bakhtin in their attempt to recover the cultural dimension of the practice of schooling. Several studies have analyzed interactions between processes occurring within schools and the surrounding social formations and have traced how regional cultures, local knowledge, and historical memory, as well as dominant ideology, are used to constitute the everyday life of schools. Finally, several studies have taken up recent trends combining historiographical and ethnographical research in order to trace the consequences of educational reforms and policies over time and to document the heterogeneity of school life in Mexico.

Three Common Themes of Ethnographic Research at the DIE

Several generations of researchers and graduate students at the DIE have worked through some of the ideas mentioned in the previous section in ethnographic studies on many facets of school life. In this section I will highlight three themes that are common to many of the studies: (a) the social construction of schools, (b) teaching as work, and (c) knowledge in social interaction. Though there are a number of other topics that cut across these ethnographies, these three allow me to give a relatively coherent view of the cumulative research done at the department.

The social construction of schooling

The metaphor of construction has been applied to education by so many authors that it is difficult to convey a particular use. The seminal book by Peter Berger and Thomas Luckmann, *The Social Construction of Reality* (1967), was widely read in Latin America, as in the English-speaking world, and contributed to our initial discussions on schooling. Nevertheless we generally did not use the categories (i.e., typification, institutionalization) privileged by these authors, but rather associated the notion of construction to other processes. Rather than stressing the internalization of shared schemes of reality, for example, the notion of construction used in many DIE studies implied negotiation among social actors who draw on different cultural resources and models. We studied the negotiation of fundamental relationships occurring in the multiple daily encounters among persons, each of whom had a substantial say regarding the actual practices they engaged in within schools.

By looking beyond the normative discourse and the highly visible routines of schooling, the ethnographic approach used by DIE researchers uncovered ways in which principals, teachers, students, and parents constantly proposed and often achieved alternative uses of the time and space of schooling, while devising strategies for dealing with official norms. We found that the ongoing interpretation of uniform official dispositions allowed considerable leeway, even though local authorities attempted to keep schools in line with their own interpretations of the norm. Because of this negotiated process of social construction, everyday school realities in Mexico, particularly at the elementary level,[23] can be quite diverse and do not always reflect the discourse of official documentation.

Ethnographers at the DIE undertook the description of this multifaceted process from several angles. The encounter among different actors emerged as particularly rich in the rural primary schools of central Tlaxcala where some of the initial research[24] was carried out, as strong local appropriations of schooling vied with successive attempts at modernization from the central government. Three interrelated studies highlighted aspects of this process.

Ruth Mercado (1987) studied the negotiation that takes place between principals and other social actors (inspectors, local authorities, committees, and parents) in promoting and financing the construction of school buildings, and showed how parents implicitly defend their right to a free school. Her research (Mercado, 1986a, 1995) set aside the neutral concept of "community" often used in ethnographies, in order to distinguish different local governing and non-governing groups that support or oppose, through shifting alliances, the successive social projects for the school. In a second study of this series, Citlali Aguilar (1991, 1995) described how teachers contribute to the material and social existence of schools through a number of time-consuming non-teaching activities, which ranged from cleaning the classrooms to organizing fund-raising events. Etelvina Sandoval (1987, 1988), exploring another facet, found that school priorities and teachers' careers are influenced and legitimized by the complicity between the national teachers' union, which in Mexico is generally controlled by the dominant political party, and the educational bureaucracy.

Within each of these studies the authors questioned certain commonsense conceptions, such as the notion that elementary education is totally free and the idea that a teacher's job is basically pedagogical. They stressed the heterogeneity of the actual experiences of schooling that result from the process of construction, by contrasting in each study two or more schools within the same district. Each study documented the interacting local forces and perspectives that determine the course of particular schools and countered the usual top-down vision of school planners.

Studies of primary schools conducted in other localities continued to open up facets of the social construction of schooling that involve parents and teachers. Carlos García (1988) traced processes leading to progressive estrangement between incoming teachers and rural parents who defended the traditions of a school constructed in Michoacán during the 1930s. Alicia Carvajal (1988) described a different dynamic in an urban marginal school, where she stressed the teachers' collective capacity to define the rules of the game. Patricia Medina (1992, 1993) examined the power play and changing alliances among groups of teachers in the everyday politics of a central urban school. Lucila Galván (1995) reexamined parents' relationships with teachers and revealed patterns of mutual influence in their work with children.

As we deepened our understanding of the social construction of schooling, we became aware of the historical dimensions that account for different school realities. Many characteristics could be traced to the way particular schools were founded or evolved (e.g. García, 1988; Medina, 1992). The transformation of rural into urban schools is particularly significant in Mexico, as shown in Maricela Olivera's study (1984). Recovering local memory in rural schools became a key to understanding present-day confrontations over school projects (Mercado, 1992) and the encounter of generations of teachers or parents holding different values and views of school practices (Aguilar, 1991).

My own subsequent research on the history of schooling in the Tlaxcala region has taken ethnographic inquiry further into the past (Rockwell, 1994, 1996) to uncover the presence of both the state and civil society in the founding of rural schools during the post-revolutionary years of 1910 to 1940.

The study shows how the construction of schools, while contributing to the formation of a centralized state, integrated the resources and demands of local populations.[25] This historical evolution furthermore left traces that explain some of the positions and practices found in present-day schools in the region. Similarly, understanding traditional beliefs concerning literacy in one village has shed light on the way teachers relate to literacy within classrooms in the region (Rockwell, 1992b), lending support to the general idea that local cultural configurations permeate schooling. The current merging of anthropological and historical approaches occurring in many fields provides a rich background for this line of research and gives a new dimension to the ethnographic understanding of cultural processes in schools.

Teaching As Work

A second theme that links these and other studies is the idea of teaching as work. Much of British and Australian ethnographic research (reviewed by Atkinson, Delamont, and Hammersley, 1988) became relevant to our research because of this interest. The everyday practice of teaching in Mexican schools was largely unknown to researchers as few studies, either quantitative or qualitative, had been done in this field. As ethnographers we insisted upon understanding teaching "on its own terms" rather than subjecting it to prescriptive or evaluative models. Gauging the quality of teaching and understanding the logic of teaching were considered two different research processes (Ezpeleta, 1986; Rockwell and Mercado, 1988), and many studies chose the latter course in order to get a sense of the complex processes that account for actual classroom practice. The research reviewed in this section approached the study of teaching through intensive observation and informal interviewing in the ordinary conditions of public schools (not in special or alternative programs) and attempted to render teaching practices intelligible within their normal institutional context.

The ethnographic analyses done at the DIE have increasingly regarded teachers as knowledgeable subjects, who generally, not just exceptionally, go about their business reflectively, appropriating and modifying the normative curriculum and teaching agenda of each school. This view of teaching contested reproduction theory while drawing on a critical theory of labor. By regarding teachers as workers, it became increasingly difficult to see them as transparent vehicles for social and cultural reproduction, though they, like all others involved in schooling, participate in these processes.

Many studies at the DIE (for example, Mercado, 1986b; Carvajal, 1988; Aguilar, 1991; Quiroz, 1991) have captured the variety of teaching and non-teaching tasks that constitute a teacher's job as constructed within particular primary and secondary schools. These studies have described how teachers are constantly negotiating the conditions and nature of their work with colleagues, principals, parents, and children. Other studies have shown how institutional conditions influence teaching. For example, Beatriz Ramírez (1980) contrasted teaching practice between the morning and afternoon shifts in an urban primary school, while Concepción Jiménez (1982) and Etelvina Sandoval (1987) analyzed teachers' resistance to the routines of in-service training sessions.

Justa Ezpeleta (1989, 1992b) has conducted comparative studies that analyze the specific constraints that multigrade and multishift schools have on the "invisible" conditions that teachers face, as well as the strategies teachers use to deal with certain administrative and curricular requirements that make little sense under those conditions. Her recent work (Ezpeleta, 1992a) has focused on the hierarchies and power relationships within the schools' technical councils. She is currently studying the background and careers of rural teachers and school inspectors. The linkage between school management and classroom pedagogy has been increasingly important for her line of research, as in studies done by her student (Pastrana, 1996).

The structure of the curriculum, as well as the organization of the school, influences teaching, particularly in post-primary levels, as is shown in Rafael Quiroz's study (1991, 1992b) of secondary schools. He has found that the secondary curriculum, which contains a great deal of highly specialized information, generates situations in which teachers and students are obliged to "simulate" the learning process and thereby become accomplices in their effort to survive through the school year. This process is particularly evident in the strategies they develop to administer and to solve the frequent tests that are typical of secondary schools. Some studies done in primary schools detected similar situations (V. Edwards, 1987; García, 1988). Nevertheless, most have stressed the teachers' relative autonomy with respect to the official syllabi and textbooks at the elementary level in Mexico (see Rockwell, 1982b; Candela, 1989, 1991; Luna, 1993; Mercado, 1994).

One of the crucial constraints on teaching is time, and not by chance the relative proportion of time allotted to various activities and subject matters captured our interest from the beginning (Gálvez, Paradise, Rockwell, and Sobrecasas, 1980). Over the years it has become evident that teachers have to deal with the constraints of time in ways that differ from other occupations, as they attempt to accommodate into the five-hour school day tasks that would normally add up to a double workday. Several studies show how these numerous tasks are variously resisted, negotiated, superimposed, or redefined to constitute the actual contents of teaching in any one school or classroom. Quiroz (1992a) has made finer qualitative distinctions in his analysis of time in secondary classes in order to show the multiple effects the temporal dimension has upon the strategies used by teachers and students.

Some researchers at the DIE have maintained that interaction with school children strongly influences teaching. María Bertely (1985) explored teachers' reactions to the emotional demands of working with preschool children. Ruth Mercado (1991, 1994) and Maria Eugenia Luna (1993, 1994) have described how primary teachers modify classroom routines and rhythms as they encounter and come to know their students. Similarly, the research project directed by Ruth Paradise in rural Mazahua (Indian) schools showed how teachers respond to the students' cultural background. It found that teachers adapt to the children's ways of learning (Paradise, 1990, 1994c; Bertely, 1992) and acknowledge an alternative use of classroom time (Robles, 1994).

Another significant facet of work in schools is the production of teacher identities in the long-term play of forces in particular institutions. This process is affected by many variables, including gender, age, training, as well as pedagogical and political preferences (Medina, 1992). Quiroz (1985, 1988) proposed that the teachers' specialized knowledge becomes a distinctive element of the occupational identity of secondary school teachers. Yet it is possible that teacher identities are malleable and change with circumstance and time. Eduardo Remedi, long interested in teacher subjectivities, has centered his recent work (1992, 1993) on the contradictory and changing identities of high school teachers recruited in the late 1960s as they survived through two decades and came to occupy administrative positions. His research, based on oral history, will open new ways of understanding the radical tradition in the public university-managed *preparatorias* in Mexico.

The everyday work of teachers has an undocumented history, reflected in the diverse and changing tasks, identities, and practices that constitute present-day teaching. Several ethnographic studies at the department have picked up on the professional traditions constructed and handed down through generations of teachers. For example, conceptions of history associated with past reforms are reflected in some of the contrasting ways teachers in rural schools presently interpret textbook lessons (Rockwell, 1988) and conduct civic ceremonies (Taboada, 1996). The collective practices that account for this sort of continuity in teaching have been examined in other studies. Ruth Mercado (1994) and Maria Luisa Talavera (1992) traced the circulation of particular resources among teachers through networks linked to personal and professional relationships. Patricia Medina (1992) linked the transmission of pedagogical traditions to everyday political alignments within the school. The teachers' uses of literacy in the workplace is a facet of this process that I have explored (Rockwell, 1992a).

Through these studies, research at the DIE has cut paths toward understanding the variable contents and conditions of teachers' work in Mexico and perhaps in other countries as well. While many of the studies stressed the structural and material constraints on teaching, the recent trend has been to examine the resources and conditions that enable teachers to carry out their work. By approaching schools as workplaces, several studies have begun to trace the collective appropriation of resources, situated within traditions kept alive or challenged by various groups of teachers. Along the way, we have questioned several assumptions that are recurrent in critical pedagogy. The frequent references to teaching as a set of routines and to the de-skilling of teachers, and the blanket indictment of "control" and "authoritarianism" found in descriptions of ordinary schooling written from a critical stance, do not seem to correspond to the complex, often contradictory, interaction constructed daily in the classrooms observed in Mexico. Rather than using the concepts of reflexivity and appropriation (Woods, 1994) to prescribe desired pedagogical practices, often exemplified by exceptional teachers, we have used these concepts as analytical tools for examining teaching as it normally occurs, under the difficult working conditions found in most schools.

From the vantage point of everyday school life it is possible to shed light on the actual incidence of curricular and administrative reforms on the qualitative dimensions of schooling and consider the conditions that enable teachers to adopt certain practices. The result is to recast discussions of educational policies that isolate the attitudes and capacities of individual teachers as a target for reform. Defining and reconstructing teaching as work has thus been crucial to gaining an understanding of the mediation between national policies and classroom realities.

Knowledge in Social Interaction

In the course of describing and analyzing interaction in numerous classrooms, DIE researchers came to stress the study of knowledge, in a broad, cultural sense. The studies generally considered knowledge as implicit in everyday practices in schools and examined ways in which it is presented, constructed, interpreted, or contextualized in everyday interaction. As we became familiar with schools in diverse settings in Mexico, we questioned the "culture conflict" thesis that was sustained in many school ethnographies in the United States.[26] We found that certain local cultural resources, rather than coming into conflict with school knowledge, were being recovered by teachers and students in the classroom.

The Geertzian insight that "the shapes of knowledge are always ineluctably local, indivisible from their instruments and their encasements" (Geertz, 1983, p. 4) gave force to the distinction between formal curricular contents and knowledge as presented in the classroom (Rockwell, 1982b). Several DIE studies have described the actual shapes, words, images, metaphors, genres, rituals, and uses that knowledge takes on as it becomes a social object, up for public viewing by students and teachers (Paradise, 1979; Rockwell and Gálvez, 1982; V. Edwards, 1987; Quiroz, 1991; Hernández, 1989; Candela, 1989, 1995a; Ortiz, 1994; Mercado, 1994; Luna, 1993). The analyses of classroom interaction tended to recover implicit and explicit meanings or contents rather than focusing on the forms and patterns of communication.

Many studies of classroom interaction at the DIE have looked not only at curricular contents taught or learned but also at the knowledge inherent in teaching and learning. The concept of appropriation, which implies active transformation (Leontiev, 1981; Rogoff, 1992) and strategic use of cultural knowledge and social institutions, became central to the conception of everyday life used in many of the studies (Ezpeleta and Rockwell, 1983). Several ethnographies thus reflect the concern with the appropriation of knowledge within a horizon bounded by the local practices and representations encountered in each school. They take into account the general context of classroom life, not only the intentional instructional interaction between teacher and students. Using this approach, my work in primary classrooms documented uses of literacy appropriated through a variety of experiences with writing in schools, even though formal instruction is restricted to a few classical forms (Rockwell, 1982a). The successive modifications—or transpositions (Chevallard, 1984)—were a key to Antonia Candela's (1989, 1995a) analysis of the appropriation of scientific concepts and experiences in the classroom.

In studying aspects of knowledge in classroom interaction, several researchers again resorted to the idea of "social construction" to refer to the ways in which meanings or representations are elaborated, negotiated, or resisted in the ongoing communication between students and teachers (Candela and Rockwell, 1991). Though sharing many of the assumptions of sociocultural research on learning that are indebted to Vygotsky, studies of interaction at the DIE have debated with the focus on control and on the gradual transfer of competencies and discourses from the teacher to the students, found in other classroom studies (Moll, ed. 1990; Wertsch, 1991; Newman, Griffin, and Cole, 1989). Thus several DIE researchers have sought to understand signs of the autonomous activity of children (V. Edwards, 1987; García, 1988; Hernández, 1989; Candela, 1990, 1991; Paradise, 1994b; Luna, 1993) as it occurs even within traditional elementary classrooms, a topic that has also drawn the attention of researchers in other countries. Similarly, my analyses of the oral mediation of literacy in classrooms (Rockwell, 1988, 1991) contrasted ways of teaching the meaning of texts that open possibilities of co-constructing interpretations. While other scholars have stressed the process that Derek Edwards and Neil Mercer (1987) identified as the construction of "common knowledge," Antonia Candela (1993, 1994, 1995b) is currently combining ethnography with the approach developed by Derek Edwards and the Discourse Analysis and Rhetoric Group at the University of Loughborough, England, to reconstruct children's argumentation of alternative interpretations of science activities within the asymmetric interaction of the classroom. The image of classroom interaction that these and other studies convey accords well with the general conceptualization of a negotiated, socially constructed, everyday school life that was sustained in other domains of DIE inquiry.

Another set of DIE ethnographies has described contrasts and interactions between out-of-school knowledge and knowledge constructed within schools, raising fundamental questions concerning the notion of "significant knowledge." Eduardo Weiss (1992) and his students Guadalupe Díaz (1992, 1993) and Claudine Levy (1990) explored this dimension in studies comparing practical agricultural knowledge with technical knowledge taught in agricultural middle schools, and showing how these two domains intersect and how they influence the pedagogical methods that teachers use. Joaquín Hernández (1989) analyzed semantic changes occurring when children use their own experience to interpret the scientific frame expressed by teachers. Quiroz (1991) used Agnes Heller's (1977) categories to argue that the specialized knowledge taught in secondary schools is appropriated by students only when it can be integrated into the structure of everyday knowledge under certain conditions rarely satisfied by school practices. Rosaura Galeana (1990) has shown some of the ways in which working children in fact do use tools learned at school as well as constructing other competencies out of school.

The idea of cultural knowledge has been used in other spheres. Ruth Paradise's (1985, 1987, 1994a) intensive study of non-verbal communication between Mazahua mothers and infants drew on the work of G.H. Mead, Garfinkel, and Giddens to study how children implicitly learn a notion of self. She has subsequently traced these cultural presuppositions into the classroom in order to examine how they influence Mazahua children's organization of learning activities (Paradise, 1991, 1994b and 1994c). Her studies suggest classroom practices may also reflect the deep Mesoamerican cultural current that Guillermo Bonfil (1987) claimed still organizes many domains of everyday life in rural Mexico.

The study of knowledge ties in to research on teachers' work, particularly through the description of cultural and professional knowledge. Ruth Mercado (1994) has drawn on Bakhtin's (1981) notion of voices and on Heller's (1977) theory to examine knowledge—in the sense of the Spanish term, *saber*—inherent and displayed in everyday practice rather than solely reported in teachers' discourse. Studies in this line analyze the teachers' ability to coordinate and modulate classwork with a heterogenous group of children (Mercado, 1991, 1994) and to construct a working relationship with students (Luna, 1993, 1994).

Implicit in our focus on knowledge is a rethinking of the concept of ideology. Some of the early work at the DIE identified several dimensions along which an ideological reading of school practices and discourses was relevant. Using the concept of hidden curriculum, several researchers turned their attention to the implicit contents of schooling. Early studies reconstructed the way school children are taught certain ways of relating to work and authority (Paradise, 1979; Bárcenas, 1982) and to knowledge (V. Edwards, 1987), which have been identified with Western capitalist and/or industrialist social formations. Josefina Granja (1988) stressed legitimation and the constitution of schooled subjectivities in tracing the complicated certification process in middle schools. Under Eduardo Remedi's direction, Ana María Cerdá (1989) examined the values and norms conveyed and resisted in high school social science classes, and Terry Spitzer (1990) explored implicit contents, linked to a professional identity, in a range of institutional and informal practices at an agricultural college. Each of these studies pointed to some of the ideological undercurrents that mold school practices.

Nevertheless, our subsequent discussions tended to stress the distinction and problematic relationship between ideology and knowledge. Though early observations yielded evidence of the conceptions of the social world that frame and fragment school knowledge, they also revealed the contradictory nature of these implicit messages. Using a Gramscian perspective, I argued that the multiple, and inevitable, ideological overtones found in classroom discourse and practice do not necessarily correspond to dominant cultural schemes. Rather, they are crossed through with personal and local values and are filtered through "folklore" and "commonsense" categories (Rockwell, 1982b, 1987b).

I would add that the DIE studies that have approached the sociocultural dimensions of knowledge—though taking seriously the challenges of careful analysis of situated talk and action—have not been exclusively concerned with the mechanisms of classroom interaction privileged by micro-ethnography. As they examine the dynamics governing what is actually taught and the response of students, they point to the broader social and political processes that occur through schooling (cf. Erickson, 1987; Foley, 1990). Furthermore, this focus on school knowledge has implied a conviction that the notions acquired through schooling are always susceptible to reinterpretation and can eventually be used against all forms of ideological inculcation. An eloquent example of this process can be found in the recent (1994) Zapatista movement in Chiapas, which has appropriated and given new meaning to the symbols of patriotism propagated particularly through schooling: the national anthem and flag.

Diverging and Converging Ethnographic Perspectives

Ethnography at the DIE has shared many concerns with other traditions of educational ethnography, and has drawn on common conceptual references. Nevertheless, it has privileged processes that may not have the same force in other countries, while perhaps leaving aside issues—such as those of gender and race[27]—that different political contexts have brought to the fore. Furthermore, the perception of relevant problems and the particular responses to the theory of reproduction constructed at the DIE during the past decades have been different from those of other groups of ethnographers in Latin America, as will be clear from the chapters included in the present volume. I must also stress that, despite the coherence I see in our past work, there have been numerous areas of debate among us. Moreover, as each researcher follows interests in particular aspects of schooling and takes into account developments in diverse fields, future ethnographies at the DIE promise to be rich and varied.

In this sense neither our past nor our future work will fit easily into the categories so freely wielded in the United States, such as micro- and macro-ethnography, or culturalist, neo-Marxist, or postmodern paradigms, among others.[28] Though we share the concern with relating "broad structural constraints" with human agency, which Gary Anderson (1989) identifies as the hallmark of critical ethnography, our perspective was constructed within a different political context, engaged in different dialogues, and contested reproduction theory on different grounds.

Ironically, part of our local history has involved overcoming the Freirian framework of the 1970s, which has gained credence, no doubt for valid reasons, in the critical pedagogy and ethnography movement in the United States and Canada. Latin American critics of the Freirian tradition (e.g., Paiva, 1982) pointed out that the movement had developed a "populist pedagogy," caught in the dilemma of attempting to recover and articulate popular culture through direct participation and, at the same time, transforming popular consciousness. Proponents of the movement—Freire's writings notwithstanding—rarely documented their field experience and often eschewed discussion of the theoretical, political, or substantive issues involved in that process. This tendency influenced much of the participatory research associated with popular education in the region. Educators in this movement often lacked the time or interest needed to reflect on the categories used to recover popular culture, or to interpret themes in relation to structural constraints and political moments. The development of ethnography in Latin America, strongly grounded in critical social theory, thus led some researchers to question the epistemology, as well as the political assumptions, associated with the Freire-inspired participatory research movement.

Though our research stems from an explicit political concern—the defense of public schools—we have come to understand the relevance of ethnographic research for the transformation of schooling in terms that are quite different from the Freirian tradition. In our view, reflexivity in ethnography should transform the researcher's own ethnocentric conceptions of other cultural formations. Thus, reflexive ethnography in education should challenge and modify our academic models and assumptions regarding life in schools. This is difficult to do if one enters a school intent upon transforming teaching practices by disseminating and confirming those same models and assumptions. Though of course attempts to influence school practices and policies may in themselves be valid,[29] ethnography inherently follows a different logic. Its strength lies in its capacity to understand how the people involved in everyday school life consciously use the available resources to accomplish their work, how they go about constructing the cultures of schooling, and how they appropriate or contest the reforms proposed from without. Rather than transforming schools, ethnography must produce texts that shed light on how transformations actually occur within schools (Rockwell, 1986b). Although it does not presume direct intervention of the researcher in the processes under study, this task has its own political relevance in the educational context I have outlined above.

Ethnography, like all research, corresponds to explicit or implicit political agendas. Ethnographic studies can influence public debates, and have done so during the past decade in Mexico. However, the terms of these debates are necessarily contingent, both in time and space. Advocacy of particular positions through research must attend to local issues, circumstances, and alliances. As our texts enter complicated political debates, we must discriminate those aspects singled out for criticism and take care before transferring the implications of ethnographic research from one context to another. To give one example, the discussion concerning textbooks is particularly sensitive in all countries, yet the analysis of the situation in the United States (e.g., Apple, 1986) is quite different from that in Mexico, where it has been necessary to defend the free, national, and relatively progressive textbooks published by the Ministry of Education.[30] Consideration of political issues such as this one has in turn influenced the topics and the discourse of our ethnographic description.

The defense of public schooling in Mexico has its own political agenda. Quantitative and comparative research has made it quite clear that the educational resources and opportunities provided to different classes and regions, in Mexico as in other countries, are extremely unequal and that these differences have increased in recent years.[31] This trend has forced us to think in terms of educational policy on a national scale, to calibrate the effects that reforms in funding, administration, curriculum, or teacher training will have on thousands of schools. It has forced us to recognize that schools are changing as a result of current state actions and, ironically, to value some of the teaching practices and existing resources that may be lost in the near future. It has also forced us to look for viable alternative practices and policies.

If ethnography is to be of value in thinking politically about education in this context, it must seek to understand the complicated processes actually occurring in schools. Research must foresee how existing classroom conditions (available time, group dynamics, teaching materials, parental involvement, working conditions) might prevent the adoption of specific proposals and how changes in those conditions might allow alternative ways of teaching to be adopted. It must gauge the strength of teaching traditions, take stock of cultural resources, trace the channels through which pedagogical knowledge circulates among teachers, describe in detail the existing practices that allow more students to learn. Moreover, ethnography must understand the negotiations taking place within the "field of contending forces" that determines school life and estimate the chances that proposed changes have of enduring within that negotiated reality. Proposals for transforming educational practice that ignore these preexisting conditions have little chance of entering schools on any significant scale and are destined to succeed at best with the lone teacher in the exceptional school.

This research agenda requires a very wide range of theoretical and methodological tools. In this sense, stressing academic paradigms may hinder the needed convergence among a variety of approaches, while a finer debate on pertinent concepts, taken from diverse theoretical legacies, may be more fruitful for understanding the processes involved in constructing school cultures.

Educational research at the DIE has followed its own course. The theoretical sources we have read, interpreted, and questioned during the past decades reflect the particular selections and mixtures that reach academic worlds at the periphery, where some references become strong even before they are widely used in mainstream research, while many remain relatively unknown due to limitations in translation and circulation. As we have advanced in the difficult task of using appropriate theoretical tools to construct ethnographic descriptions, we have analyzed specific concepts, establishing differences between key authors that are often grouped together.[32] We have progressively come to value research developed in such fields as culture, literacy, and cognition, comparative studies on the culture and social history of schooling and teaching, or the analysis of discourse in domains other than schooling.[33] Ethnographies that delve deeply into the particular processes that occur in distant places—such as Hammerstown, Trackton, or Northtown—have become more useful for this search than the abstract, presumably universal schemes so often espoused in education. Studies by researchers from other countries working in Mexico[34] have brought in new terms of reference, at times nearer to debates at home than to local concerns, though they nevertheless reveal facets of schooling and culture not easily seen from within. Perhaps the priorities and perceptions of our research may begin to make sense as well in the English-speaking world. In any case, ethnographic research, while responding to local knowledge, will become increasingly relevant across borders as the destinies of schooling north and south gradually converge.

Notes

I wish to thank my colleagues Antonia Candela, Ruth Mercado, and Ruth Paradise for comments on previous versions. I take full responsibility, however, for errors in the present account of work at the DIE.

1. Pronounced dee-eh. Departamento de Investigaciones Educativas, Centro de Investigación y de Estudios Avanzados, Instituto Politécnico Nacional (DIE-CINVESTAV-UPN), México, D.F. FAX (525) 575–0320.

2. Some representative works are: Aguirre Beltrán (1953); Julio de la Fuente (1964); Sáenz (1966).

3. Centro de Investigación y Estudios Superiores de Antropología Social (formerly Centro de Investigación Social del Instituto Nacional de Antropología e Historia, CISINAH), where during the mid-1970s Guillermo de la Peña conducted a seminar on educational ethnography with students from several institutions. Ethnography has since spread to many other institutions, notably the Ibero-American University (UIA); the National School of Anthropology and History (ENAH); the National Pedagogic University (UPN); and the National Autonomous University of Mexico (UNAM). UNAM's Center for Research and Educational Services (CISE) deserves credit for networking ethnographers in Mexico, Latin America, and the United States, through the yearly seminars organized with the University of New Mexico. See Bertely and Corenstein, in this volume.

4. When the Master's program in educational research began in 1975, there were no other interdisciplinary graduate programs in educational research in Mexico. Many of the studies reported in this review are master's theses; however, these were more demanding than those usually done in the United States, as they required extensive fieldwork at one site, in-depth analysis, and a written monograph averaging 200 pages. Since possibilities for publication of such studies in Mexico has been very limited, the DIE has issued noncommercial editions of the best work in its series TESIS DIE.

5. Academic exchange with South American researchers was made possible through the International Development Research Center's (Canada) sponsorship of a network between 1980 and 1986 (Red Latinomericana de Investigación Cualitativa de la Realidad Escolar), which held workshops and symposia and published a quarterly, *Dialogando*. Additionally, several U.S. scholars associated with the DIE through Fulbright fellowships during these years came to know and helped disseminate our work. Mary Kay Vaughan (U. of Illinois-Chicago), Bradley Levinson (Indiana University), and Susan Street (now at CIESAS) deserve special mention in this respect.

6. On our methodological discussions of ethnography, see Ezpeleta and Rockwell (1986) and Rockwell (1987a).

7. In Latin America, as in other parts of the world, the term *popular education* originally (19th century) referred to a free, universal, public school system. Many educators formerly involved in non-formal popular education of the 1960s and 1970s, including Freire himself, later influenced or headed reform movements in the public school systems, particularly in Brazil, Chile, Bolivia, Ecuador, and Colombia.

8. I include Foucault—a poststructuralist—since his most influential work at the time (1976), *Discipline and Punish*, was read as an argument for the reproductivist thesis.

With few exceptions (e.g., Jules Henry, Philip Jackson), the works of the ethnographic tradition of the United States and the English New Sociology of Education were not translated into Spanish until the mid-1980s.

9. This history has been well documented by Michael Apple, Henry Giroux, Lois Weis, Philip Wexler, and others. The ethnographic work of Jean Anyon, Hugh Mehan, and Robert Connell, which stressed the socially constructed and differential practices and student careers within schools, was important in countering the determinism—cultural as well as economic—of some early versions of reproduction theory.

10. See particularly Willis (1977); Giroux (1983); Erickson (1987); and Foley (1990). The related theory developed by Ogbu (1987) is discussed by Foley (1991) and Levinson (1992).

11. See reviews on critical ethnography by Simon and Dippo (1986); Anderson (1989, 1994); Levinson (1992); and several chapters in LeCompte, Millroy, and Goetz (1992).

12. See Wexler (1987) and Anyon (1994) for relevant discussions.

13. Some important early references are: Germán Rama (1984); Dermeval Saviani (1984); Juan Carlos Tedesco (1983, 1987); María de Ibarrola and Elsie Rockwell (Eds.) (1985); Felicia Madeira and Guiomar Namo de Mello (Eds.) (1985).

14. Among the scholars who were most influential for our work in education are Carlos Pereyra, José Aricó, Carlos Monsiváis, and Guillermo Bonfil.

15. Unlike the Asian and African regions, Latin America in general had achieved nearly equal school attendance for girls as for boys, even through the secondary level. In Mexico coeducation and the non-religious curriculum have countered the strong gender differentiation and patriarchal relationships found generally in the society. See Levinson (1993) for further discussion of these issues.

16. *Appropriation* is a term widely used in the Marxist tradition by authors such as Leontiev (1981); Heller (1977); and Bakhtin (1981) and taken up by researchers such as Barbara Rogoff (1992) and Roger Chartier (1987). The concept has been increasingly used in the field of education, though often with different meanings.

17. Tadeu da Silva (1988) discusses these alternative explanations.

18. It was recognized, for example, that it would be impossible to achieve full adult literacy through small-scale popular education programs, if the retention rates and quality of formal schooling were not modified to prevent the large-scale production of illiterates. The pedagogical legacy of popular education has been used, however, in the development of innovative programs for formal schooling.

19. See, for example, the collection of papers in Ezpeleta and Furlán (Eds.), (1992).

20. This should not be confused with the "back to basics" trend, which recommends training in functional skills. The idea of "relevant basic knowledge" insists upon comprehension as well as competence and stresses conceptual development in science and social science as well as in language and math. The definition of relevant curricular contents for universal education has been a key point in the debate.

21. In Mexico most of the educational system has been under federal administration since the 1930s. See Vaughan (1982) and Meneses (1986–91) on this history. In 1992 the central government began to decentralize the administration of primary and secondary education, though it still controls funding and establishes a uniform curriculum.

22. I recognize that there are significant differences among the American authors I have cited and that I have oversimplified their theses in order to stress the contrast. Moreover, other American ethnographers, such as George and Louise Spindler and Katherine Anderson-Levitt, have pointed to the effects of social and cultural contexts on schooling.

23. The secondary level (grades 7–9) schools tend to be more homogeneous, for several reasons. See Levinson (1993); Quiroz (1992b).

24. These studies were part of a collective project, "Teaching practice and its institutional context," which I coordinated with Justa Ezpeleta between 1980 and 1985. Ruth Mercado, Etelvina Sandoval, Citlali Aguilar, Concepción Jiménez, and Gerardo López participated in the joint fieldwork, each focusing on different aspects of schooling.

25. Similar conclusions have been reached by Ben Eklof (1990); Deborah Reed-Danahay (1987); and Mary K. Vaughan (1993).

26. Important discussions of the culture conflict thesis were expressed by several authors, for example, Ogbu (1981); Atkinson, Delamont, and Hammersley (1988); Foley (1991). For discussion by DIE researchers, see Paradise (1990); Rockwell (1995b).

27. This of course does not mean that there are no problems with gender and race in Latin America, though their manifestation in schooling may be different from what occurs in the English-speaking world. For a recent analysis of the implications of race in Mexico, see Lomnitz-Adler (1992). Gender is now becoming an important focus for educational researchers, such as Gabriela Delgado Ballesteros and Etelvina Sandoval, in other Mexican institutions.

28. Examples of some early classifications are found in Ogbu (1981) and Jacob (1987) and are discussed by Atkinson, Delamont, and Hammersley (1988). The more recent classification is well documented in LeCompte, Millroy, and Goetz (Eds.) (1992). See also Anderson (1994) and Anyon (1994).

29. Most ethnographers at the DIE have also been involved over the years in a number of large-scale projects for developing, in many cases with participatory methods, alternative educational programs, textbooks, and teacher training materials. They have also participated in and influenced the public debate on educational policy. These actions have both influenced and been influenced by ethnographic research, but are separate tasks.

30. See Macías (1990) on the Mexican primary school curriculum.

31. An important recent study in this sense was coordinated by Sylvia Schmelkes (1993), and ongoing quantitative analysis in the Center for Educational Studies (CEE) shows tendencies reversing previous gains in the poorer regions of the country.

32. For example: Bourdieu, Foucault, Gramsci, Bakhtin and Vygotsky.

33. There are too many important references to list, but I would mention as examples of the range of interests, the work of Katie Anderson-Levitt, Stephen Ball, Michael Billig, Roger Chartier, Robert Connell, Derek Edwards, Frederick Erickson, Douglas Foley, Shirley Heath, Dorothy Holland, Jean Lave, Neil Mercer, Barbara Rogoff, James Scott, Brian Street, James Wertsch, Peter Woods.

34. This is also a growing set, and includes Gary Anderson, Marcia Farr, Mark Ginsburg, Bradley Levinson, José Macías, Chris Martin, among others.

References

Aguilar, C. (1991). El trabajo de los maestros: Una construcción cotidiana. (Tesis DIE 5). México, D.F.: Departamento de Investigaciones Educativas, Centro de Investigación y de Estudios Avanzados del Instituto Politécnico Nacional (in future references, DIE-CINVESTAV-IPN).

Aguilar, C. (1995). El trabajo extra-enseñanza y la construcción social de la escuela. In E. Rockwell (Ed.), La escuela cotidiana. México, D.F.: Fondo de Cultura Económica.

Aguirre Beltrán, G. (1953). Teoría y práctica de la educación indígena. México, D.F.: Instituto Nacional Indigenista.

Althusser, L. (1979). La filosofía como arma de la revolución. México, D.F.: Pasado y Presente.

Anderson, G.L. (1989). Critical ethnography in education: Origins, current status and new directions. Review of Educational Research, 59(3), 249–270.

Anderson, G.L. (1994). The cultural politics of qualitative research in education: Confirming and contesting the canon. Educational Theory, 44(2), 225–237.

Anderson-Levitt, K. (1987). Cultural knowledge for teaching first grade: An example from France. In G. Spindler and L. Spindler (Eds.), Interpretive ethnography of education at home and abroad. Mahwah, NJ: Lawrence Erlbaum.

Ansión, J. (1990). La escuela y la comunidad campesina. Lima, Peru: Proyecto escuela, ecología y comunidad campesina.

Anyon, J. (1994). The retreat of Marxism and socialist feminism: Postmodern and poststructural theories in education. Curriculum Inquiry, 24(2), 115–133.

Apple, M. (1983). Ideology and practice in schooling: A political and conceptual introduction. In M. Apple and L. Weis (Eds.), Ideology and practice in schooling. Philadelphia: Temple University Press.

Apple, M. (1986). *Teachers and texts.* New York: Routledge and Kegan Paul.

Aricó, J. (1982). *Marx y América Latina.* México, D.F.: Alianza.

Atkinson, P., Delamont, S., and Hammersley, M. (1988). Qualitative research traditions: A British response to Jacob. *Review of Educational Research,* 58(2), 231–250.

Bakhtin, M. (1981). *The Dialogic Imagination.* Essays edited by M. Holquist. Austin: University of Texas Press.

Bárcenas, M.G. (1982). *La educación preescolar como instancia socializadora: Institución y práctica pedagógica.* Unpublished master's thesis, DIE-CINVESTAV-IPN, México, D.F., México

Baudelot, C. and Establet, R. (1975). *La escuela capitalista.* México, D.F.: Siglo XXI.

Berger, P. and Luckmann, T. (1967). *The Social Construction of Reality.* New York: Doubleday.

Bertely, M. (1985). *La realidad emocional y sensual en la familia y el jardín de niños.* Unpublished master's thesis, DIE-CINVESTAV-IPN, México, D.F., México.

Bertely, M. (1992). Adaptaciones docentes en una comunidad mazahua. *Nueva Antropología,* 42, 101–120.

Bonfil, G. (1987). *México profundo: Una civilización negada.* México, D.F.: Centro de Investigación y Estudios Superiores de Antropología Social y Secretaría de Educación Pública.

Bourdieu, P. and Passeron, J.C., (1977). *La reproducción: Elementos para una teoría del sistema de enseñanza.* Barcelona: Laia.

Bowles, S. and Gintis, H. (1976). *Schooling in capitalist America.* New York: Basic Books.

Broccoli, A. (1977). *Antonio Gramsci y la educación como hegemonía.* México, D.F.: Nueva Imagen.

Candela, A. (1989). *La necesidad de entender, explicar y argumentar: Los alumnos de primaria en la actividad experimental.* Unpublished master's thesis, DIE-CINVESTAV-IPN, México, D.F., México.

Candela, A. (1990). Investigación etnográfica en el aula: El razonamiento de los alumnos en una clase de Ciencias Naturales en la escuela primaria. *Investigación en la Escuela (Sevilla),* 11, 13–23.

Candela, A. (1991). Argumentación y conocimiento científico escolar. *Infancia y Aprendizaje (Madrid),* 55, 13–28.

Candela, A. (1993). La construcción discursiva de la ciencia en el aula. *Investigación en la Escuela (Sevilla),* 21(7), 11–26

Candela, A. (1994). La enseñanza de la ciencia y el análisis del discurso. In M. Rueda Beltrán, G. Delgado Ballesteros, and Z. Jacobo (Eds.), *La etnografía en educación: panorama, prácticas y problemas.* (pp. 149–169) México, D.F.: UNA México and University of New Mexico.

Candela, A. (1995a). La transformación del conocimiento científico en el aula. In E. Rockwell (Ed.), *La escuela cotidiana.* Mexico, D.F.: Fondo de Cultura Económica.

Candela, A. (1995b). El discurso en el aula: La construcción de un contexto argumentativo. *Infancia y Aprendizaje (Madrid).* 59, 6–13 (theme issue edited by C. Coll).

Candela, A. and Rockwell, E. (1991). Construcción social del conocimiento en el aula: Un enfoque etnográfico. *Infancia y Aprendizaje,* 55, 5–12.

Carvajal, A. (1988). *El margen de acción y las relaciones sociales entre los maestros: Un estudio etnográfico en la escuela primaria.* Unpublished master's thesis, DIE-CINVESTAV-IPN, México, D.F., México.

Cerdá, A.M. (1989). *Normas, principios y valores en la interacción maestro-alumnos: El caso del Colegio de Ciencias y Humanidades.* Unpublished master's thesis, DIE-CINVESTAV-IPN, México, D.F., México.

Chartier, R. (1987). Introduction. In R. Chartier (Ed.), *The culture of print.* Princeton, NJ: Princeton University Press.

Chevallard, I. (1984). *La transposición didactique.* Paris: La Pensée Sauvage.

Connell, R.W. (1983). *Which way is up? Essays on class, sex and culture.* London: Allen and Unwin.

Díaz, G. (1992). *El saber técnico en la enseñanza agropecuaria.* Unpublished master's thesis, DIE-CINVESTAV-IPN, México, D.F., México.

Díaz, G. (1993). El saber técnico en la enseñanza agropecuaria. *Revista Latinoamericana de Estudios Educativos (Mexico)*, 22(2), 121–134.

Edwards, D. and Mercer, N. (1987). *Common knowledge: The development of understanding in the classroom.* London: Routledge and Kegan Paul.

Edwards, V. (1987). *Los sujetos y la construcción social del conocimiento en primaria.* Unpublished master's thesis, DIE-CINVESTAV-IPN, México, D.F., México. (Also published in Santiago, Chile: Programa Interdisciplinario de Investigación Educativa).

Edwards, V. (1995). Las formas del conocimiento en el aula. In E. Rockwell (Ed.), *La escuela cotidiana.* Mexico: Fondo de Cultura Económica.

Eklof, B. (1990). Peasants and schools. In B. Eklof and S.P. Frank (Eds.), *The world of the Russian peasant* (pp. 115–132). Boston: Unwin and Hyman.

Erickson, F. (1987). Transformation and school success: The politics and culture of educational achievement. *Anthropology and Education Quarterly*, 18(4), 335–356.

Everhart, R. (1983). *Reading, writing and resistance: Adolescence and labor in a junior high school.* London: Routledge and Kegan Paul.

Ezpeleta, J. (1986). *La escuela y los maestros: Entre el supuesto y la deducción.* (Cuaderno de Investigación 20). México, D.F.: DIE-CINVESTAV-IPN.

Ezpeleta, J. (1989). *Escuelas y Maestros: Condiciones del trabajo docente en Argentina.* Santiago, Chile: OREALC-UNESCO.

Ezpeleta, J. (1992a). El Consejo Técnico: Eficacia pedagógica y estructura de poder en la escuela primaria mexicana. *Revista Latinoamericana de Estudios Educativos (Mexico)*, 4(4), 56–74.

Ezpeleta, J. (1992b). El trabajo docente y sus condiciones invisibles. *Nueva Antropología, 42*, 27–42.

Ezpeleta, J. and Furlán, A. (Eds.). (1992). *La gestión pedagógica de la escuela.* Santiago de Chile: OREALC-UNESCO.

Ezpeleta, J. and Rockwell, E. (1983). Escuela y clases subalternas. *Cuadernos Políticos (Mexico)*, 37, 70–80.

Ezpeleta, J. and Rockwell, E. (1986). *Pesquisa participante.* São Paulo, Brazil: Cortez Editora Autores Asociados.

Foley, D. (1990). *Learning capitalist culture: Deep in the heart of Tejas.* Philadelphia: University of Pennsylvania Press.

Foley, D. (1991). Reconsidering anthropological explanations of ethnic school failure. *Anthropology and Education Quarterly*, 22(1), 60–86.

Foucault, M. (1976). *Vigilar y castigar.* México, D.F.: Siglo XXI.

Freire, P. (1972). *Pedagogy of the oppressed.* Harmondsworth, U.K.: Penguin.

Fuente, Julio de la. (1964). *Educación, antropología y desarrollo de la comunidad.* México, D.F.: Instituto Nacional Indigenista.

Galeana, R. (1990). *El trabajo infantil y adolescente como instancia socializadora y formadora en, para y por la vida.* Unfinished master's thesis, DIE-CINVESTAV-IPN, México, D.F., México.

Galván, L. (1995) *El trabajo conjunto de padres y maestros relativo al salón de clase: Estudio etnográfico.* Unpublished master's thesis. México, D.F.: DIE-CINVESTAV-IPN.

Gálvez, G., Paradise, R., Rockwell, E., and Sobrecasas, S. (1980). *El uso del tiempo y los libros de texto en primaria.* (Cuadernos de Investigación Educativa 1). México, D.F.: DIE-CINVESTAV-IPN.

García, C. (1988). La escuela DPR 160720-5: Crónica de un desentrañamiento. Unpublished master's thesis, DIE-CINVESTAV-IPN, México, D.F., México.

Geertz, C. (1983). *Local knowledge.* New York. Basic Books.

Giddens, A. (1984). *The constitution of society.* Berkeley: University of California Press.

Giroux, H. (1983). Theories of reproduction and resistance in the new sociology of education. *Harvard Educational Review*, 53(3), 257–280.

Gramsci, A. (1975). *Cuadernos de la Carcel*, 6 volumes. México, D.F.: Juan Pablos.

Granja, J. (1988). *Los procesos de legitimación de los aprendizajes escolares: Rituales normativos, saberes legítimos y sujetos constituidos.* Unpublished master's thesis, DIE-CINVESTAV-IPN, México, D.F.: México.

Heller, A. (1977). *Sociología de la vida cotidiana*. Barcelona: Península.

Henry, J. (1963). *Culture against man*. New York: Vintage.

Hernández, J. (1989). *La enseñanza de las ciencias naturales: Entre una redescripción de la experiencia cotidiana y una resignificación del conocimiento escolar*. Unpublished master's thesis, DIE-CINVESTAV-IPN, México, D.F., México.

Holland, D. and Eisenhart, M. (1990). *Educated in romance: Women, achievement and college culture*. Chicago: University of Chicago Press.

Holloway, J. (1980). El estado y la lucha cotidiana. *Cuadernos Políticos*, 24: 8–28.

Ibarrola, M. and Rockwell, E. (Eds.). (1985). *Educación y clases populares en América Latina*. México, D.F.: DIE-CINVESTAV-IPN.

Jackson, P.W. (1968). *Life in classrooms*. New York: Holt, Rinehart & Winston.

Jacob, E. (1987). Qualitative research traditions: A review. *Review of Educational Research*, 57(1), 1–50.

Jiménez, C. (1982). *Cómo participan los maestros en los proyectos de reforma educativa*. Paper presented at the Forum of the Movimiento Revolucionario del Magisterio, Chihuahua, México.

Labarca, G. (1977). *La educación burguesa*. México, D.F.: Nueva Imagen.

LeCompte, M., Millroy, W., and Goetz, J. (Eds.). (1992). *The handbook of qualitative research in education*. San Diego, CA: Academic Press.

Leontiev, A.N. (1981). *Problems in the development of mind*. Moscow: Progress Publishers.

Levinson, B. (1992). Ogbu's anthropology and the critical ethnography of education: A reciprocal interrogation. *Qualitative Studies in Education*, 5(3), 205–225.

Levinson, B. (1993). *Todos somos iguales: Cultural production and social difference at a Mexican secondary school*. Unpublished doctoral dissertation, University of North Carolina, Chapel Hill.

Levy, C. (1990). *El saber técnico en las escuelas agropecuarias*. Unpublished master's thesis, DIE-CINVESTAV-IPN, México, D.F., México.

Lomnitz-Adler, C. (1992). *Exits from the labyrinth: Culture and ideology in the Mexican national space*. Berkeley, CA: University of California Press.

Luna, M.E. (1993). *Los alumnos como referente básico de la organización cotidiana del trabajo del aula*. Unpublished master's thesis, DIE-CINVESTAV-IPN, México, D.F., México.

Luna, M.E. (1994). Los maestros y la construcción del expediente cotidiano. *Investigación en la Escuela (Seville)*, 22, 105–114.

Macías, J. (1990). Scholastic antecedents of immigrant students: Schooling in a Mexican immigrant-sending community. *Anthropology and Education Quarterly*, 21(4), 291–318.

Madeira, F. and Namo de Mello, G. (Eds.). (1985). *Educaçao na América Latina, Os modelos teóricos e realidade social*. São Paulo, Brazil: Cortez Editora y Editora Autores Asociados.

Mariategui, J.C. (1979). *Siete ensayos de interpretación de la realidad peruana*. México, D.F.: ERA (originally published in 1928).

Medina, P. (1992). *Ser maestra, permanecer en la escuela: La tradición en una escuela urbana*. Unpublished master's thesis, DIE-CINVESTAV-IPN, México, D.F., México.

Medina, P. (1993). Ser maestra, permanecer en la escuela: Las estrategias de acción cotidiana. In M. Rueda Beltrán, G. Delgado Ballesteros, and Z. Jacobo. (Eds.), *La etnografía en educación: Panorama, prácticas y problemas*. (pp. 389–435) México, D.F.: UNAMéxico and University of New Mexico.

Meneses, E. (1986–1991). *Tendencias Educativas Oficiales en México*, 4 volumes. México, D.F.: Centro de Estudios Educativos.

Mercado, R. (1986a). Una reflexión crítica sobre la noción de "escuela-comunidad." In E. Rockwell and R. Mercado (Eds.), *La escuela: Lugar del trabajo docente* (pp. 47–55). México, D.F.: DIE-CINVESTAV-IPN.

Mercado, R. (1986b). El trabajo cotidiano del maestro en la escuela primaria. In E. Rockwell and R. Mercado (Eds.), *La escuela, lugar del trabajo docente* (pp.55–61). México, D.F.: DIE-CINVESTAV-IPN.

Mercado, R. (1987). *La escuela primaria gratuita, una lucha popular cotidiana*. Unpublished master's thesis, DIE-CINVESTAV-IPN, México, D.F., México.

Mercado, R. (1991). Los saberes docentes en el trabajo cotidiano de los maestros. *Infancia y Aprendizaje (Madrid)*, 55, 59–72.

Mercado, R. (1992). La escuela en la memoria histórica local: Una construcción colectiva. *Nueva Antropología (México)*, 42, 73–87.

Mercado, R. (1994). *Saberes* and social voices in teaching. In A. Alvarez and P. del Rio (Eds.), *Education as cultural construction* (pp. 112–139). Madrid: Infancia y Aprendizaje Foundation.

Mercado, R. (1995). Procesos de negociación local para la operación de las escuelas. In E. Rockwell (Ed.), *La escuela cotidiana*. México, D.F.: Fondo de Cultura Económica.

Modiano, N. (1974). *La educación indígena en Los Altos de Chiapas*. México, D.F.: Instituto Nacional Indigenista.

Monsiváis, C. (1987). *Entrada libre*. México, D.F.: ERA.

Newman, D., Griffin, P., and Cole, M. (1989). *The construction zone: Working for cognitive change in school*. New York: Cambridge University Press.

Ogbu, J. (1981). School ethnography: A multilevel approach. *Anthropology and Education Quarterly*, 12(1), 3–29.

Ogbu, J. (1987). Variability in minority school performance: A problem in search of an explanation. *Anthropology and Education Quarterly*, 18(4), 312–334.

Olivera, M. (1984). *De escuela rural a escuela urbana: La modernización de la primaria en San Pedro Tultepec*. Unpublished master's thesis, DIE-CINVESTAV-IPN, México, D.F., México.

Ortiz, J. (1994). *Ritos de pasage en la matemática universitaria*. Unpublished master's thesis, DIE-CINVESTAV-IPN, México, D.F., México.

Paiva, V. (1982). Populismo católico y educación. *Cuadernos Políticos (México)*, 34, 23–39.

Paradise, R. (1979). *Socialización para el trabajo: La interacción maestro-alumnos en la escuela primaria*. Unpublished master's thesis, DIE-CINVESTAV-IPN, México, D.F., México.

Paradise, R. (1985). Un análisis psico-social de la motivación y participación emocional en un caso de aprendizaje individual. *Revista Latinoamericana de Estudios Educativos (México)*, 15(1), 83–93.

Paradise, R. (1987). *Learning through social interaction: The experience and development of the Mazahua self in the context of the market*. Unpublished doctoral dissertation, University of Pennsylvania, Philadelphia.

Paradise, R. (1990). *Pasos hacia la comunicación intercultural: Las adaptaciones de niños Mazahuas y sus maestros en la práctica dentro del aula*. Paper presented at the Seminar on Culture and Education. Consejo Nacional para la Cultura y las Artes, México, D.F., November.

Paradise, R. (1991). El conocimiento cultural en el salón de clases: Niños indígenas y su orientación hacia la observación. *Infancia y Aprendizaje*, 55, 83–85.

Paradise, R. (1994a). Interactional style and nonverbal meaning: Mazahua children learning how to be separate-but-together. *Anthropology and Education Quarterly*, 25(2), 1–17.

Paradise, R. (1994b). The autonomous behavior of indigenous students in classroom activities. In A. Alvarez and P. del Río (Eds.), *Education as cultural construction*. Madrid: Infancia y Aprendizaje Foundation.

Paradise, R. (1994c). Spontaneous cultural compatibility: Mazahua students and their teachers constructing trusting relations. *Peabody Journal of Education*, 69(2), 60–70.

Pastrana, L. (1996). *Organización dirección y gestión en la escuela primaria*. Unpublished master's thesis, DIE-CINVESTAV-IPN, México, D.F., México.

Pereyra, C. (1984). *El sujeto de la historia*. Madrid: Alianza.

Ponce, A. (1974). *Educación y lucha de clases*. México, D.F.: Cartago.

Quiroz, R. (1985). El maestro y la legitimación del conocimiento. In E. Rockwell (Ed.), *Ser maestro: Estudios sobre el trabajo docente* (pp. 27–37) México: El Caballito.

Quiroz, R. (1988). El maestro y el saber especializado. *DIDAC (México)*, 12, 7–15.

Quiroz, R. (1991). Obstáculos para la apropiación de los contenidos académicos en la escuela secundaria. *Infancia y Aprendizaje (Madrid)*, 55, 45–58.

Quiroz, R. (1992a). El tiempo cotidiano en la escuela secundaria. *Nueva Antropología (México)*, 42, 89–100.

Quiroz, R. (1992b). La gestión pedagógica del currículo formal en las escuelas secundarias. In J. Ezpeleta and A. Furlán (Eds.), *La gestión pedagógica de la escuela* (pp. 312–224). Santiago, Chile: OREALC-UNESCO.

Rama, G. (1984). Educación y democracia. In R. Nassis, J.C. Tedesco, and G. Rama (Eds.), *El sistema educativo en América Latina* (pp. 4–21). Buenos Aires: Kapelusz-UNESCO.

Ramírez, B. (1980). La enseñanza diferencial de la lectura y su relación con factores socioeconómicos. In B. Calvo (Ed.), *Simposio sobre el magisterio nacional.* México, D.F.: Centro de Investigación y de Estudios Avanzados de Antropología Social.

Reed-Danahay, D. (1987). Farm children at school: Educational strategies in rural France. *Anthropological Quarterly,* 60(2), 83–89.

Remedi, E. (1992). Desorden, sentidos y signos de la gestión: Voces de los sujetos. In J. Ezpeleta and A. Furlán (Eds.), *La gestión pedagógica de la escuela* (pp.175–201). Santiago, Chile: OREALC-UNESCO.

Remedi, E. (1993). *Profesión docente e identidades culturales: Trayectorias y saberes movilizados.* Paper presented at the XIII International Congress of Anthropological and Ethnological Sciences, México, D.F., México.

Robles, A. (1994). *Diálogo cultural: Tiempo Mazahua en un jardín de niños rurales.* Unpublished master's thesis, DIE-CINVESTAV-IPN, México, D.F., México.

Rockwell, E. (1982a). Los usos escolares de la lengua escrita. In E. Ferreiro and M. Gómez-Palacio (Eds.), *Nuevas perspectivas sobre los procesos de la lectura y la escritura* (pp. 296–320), México, D.F.: Siglo XXI.

Rockwell, E. (1982b). *De huellas, bardas y veredas: Una historia cotidiana en la escuela.* (Cuadernos de Investigación 4). México, D.F.: DIE-CINVESTAV-IPN.

Rockwell, E. (1986a). Cómo observar la reproducción. *Revista Colombiana de Educación (Bogotá),* 17, 109–125.

Rockwell, E. (1986b). La relevancia de la etnografía para la transformación de las escuelas. In *Memorias del Tercer Seminario de Investigación Educativa.* Bogotá, Colombia: ICPES-Centro de Investigación de la Universidad Pedagógica.

Rockwell, E. (1987a). *Reflexiones sobre el proceso etnográfico.* (DIE research monograph). México, D.F.: DIE-CINVESTAV-IPN.

Rockwell, E. (1987b). *Repensando institución: Una lectura de Gramsci.* (DIE research monograph). México, D.F.: DIE-CINVESTAV-IPN.

Rockwell, E. (1988). Procesos cotidianos, lenguaje y conocimiento en el aula. *Colección Pedagógica Universitaria (Jalapa),* 15, 25–40.

Rockwell, E. (1991). Palabra escrita, interpretación oral: Los libros de texto en la clase. *Infancia y Aprendizaje (Madrid),* 55, 29–43.

Rockwell, E. (1992a). Los usos magisteriales de la lengua escrita. *Nueva Antropología (México),* 42, 43–56.

Rockwell, E. (1992b). Tales from Xaltipan: Documenting orality and literacy in rural México. *Cultural Dynamics,* 5(2), 156–175.

Rockwell, E. (1994). Schools of the revolution: Enacting and contesting state forms in Tlaxcala (1910–1930). In G. Joseph and D. Nugent (Eds.), *Everyday forms of state formation: Revolution and the negotiation of rule in modern Mexico* (pp. 170–208). Durham, NC: Duke University Press.

Rockwell, E. (1995a). La dinámica cultural en la escuela. In A. Alvarez and P. del Río (Eds.). *Hacia un curriculum cultural: un enfogue Vygotskiano* (pp. 101–132), Madrid: Infancia y aprendizaje.

Rockwell, E. (Ed.). (1995b). *La escuela cotidiana.* México, D.F.: Fondo de Cultura Económica.

Rockwell, E. (1996). Keys to Appropriation: Revolution and Rural Schools. In B. Levinson and D. Foley (Eds.), *The cultural production of the educated person: Critical ethnographies of schooling and local practice* (pp. 301–324). Albany: State University of New York Press.

Rockwell, E. and Ezpeleta, J. (1985). La escuela: Relato de un proceso de construcción inconcluso. In F. Madeira and G. Namo de Mello (Eds.), *Educaçao na América Latina, Os modelos teóricos e a realidade social* (pp. 151–172). São Paulo, Brazil: Cortez Editora y Editora Autores Asociados.

Rockwell, E. and Gálvez, G. (1982). Formas de transmisión del conocimiento científico: Un análisis cualitativo. *Educación (México),* 42, 97–139.

Rockwell, E. and Mercado, R. (1988). La práctica docente y la formación de maestros. *Investigación en la Escuela (Seville),* 4, 65–78.

Rogoff, B. (1992). *Observing socio-cultural activity on three plains: Participatory appropriation, guided participation, apprenticeship.* Paper presented at the Conference for Socio-Cultural Research, Madrid, Spain.

Sáenz, M. (1966). *Carapan.* Morelia, México: Gobierno del Estado de Michoacán.

Sandoval, E. (1987). *Los maestros y su sindicato: Relaciones y procesos cotidianos.* Unpublished master's thesis, DIE-CINVESTAV-IPN, México, D.F., México.

Sandoval, E. (1988). La construcción cotidiana de la vida sindical de los maestros de primaria. *Revista Latinoamericana de Estudios Educativos,* 8(1), 45–58.

Sandoval, E. (1995). Relaciones y saberes docentes en los cursos de actualización. In E. Rockwell (Ed.), *La escuela cotidiana.* México, D.F.: Fondo de Cultura Económica.

Saviani, D. (1984). Las teorías de la educación y el problema de la marginalidad en América Latina. *Revista Colombiana de Educación,* 13, 9–33.

Schensul, J.J. (1976). *Enseñanza para el futuro y el futuro de la enseñanza.* México, D.F.: Secretaría de Educación Pública.

Schmelkes, S. (1993). *La calidad de la educación primaria: Estudio en cinco regiones del estado de Puebla.* México, D.F.: Centro de Estudios Educativos.

Schütz, A. (1970). *On phenomenology and social relations.* Chicago: University of Chicago Press.

Simon, R. and Dippo, D. (1986). On critical ethnographic work. *Anthropology and Education Quarterly,* 17(4), 195–202.

Spindler, G. and L. Spindler (Eds.). (1987). *Interpretive Ethnography of Education at Home and Abroad.* Mahwah, NJ: Lawrence Erlbaum.

Spitzer, T. (1990). *El proceso de socialización del estudiante en la Universidad Autónoma de Chapingo: Hacia la internalización de un rol profesional.* Unpublished master's thesis, DIE-CINVESTAV-IPN, México, D.F., México.

Taboada, E. (1996). Las ceremonias cívicas: ¿Un curriculum paralelo de la enseñanza de la historia? (Cuadernos de Investigacion). México, D.F.: DIE-CINVESTAV-IPN.

Tadeu da Silva, T. (1988). Distribution of school knowledge and social reproduction in a Brazilian urban setting. *British Journal of Sociology of Education,* 9(1), 55–79.

Talavera, M.L. (1992). *Construcción y circulación de recursos docentes en primer grado: Estudio etnográfico.* Unpublished master's thesis, DIE-CINVESTAV-IPN, México, D.F., México.

Tedesco, J.C. (1983). Crítica al reproductivismo educativo.*Cuadernos Políticos (México),* 37, 59–69.

Tedesco, J.C. (1987). Paradigms of socioeducational research in Latin America. *Comparative Education Review,* 31(4), 509–532.

Thompson, E.P. (1966). *The making of the English working class.* New York: Random House.

Vasconi, T. (1973). Ideología, lucha de clases y aparatos educativos en el desarrollo de America Latina. *Cuadernos de Educación (Caracas),* 4, 12–13.

Vaughan, M.K. (1982). *The state, education, and social class in Mexico, 1889–1928.* De Kalb, IL: Northern Illinois University Press.

Vaughan, M.K. (1993). The construction of patriotic festivals in central Puebla (1900–1946). In W. Beezley, C.E. Martin, and W.E. French (Eds.), *Rituals of rule, rituals of resistance* (pp. 101–130). Wilmington, DE: Scholarly Resources.

Weis, L. (1984). *Between two worlds.* London: Routledge and Kegan Paul.

Weiss, E. (1992). Saber técnico y saber extraescolar campesino. In M.A. Gallart (Ed.), *Educación y Trabajo,* Vol. 2 (pp. 275–292). Buenos Aires: CIID-CENEP.

Wertsch, J. (1991). *Voices of the mind.* Cambridge, MA: Harvard University Press.

Wexler, P., Whitson, T., and Moskowitz, E.J. (1981). Deschooling by default: The changing social functions of public schooling. *Interchange,* 12(2–3), 133–150.

Wexler, P. (1987). *Social analysis of education.* London: Routledge and Kegan Paul.

Williams, R. (1981). *The Sociology of Culture.* New York: Schocken Books.

Willis, P. (1977). *Learning to labour.* London: Saxon House.

Willis, P. (1981). Cultural production is different from cultural reproduction is different from social reproduction is different from reproduction. *Interchange,* 12(2–3), 48–67.

Willis, P. (1990). Forward. In D.E. Foley, *Learning capitalist culture: Deep in the heart of Tejas* (pp. vii–xii). Philadelphia: University of Pennsylvania Press.

Woods, P. (1994). Teachers under siege: Resistance and appropriation in English primary schools. *Anthropology and Education Quarterly,* 25(3), 250–265.

Chapter Two
Appropriating Ethnography for Research in Education
Reflections on Recent Efforts in Argentina and Chile

Graciela Batallán

For anthropologists the term *ethnography* means both process and product; that is, a specific methodological approach and, originally, a descriptive monograph or, following Geertz (1987), a "thick" description. From his interpretivist perspective on the study of culture, Geertz describes how the true ethnographic account is constructed. First there is direct documentation of the processes that characterize specific "ways of life" whose genesis is difficult to capture through an objectifying methodological approach. Moreover, this documentation's texture or "thickness" is recognizable as ethnographic to the extent that theory is sustained at the level of the conceptual world "our subjects inhabit" (Geertz, 1987). Finally, an ethnographic study should reflect the discipline's cultural approach and analysis.

This holistic tradition, along with the problematic issues it raises for anthropology, has been integrated into Malinowski's (1986) methodological approach, which posits that understanding exotic worlds, alien to the scientist's Western world, is possible only through comprehending the modes of speech that express the meaning of the behavior being observed. Since it is not feasible for outsiders to utilize their own systems of logic to classify the rules governing a different way of life, becoming a participant observer is one way to understand the logic implicit in subjects' actions. The researcher who enters into dialogue and has long-term contacts with subjects may be able to find the keys to the conceptual world, which provides a rationale for the actions observed.

Thus anthropology, with its corpus of ethnographic reconstructions, has sought to know and make known other social worlds through understanding them. Avoiding value judgments, anthropology has created the concept of cultural relativism, making peoples—"the other"—worthy of being perceived in ways that preclude condemnation and discrimination.

In recent years the connection between the traditional empirical account and methodological issues has become more complex. However, anthropology's unique mission—to ensure the production of reliable primary-source "documents"—still exists. Therefore field work needs to be done, and the discipline's methods and techniques need to be employed (Schütz, 1974). Anthropology, in spite of controversy, retains its classic style. It has produced descriptive reconstructions of exotic realities that were addressed only in limited ways by other disciplines. With its own particular methods and goals, anthropology diverges from the predictive and social engineering emphasis of mainstream social science, which focuses on analyzing social problems recognized as such officially and whose conclusions are expected to lead to workable policies.

Because of its concern with validating the vision of the subjects, anthropology finds itself—explicitly or implicitly—with a viewpoint diametrically opposite that now dominating research on contemporary society, a fact which may well explain why anthropologists have until fairly recently been excluded from or uninterested in debating issues of method with the hegemonic paradigm (Rockwell, 1987). Dialogue with other disciplines on questions of theory is hindered also by the form of ethnographic writing, with its resemblance to the story, the chronicle, or the essay.

Indeed, anthropologists rarely participate in epistemological debates taking place outside their field. When anthropology is brought into the general discussion, it is not because members of the anthropological community are raising questions, but rather it is an effort to argue against methodological monism.

Anthropology and the Study of Schooling in Latin America

If we accept the above brief characterization of the current state of ethnography and the social sciences, the idea of anthropology entering the terrain of formal education appears somewhat peculiar. Few institutions seem to belong to the established social order as much as the school. Its administration and bureaucratic structure are totally devoid of exoticism. Seemingly, there is nothing easier to approach through traditional social science methods than the school.

In Latin America ethnography was until quite recently unrecognized (especially in the field of educational research), or scorned as mere fad or the "latest intellectual import" (García Huidobro, 1984). Mexico was a notable exception, since educational ethnography there already had a theoretical apparatus independent of work done in North America.

It is no mystery why the ethnographic perspective should have caused such uneasiness in Argentina and Chile, where academic opinion had been firmly fixed in an environment almost totally hegemonized by "quantitative" sociology and to some extent by the tradition of qualitative sociology. The latter, although taking note of cultural differences, remained within the traditional methodological canons, especially in regard to accepted criteria of representativeness and validity.

We can presume that the increasing acceptance of anthropological research in formal education has not come about only because of a recognition that a different perspective and a different way of posing questions might lead to a better understanding of schools. Rather, ethnography has been introduced primarily because of the continuing crisis in education— a crisis that the instrumental predictions of traditional educational research have not resolved.

Thus in recent years a dialogue with ethnography became possible when an acceptance of the gravity of the educational crisis (mainly for social sectors with limited resources in basic education) led experts to acknowledge the emergence of a "new paradigm" for research in education (Tedesco, 1987). Such a paradigm would combine Latin American contributions in popular education and variants on North American symbolic interactionism, both of which contained elements of an ethnographic approach to analyzing classroom relationships.[1]

Acknowledging the ethnographic approach made it possible to set aside rigid models of social reproduction. There was also a growing interest in foci that were "more processual and grasped the complexity of the forces at work and the role played by people in relation to those forces [of social reproduction]" (Tedesco, 1987, p. 131). This shift was significant, since up until the early 1980s studies of children of the poorer classes had concluded that low achievement, poor attendance, and lack of integration into the educational system were the result of conditions outside the school, primarily those of an economic nature. The psychological and cultural effects of these conditions, manifested in the behavior of pupils and their parents, were thought to make the schools' efforts futile.

The hypothesis that school failure could also be explained by relationships and behaviors within the school setting led to shifting the emphasis to the connection between school problems and the quality of education, as could be seen by educational reforms undertaken in some countries. However, focusing on the need to improve the quality of education did not bring into question the basic conceptualizations around which formal learning is structured: conceptualizations of what is traditionally considered "knowledge" by the school, the complex ways that students appropriate that knowledge, how the teacher's role is defined, and so on.

Academic thinking in Latin America reflects the shift in educational concerns outlined above. In 1988 a survey of trends in Latin American educational research noted that in the previous ten years the percentage of studies using qualitative methodology had increased from 10 percent to 43.6 percent. Also, a significant increase in the ratio of theoretical studies to empirical ones (18.5 percent to 38.4 percent) was developing into the beginnings of a regional school of thought on education (García Huidobro et al., 1988).

A First Generation of Latin American Educational Ethnography

Before examining how it is now being utilized, we must trace Latin American ethnographic research in education back to its beginnings. The initial orientation came from the influential studies done by Elsie Rockwell and her associates at the Department of Educational Research (DIE) of Mexico's Polytechnic University. Subsequent branching out into interdisciplinary research was made possible by the formation of the Latin American Network of Qualitative Research on Schools (RINCUARE). Sponsored by the Canadian International Center for Research and Development, RINCUARE was created to foster continuing interchanges among researchers and research teams trained at the 1980 Seminar on Ethnography and Education held in Austin, Texas, and Mexico City.[2]

In her approach to "qualitative" research in education Rockwell has been strongly influenced by the writings of Clifford Geertz. She has focused on coordinating theory and practice so that neither operates in isolation nor acts to neutralize the other. Fieldwork methods are consistent with epistemological principles and theoretical concepts. The holistic tradition of classical anthropology is brought to the school setting with the premise that "documenting the undocumented" could reveal the contents of education's "black box," inside of which are hidden complex processes that play a significant role in teaching-learning interactions and encompass more than the strictly pedagogical.

According to Rockwell, reconstructing the complex configuration of the day-to-day world of school within its local contexts could also make it possible to define the limits of effective state participation in education (Rockwell and Ezpeleta, 1983). By looking at the school from "below," the ethnographic approach could change significantly the evaluative perspective inherent in the standards of traditional pedagogy and thus make an important contribution to the field of education.

By answering seemingly simple questions such as, What is a school? and What goes on there?, ethnography at its descriptive level penetrates deeply into the school, untangling the web of relationships that make this institution a special world, far more intricate than would appear when viewed from above.

The approach developed by Rockwell and her research team was based on the holistic tradition of functionalist cultural anthropology reexamined from a theoretical point of view, and it included a reevaluation of Marxist structural theses of schooling. Rockwell's methodological approach embraces a holistic perspective that aims to capture processes rather than behaviors and to regard them as constituent elements of established structures of meaning (Geertz, 1987) or historical sedimentations (Gramsci, 1973). In outlining a reexamination of the concept of culture, Rockwell (1980b) interrogates the discipline's central concept and argues that replacing it with Gramsci's notion of "common sense" and the "everyday life" category developed by philosopher Agnes Heller (1987) would enable researchers to break away from the overdetermination of both functionalist cultural analysis and Marxist structuralism.[3]

According to Rockwell (1980a), the social processes at work in the school setting are coercion, negotiation, and resistance; the forms they take set apart and historicize each school (Rockwell, 1980a). Reconstructing the daily school routine from the participants' viewpoint assumes the intention and possibility of achieving in-depth descriptions of different aspects of school life. The "social categories" that subjects use to describe their world strain the limits of the researcher's theoretical categories of interpretation. Anthropological documentation of the school—or any other contemporary institution—requires that the researcher reverse the usual procedure for understanding how others live—the aim of traditional anthropology—and instead transform the familiar into the exotic (Da Matta, 1983).

Ethnographic reconstruction requires continuous reflexivity in which the researcher checks the initial hypothesis against the ongoing development of "social categories" (Malinowski's "internal categories") derived from data analysis in the field. The researcher's underlying assumptions (Gouldner, 1979) and unspoken rules or "reflexivity" necessarily lead to prejudging; but if such assumptions are examined hand-in-hand with carrying out ethnographic research, the ethnographer's capacity to perceive is greatly increased (Rockwell, 1987; Willis, 1984).

Guidelines for fieldwork and for the analysis of field notes are in accordance with the conceptual framework described above, which, while influenced by Geertzian interpretativism, attempts to break away from interpretativism by establishing a dialectical tension between the day-to-day social processes encountered in local schools (Rockwell and Ezpeleta, 1983) and a social-historical framework defined and limited by the schools' social class structure.

It is also assumed that the mediating categories that emerge from ethnographic reconstructions reflect the heterogeneity of the subjects' actions, thus leading to the development of a theoretical basis for research on schools that moves away from the determinism of social reproduction and the constructivism of phenomenological models.

Educational Ethnography in Argentina and Chile

The above summarizes (and of course, interprets) the point of departure for those in Argentina and Chile utilizing an ethnographic approach to educational research. I shall now turn to an overview of developments in educational ethnography, with a focus on local contexts, the production of original research, and the growing interest in the field. In an effort to broaden and enrich our common theoretical-methodological approach, I shall conclude by suggesting areas of possible controversy.

As I indicated above, the Seminar on Ethnography and Education that took place in Austin, Texas, and Mexico City in 1980 and the subsequent formation of RINCUARE were the first milestones in the adoption of the ethnographic approach.[4] With the end of the Network and its graduate program, DIE continued hosting researchers and fellows, who would return to Argentina and Chile to join the early research teams or set up their own projects.

As Rockwell (this volume) points out, those participating in the formative stages shared a background of common experiences. The eras of dictatorship in Argentina (1976–1983) and Chile (1973–1989) severely restricted all aspects of academic work in the universities and also affected school systems, which became enmeshed in authoritarian teaching policies and strict control and surveillance of teachers.

Among the Chilean and Argentinean members of the Network were researchers with anthropological training and previous experience in studying popular education. There was general support, in principle and practice, for teachers' efforts to organize school reform movements and create stronger teachers' unions.

Most of the members of the early research teams in Chile had received their professional training in education or psychology. For them ethnographic studies provided answers to questions about school failure, which the quantitative studies then in vogue had been unable to do. As a result of their interchanges with Mexico, Chilean researchers began to specialize in ethnography; eventually, some entered graduate programs in England or the United States.

In Argentina the first research teams were interdisciplinary, with ideas from anthropology, philosophy, education, psychology, and social psychology. Such a broad perspective meant that the ethnographic approach would be used in a wide variety of research projects, primarily those whose main purpose was to understand the teaching–learning process.

Bringing in Teachers: The Workshops for Educators

It should be noted that the style of participatory research then taking shape in Argentina had as its model the Workshops for Educators set up in 1976 by Rodrigo Vera and Manuel Argumedo (1976). The workshops were designed to provide advanced training for teachers, using a method that combined social research with teachers' thoughts and ideas on their work. Teaching the basics of classroom management and socio-educational analysis, the workshop leaders hoped to develop critical thinking about standard teacher training methods, which they felt contributed to the reproduction of traditional teaching practices.[5]

The workshops became the basis for a collaborative Chilean–Argentinean research program set up in 1980, which later followed different paths. In Chile the approach came to be called "participatory research" (*investigación protagónica*), moving away from ethnographic research as such and playing a significant role in the educational reform movement, which was a reaction to authoritarian policies of the military government. The Workshops for Democratic Education (TED), based on the principles of participatory research, were directed (and continue to be today) by members of the research team trained at the center that first organized the workshops. Thus there has been continuing dialogue between researchers' findings and the orientation of teacher-training programs toward changing school culture.

Chilean Studies of School Failure

As I have indicated above, Chilean ethnographers focused mainly on school failure. The translated title of one of their representative works is *School Culture, Responsible for Failure?* (López et al., 1984). According to the authors, long-term, comparative observation of academic settings with the highest dropout and failure rates—public schools in poor districts—demonstrates the existence of a culture of school failure. Through systematic documentation of differing school behaviors, especially in the classroom, researchers concluded that the culture of failure was generated through daily interactions. When manifestations of "popular culture" did not fit in with school discipline practices or established forms of scholastic knowledge, they were disparaged and rejected; the resulting misunderstandings and conflicts led to failure in the classroom.

Using Bourdieu and Passeron's (1977) theory of cultural capital as a conceptual basis for cultural analysis, the Chilean researchers have been able to highlight the hierarchical control and conformity imposed by the state educational system in their country. Subsequent studies have supported the social reproduction thesis of socialization by determining "the ideal discourse," which is a combination of meanings shared by the school culture (educators) and the informants from the popular culture (students and parents). The researchers found that because of the "solid citizen" ideal, which stems from the school's concept of "normalcy," school failure tends to be morally sanctioned and internalized by its victims (Assaél et al., 1989).

Framing studies with theories of reproduction and socio-historical context does not preclude providing examples and descriptions of particular situations. These examples can be based on the observation of teaching methods or daily disciplinary techniques and through noting the expressions, linguistic codes, and categories used to convey cultural meanings. These ethnographic studies focus on documenting the everyday mechanisms by which schools simultaneously marginalize and socialize the popular classes.

Edwards's (1989) ethnography takes on a more specific theme, "forms of school knowledge." The greater complexity of her work and its departure from previous theoretical orientations signal a second stage of development in Chilean ethnographic research. Edwards has created descriptive categories that suggest a critique of social definitions of "valid knowledge" in the school. With its documentation of the varieties of resistance displayed by students and the corresponding diversity of approaches among teachers, this ethnography moves away from former theories of social reproduction by using the category of "appropriation" (Heller, 1987) to avoid structuralist determinism and to understand more fully the complexities of classroom life.

The prolific work of Edwards's team now has an audience both in and out of Chile because of their research findings and their active role in teacher training.[6] The team's efforts have created conceptual guidelines for policies, strategies, and methodologies that contribute to improving Chilean education.

A recent study on work and socialization practices in the middle school (Edwards et al., 1993), has provoked a debate among ethnographers at the national level. The government-sponsored study covers eighteen educational institutions of different types (city-run, private, subsidized) in five regions of Chile. The authors use ethnographic description to closely examine both the prevailing ways of transmitting knowledge and alternative methods that view learning as a constructivist process.

The study extends the view of the middle school's culture and hidden curriculum by describing the socialization process and teaching methods found in these institutions and the forms of resistance employed by today's youth. Categories such as humor, punishment, labeling, gender and ethnic discrimination, along with the importance of "the culture of success," reveal the role played by the secondary school in creating an identity for the contemporary Chilean adolescent.

Although it is not possible to examine their work in detail here, other researchers in Chile work from an educational anthropology perspective. At universities anthropologists, some of whom did graduate work in Mexico City or the United Kingdom, are beginning to produce writings that delve into educational matters, approaching critically the homogeneity of Chile's educational system and insisting that ethnic and social diversity be recognized. Current activity in teaching, seminars, and exchanges among researchers encourages us to predict that educational ethnography will one day be a field of major academic importance in Chile.

Incorporating the Perspectives of Argentinean Teachers: Teachers As "Powerful Subordinates"

In Argentina the ethnographic approach also was developed initially in workshops for educators, which included research on in-service teacher training (Batallán et al., 1982). Some features of the participatory research method were introduced in training educators to analyze their own teaching practices. Teachers attending workshops were asked to become partners in a research project on the meaning of teaching; participation was voluntary, with the only incentive the opportunity to learn the basics of anthropological fieldwork.

The workshops focused on understanding schooling through the eyes of the teachers (Batallán, 1983). A basic premise of the year-long training period was that only through the commitment and participation of the teachers themselves would it be possible to understand the linkages between day-to-day classroom practices and the roles assigned to teaching by tradition and the state.

Data from the workshops along with the field notes of the researchers and the teachers (who were gradually developing skills in ethnography) support the contention that the insight gained from this kind of approach develops in spiral fashion. The first moment is called "problematization," in which the ideological meanings of educational practices are identified. In the second moment, "ideological deconstruction," a particular ideology is subject to close scrutiny and critical analysis through the research process. Finally, during a third moment, "conceptual reconstruction" makes it possible to seek other explanations, more complex than those currently accepted on the basis of "common sense." The new thinking which may result is then put into practice by the teachers, now able to coordinate research procedures while working with students in the classroom (Batallán, García, and Morgade, 1988).

The theoretical contributions of the research done at the Latin American School of Social Sciences (FLACSO) between 1983 and 1986 have brought about a critical examination of the following: (a) the concept of childhood implicit in the definition of school knowledge; (b) the structural characteristics of the teaching process as currently defined; and (c) the institutional legitimization of the knowledge transmitted in schools (Batallán, García, and Saleme, 1986).

Several studies have had an impact on educational policies and practices in the region. Batallán and Morgade (1987) applied the critique of knowledge as transmission to the teaching of social studies, and their work subsequently became the basis for curriculum change in the Buenos Aires School District (Municipalidad de la Ciudad de Buenos Aires, 1989). Morgade's (1990, 1991) exploration of gender issues in teaching has influenced government guidelines used in national teacher training programs.

The notion of research which emphasizes understanding schools in order to change them assumes that teaching, because it is at the center of any definition of the school, is a focal point of school change. The position of power held by the classroom teacher as the leader in the teaching–learning relationship allows, and indeed creates, alternative practices with the potential of challenging established norms. The meaning of teaching, however, is strongly influenced by the conditions that are imposed on teachers as functionaries in a bureaucracy. The resulting characterization of teachers as "powerful subordinates" underlines the tension that allows educators a wide margin for action and makes them key subjects in the possible transformation of the school (Batallán and Morgade, 1987).

In an examination of the concept of ideology in research on schooling, García (1986) locates the theoretical foundations within the critical theory of the Frankfurt School and takes issue with the Marxist structuralist concept of ideology as false consciousness. Another significant milestone in the theoretical-methodological thinking on school research is the connection made between school knowledge, as an adaptation of what society wants transmitted, and the democratization process in Latin American countries. (Batallán and García, 1992b; Schmukler, 1992)

Researchers at the University of Buenos Aires have begun a study of the social construction of the teaching profession, examining from the teachers' perspective the meaning of their work. This research program examines the teachers' union struggles during various periods in Argentinean history and the problem of creating an independent identity for the teaching profession, whose members have traditionally been functionaries of the state in Latin America. The tradition of teacher as "change agent" (that is, someone for whom school change is a direct result of classroom practice) has produced a debate among teachers as to how teachers can play a significant role in school change (Batallán and García, 1986).

Pursuing this line of research, Batallán et al. (1993) looked at the system of teacher evaluations as one of the obstacles facing the construction of a professional identity. They found that the methods for evaluating what teachers do in the classroom infantilize them and represent an extension of the methods used to evaluate their students. Various notions of teacher evaluation have been reconstructed by studying teacher work histories and by exploring how teachers weigh administrative directives against the daily realities of life in the classroom (Batallán et al., 1993).

As we look at the direction this research has taken, it is important to emphasize the increasing use of the ethnographic approach among the groups of teachers participating in the various workshop experiments. A number of these educators, already trained in their own fields, have directed teacher training projects in non-governmental institutions and in government-sponsored sessions. Although much of their work has not been recorded, Dente, Di Santo, and Visintin (1993) have reported on their research on kindergarten classrooms in low-income neighborhoods, and Maddonni and López (1993) report a modification in the approach to in-service teacher training in which they were involved.

Once the first research on teaching had been set in motion with the encouragement of the Network (RINCUARE), other groups gradually began working on their own in other parts of Argentina. For example, using the workshop method, Achilli, Ageno, and Ossana (1987) studied the meaning of state-promoted school democratization, focusing on understanding the teachers' view of vertically imposed democracy. Using a more specifically anthropological approach, Achilli (1989) observed the daily school routine, finding certain codes in school life that limit the democratization process. More recently, and independently of the influence of the initial group, Justa Ezpeleta (1989) has examined teaching by emphasizing working conditions as a factor in how educators view their profession.

In 1987 a Department of Anthropology and Education was established at the Institute of Anthropology of the University of Buenos Aires, marking the beginning of a program to introduce graduates in anthropology and education to the new field. As a result of seminars and fellowship programs, subjects of interest have become more diversified and the field has become more widely known in academic circles in Argentina.

An important milestone was reached when the Second National Congress of Social Anthropology devoted a special session to papers on anthropology and educational research. The introduction to the published papers summarizes the theoretical background and discusses the problem of possible personal bias in ethnographic reconstructions (Batallán and Neufeld, 1988). The introduction also stresses that the leitmotif running through all the papers is the enduring nature of authoritarian social processes in formal education, which are reinforced by the adversarial relationship between family and school (Schmuckler and Savigliano, 1988).

There is a growing interest in the relationship between the popular sectors (marginal urban groups and rural populations) and formal education. Researchers are describing strategies of upward mobility through school choice, which are being used to avoid the discrimination that comes from attending a school classified as marginal (Neufeld, 1992).

Research with a more traditional ethnographic approach is focusing on the reconstruction of daily life in popular-sector schools and on constructing "from within" mediating categories which can elucidate the meaning of "participation" as an idealization of democracy in these settings. One of the ideas being examined here is that schools in popular sectors, by assuming a social welfare function as part of their services, actually hinder participation in any real sense (Padawer, 1991).

Díaz (1992) did an ethnographic study of the elementary school's role in strengthening or weakening national identity. The researcher monitored classroom interaction relating to the teaching of social sciences and the learning of significant national dates and patriotic symbols, and did a comparative analysis of school ceremonies celebrating national leaders. The data were examined in the context of a historical reconstruction of the educational policy debate over the school's role in inculcating concepts of nationality (Díaz, 1992).

Conclusion

In conclusion, we can state that the anthropological tradition in qualitative research is now a recognized presence in Argentina and Chile. Its acceptance is demonstrated by the changes which have occurred in teaching and by the use of its findings in formulating educational policy in both countries.

Within the academic community there will continue to be dialogue and debate around issues such as a deeper questioning of the traditional criteria for doing ethnographic fieldwork. As participatory research becomes more popular, traditional criteria based on the researcher as outsider will have to be rethought as "insiders" begin doing their own field research (Batallán and García, 1992a). This makes many ethnographic researchers nervous, as traditionally ethnographers sought "natural settings" to study and worked hard to keep their presence in the setting from creating "reactivity" on the part of informants (Assael et al., 1992).

The anthropology of education in Argentina and Chile has experimented with topics and methods that depart to some extent from the anthropological tradition. One of the limitations in this sense is the difficulty in writing up ethnographic accounts of producing the kind of thick description that is called for by current ethnographic practice. Furthermore, the scarcity of school ethnographies and the general lack of studies that depart from traditional "research reports" are due, in part to the need for educational researchers to gain legitimacy in a field suspicious of narrative styles of representation that challenge accepted notions of internal and external validity. Moreover, the requirements of international agencies that support research seldom favor qualitative studies.

Finally, the challenge of generating theory grounded in the interpretations of informants themselves has produced a series of interesting dilemmas with regard to linking theory, epistemology, and method. In this sense we share in the contemporary crisis that all social scientists are experiencing with regard to the complex task of interpreting and representing social phenomena.

Notes

Many thanks to the colleagues with whom I discussed the state of fieldwork in anthropology and education: Jenny Assaél and Verónica Edwards of PIIE; in Santiago, Raúl Díaz and María Rosa Neufeld; and researchers from the Department of Education and Anthropology of the Philosophy and Letters Faculty at the University of Buenos Aires. Special appreciation to Silvina Campini for her insights and to José Fernando García for his help in editing the manuscript.

1. The ethnographic approach must be distinguished from those known as micro-ethnography. The latter have been employed by sociologists, psychologists, and anthropologists doing research from various empirical perspectives. The purpose of micro-ethnographic studies is descriptive. They have been used most often to trace the genesis of discriminatory stereotypes in the classroom. Briones (1990) places micro-ethnographies within a "subjective-interpretative paradigm." An earlier work by Rockwell (1980a) offers a critique of such studies.

2. The intensive training provided at the 1980 seminar included both theory and practice. Elsie Rockwell directed the month-long program in Mexico held at the DIE. Participating were: Araceli de Tezanos (Colombia), Gabriela López (Chile), Maritza Balderrama de Crespo (Bolivia), Irma Hernández (Venezuela), Beatriz Diconca (Uruguay), and Graciela Batallán (Argentina). The establishment of the Network led to the creation of new research teams in centers and universities in Buenos Aires, Córdoba, Río Negro, Neuquén, and Rosario, all in Argentina. In Chile most work has been done in institutions such as PIIE and the Center for Educational Research and Development (CIDE).

3. "Culture does not explain, but rather describes in specific and concrete form peoples' actions. These actions are determined, institutionally through hegemonic apparatuses charged with socialization, and also by social class identification and the historical stage of the social struggle. If the term 'culture' has to be used, it should be limited to the very concrete, descriptive level of the day-to-day forms through which processes of production and reproduction occur, and the day-to-day thoughts of subjects about their world" (Rockwell, 1980b, p. 11).

4. The role played by the following in setting up RINCUARE should not be forgotten: Beatriz Avalos, Sheldon Shaeffer, Nelly Stromquist, Elizabeth Fox, and especially Rodrigo Vera, the academic coordinator. Besides organizing meetings, conferences, and academic exchanges, the Network put out two publications: *Dialogando*, a quarterly, and *Cuadernos de formación para investigadores*, which came out twice a year. The Network's three years of activity and hard work led to the creation of research teams in several countries in the region.

5. Theoretical work on group processes was initiated in Argentina by Enrique Pichón Riviere (1983), founder of the Argentinean School of Social Psychology. His vast influence in Argentina and other Latin American countries has proved productive in several disciplines. In education the concept of "operative groups," which is rooted in Freudian psychoanalysis, has contributed to the thinking that has led to the development of antiauthoritarian practices in the schools.

6. The findings in this area, as well as the methodologies developed, have been used in Chile and other Latin American countries; e.g., the Colombian Ministry of Education, innovations sponsored by UNESCO, and various teachers' organizations in the region.

References

Achilli, E. (1989). Escuela y democratización: Para debatir un enfoque antropológico. *Cuadernos de formación docente de La Universidad Nacional de Rosario*, 10, 2–31.

Achilli, E., Ageno, R., and Ossana, E. (1987). *La significación en la escuela de las propuestas estatales de participación y democratización*. Rosario, Argentina: Centro Rosario de Investigaciones en Ciencias Sociales (CRICSO).

Assaél, J., Edwards, V., and López, G. (1992). *Apuntes sobre el proceso de construcción etnográfica en la investigación educativa*. Santiago, Chile: Programa Interdisciplinario de Investigaciones en Educación (PIIE).

Assaél, J., Edwards, V., López, G., and Adduard, A. (1989). *Alumnos, padres y maestros: La representación de la escuela*. Santiago, Chile: Programa Interdisciplinario de Investigaciones en Educación (PIIE).

Batallán, G. (1983). *Talleres de educadores. Capacitación por la investigación de la práctica. Síntesis de fundamentos. Documentos de trabajo*. Buenos Aires: Facultad Latinoamericana de Ciencias Sociales (FLACSO).

Batallán, G. and García, J.F. (1986). Trabajo docente, democratización y conocimiento. *Revista Paraguaya de Sociología*, 65(1), 31–47.

Batallán, G. and García, J.F. (1992a). Antropología y participación: Contribución al debate metodológico. *Revista Publicar en antropología y ciencias sociales*, 1(1), 73–96.

Batallán, G. and García, J.F. (1992b). La especificidad del trabajo docente y la transformación escolar. In J. Miño and A. Dávila (Eds.), *Maestros, formación, práctica y transformación escolar* (pp. 123–150). Buenos Aires: Nueva Visión.

Batallán, G., García, J.F., Dente, L., Maddonni, P., and López, D. (1993). *La construcción social de la carrera docente: Un enfoque antropológico*. Unpublished manuscript, La Universidad de Buenos Aires, Argentina.

Batallán, G., García J.F., and Morgade, G. (1988). El trabajo docente y su significación en la perspectiva del cambio de la escuela. In *Curso de metodología de la investigación en ciencias sociales*. Rosario, Argentina: Instituto Rosario de Investigación en Ciencias de la Educación (IRICE).

Batallán, G., García, J.F., and Saleme, M. (1986). *El mundo del niño y el aprendizaje escolar: Su incidencia en la reformulación del rol docente*. Buenos Aires: Facultad Latinoamericana de Ciencias Sociales (FLACSO).

Batallán, G. and Morgade, G. (1987). El niño y el conocimiento social en la escuela. In N. Elichiry (Ed.), *El niño y la escuela* (pp. 38–57). Buenos Aires: Nueva Visión.

Batallán, G. and Neufeld, M.R. (1988). Problemas de la antropología y la investigación educacional en América Latina. *Cuadernos de Antropología Social*, 2, 33–58.

Batallán, G., Raymundo, O., and De Carli, G. (1982). *Talleres de educadores como modalidad de perfeccionamiento operativo: Informe de investigación, Centro de Investigaciones en Educación*, Volumes I and II. Buenos Aires: Centro de Investigaciones Educativas.

Bourdieu, P. and Passeron, J.C. (1977). *La reproducción*. Barcelona: Laia.

Briones, G. (1990). *La investigación educativa en Chile: Generación y utilización del conocimiento*, Volume I. Santiago, Chile: Facultad Latinoamericana de Ciencias Sociales (FLACSO).

Da Matta, R. (1983). Um introduçao a Antropología social. *Voces*, 1, 24–40.

Dente, L., Di Santo, B., and Visintin, M. (1993). *Jardines infantiles populares comunitarios: Una estrategia pedagógica y organizativa de atención a la infancia*. Buenos Aires: Centro de Investigación y Promoción Educativa y Social (CIPES).

Díaz, R. (1992). *Las ideas de nacionalidad en la escuela primaria*. Unpublished manuscript, Universidad de Buenos Aires, Argentina.

Edwards, V. (1989). *Los sujetos y la construcción del conocimiento escolar en primaria: Un estudio etnográfico*. Santiago, Chile: PIIE.

Edwards, V., Calvo, C., Conde, A., Inoztroza, G., and Gomez, V. (1993). *Prácticas de trabajo y socialización en establecimientos de educación media*. Santiago, Chile: PIIE.

Ezpeleta, J. (1989). *Escuela y maestros: Condiciones del trabajo docente en Argentina*. Santiago, Chile: UNESCO.

García, J.F. (1986). El concepto de ideología y la transformación de la escuela. *Revista Colombiana de Educación*, 17, 57–79.

García Huidobro, J.E. (1984). *Orientaciones de la investigación educacional en América Latina*. Santiago, Chile: IDRC.

García Huidobro, J.E., Ochoa, J., and Tellez, F. (1988). *Tendencias de la investigación educativa en América Latina*. Santiago, Chile: Centro de Investigación y Desarrollo Educativo (CIDE).

Geertz, C. (1987). *La interpetación de las culturas*. México, D.F.: Gedisa.

Gouldner, A. (1979). *La crisis de la sociología occidental*. Buenos Aires: Amorrurtu.

Gramsci, A. (1973). *El materialismo histórico y la filosofía de Benedetto Crocce*. Buenos Aires: Nueva Visión.

Heller, A. (1987). *Sociología de la vida cotidiana*. Barcelona: Península.

López, G., Assaél, J., and Neumann, E. (1984). *La cultura escolar: ¿Responsable del fracaso?*. Santiago, Chile: PIIE.

Maddonni, P. and López, D. (1993). *Diálogo sobre la capacitación en servicio: El enfoque etnográfico en el análisis de la institución educativa*. Buenos Aires: Secretaría de Educación de la Municipalidad de la ciudad de Buenos Aires (MCBA).

Malinowski, B. (1986). *Los argonautas del Pacífico Occidental*. Barcelona: Planeta-Agostini.

Morgade, G. (1990). *El determinante de género en el trabajo docente en la escuela primaria*. Unpublished master's thesis, FLACSO, Buenos Aires, Argentina.

Morgade, G. (1991). *La feminización de la escuela primaria argentina: Políticas educativas y significación del trabajo (1870–1930)*. Buenos Aires: Instituto de Ciencias de la Educación de La Universidad de Buenos Aires, Consejo Nacional de Investigaciones Cientítificas y Técnicas (CONICET).

Municipalidad de la Ciudad de Buenos Aires (1989). Objetivos en Ciencias Sociales primer nivel. In *Diseño curricular para la educación inicial* (pp. 78–90). Buenos Aires, Argentina.

Neufeld, M.R. (1992). Subalternidad y escolarización: Acerca de viejos y nuevos problemas de las escuelas de islas. *Etnia*, 36/37, 29–41.

Padawer, A. (1991). *La participación y el asistencialismo en escuelas de sectores populares*. Unpublished bachelor's thesis, Universidad de Buenos Aires, Buenos Aires, Argentina.

Pichón Rivière, E. (1983). *El proceso grupal: Del psicoanálisis a la psicología social*. Buenos Aires: Nueva Visión.

Rockwell, E. (1980a). *Etnografía y teoría en la investigación educativa*. (DIE research monograph). México, D.F.: DIE-CINVESTAV-IPN.

Rockwell, E. (1980b). *Antropología y educación: Problemas del concepto de cultura*. (DIE research monograph). México, D.F.: DIE-CINVESTAV-IPN.

Rockwell, E. (1987). *Reflexiones sobre el proceso etnográfico*. (DIE research monographs). México, D.F.: DIE-CINVESTAV-IPN.

Rockwell, E. and Ezpeleta, J. (1983). Escuela y clases subalternas. *Cuadernos Políticos*, 37, 24–69.

Schmukler, B. (1992). Women and the microsocial democratization of everyday life. In N. Stromquist (Ed.), *Women and education in Latin America* (pp. 246–263). Boulder, CO: Lynne Rienner.

Schmukler, B. and Savigliano, M. (1988). Cooperación o autoritarismo en el vínculo familias y escuela: Las contradicciones de una socialización compartida. *Cuadernos de Antropología Social*, 1(2), 34–49.

Schütz, A. (1974). *Estudios de teoría social*. Buenos Aires: Amorrortu.

Tedesco, J.C. (1987). Paradigmas de la investigación socio-educativa. *Revista latinoamericana de estudios educativos,*15(2), 11–41.

Vera, R. and Argumendo, M. (1976). *Los talleres de educadores como modalidad de perfeccionamiento operataivo*. Buenos Aires: CIE.

Willis, P. (1984). Notas sobre el método. *Dialogando: Revista de la Red de Investigacion Cualitativa para la Realidad Escolar,* 3, 4–12. (Trans. Gabriela López).

Chapter Three
An Overview of Ethnographic Research in Mexico
An Approach to Educational Problems

María Bertely and Martha Corenstein

Educational ethnographic research[1] in Mexico emerged from qualitative or interpretative approaches associated with the traditions of anthropology and sociology and their detailed descriptions of what occurs in natural social and cultural situations.

Ethnographic research became prevalent in Mexico during the late 1970s, though it had previously been part of the field tradition in anthropology.[2] During the next fifteen years, due to a growing interest and considerable expansion in ethnographic research, projects encompassing various aspects of the educational process were undertaken at various institutions throughout the country.

Studies using an ethnographic perspective were specifically undertaken by institutions like the Departamento de Investigaciones Educativas (DIE, Department for Educational Research of the Polytechnic University); the Centro de Investigaciones y Estudios Superiores en Antropología Social (CIESAS, Center for Research and Higher Education in Social Anthropology); various departments of the Universidad Nacional Autónoma de México (UNAM, National Autonomous University of Mexico); the Universidad Pedagógica Nacional (UPN, National Pedagogic University); the Instituto Superior de Ciencias de la Educación del Estado de México (ISCEEM, Universidad Iberoamericana); the Escuela Nacional de Antropología e Historia (ENAH, National School of Anthropology and History); various state universities; and several teacher training schools. Inter-institutional workshops or seminars were organized by the National Council for Culture and the Arts; the Universidad Autónoma del Estado de México (UAEM, Autonomous University of the State of Mexico); and the UNAM's Centro de Investigaciones y Servicios Educativos (CISE, Center for Educational Research and Services).

The expansion of ethnographic research within these institutions is, without doubt, proof of the growing concern for diverse issues at all educational levels within the national education system. In particular, the emphasis has been basic elementary education and post-secondary education. But just as varied as the expansion of ethnographic research has been, approaches with an ethnographic perspective have also been as diverse as the institutions that use them. This is evident in the variety of topics, theoretical articulations, methodological approaches—ranging from descriptive and anecdotal studies of an empirical nature to research involving broad social concepts—that attempt to bridge the gap between micro and macro-levels of analysis.

The purpose of this chapter is to document the evolution of ethnographic research[3] during the last decade and a half in Mexico, focusing on three basic issues: (1) the major research traditions encompassed by ethnography during this period and the general context from which they derive meaning; (2) the epistemological debates influencing ethnographic research; and (3) the educational analytic dimensions involved. By exploring these issues not only can the current status of ethnographic research in Mexico be described but, more importantly, some of the limits and potential of social practices in schools, and also some of the challenges facing educational policy can be identified.

Traditions in Educational Research and the Ethnographic Perspective

From its inception the application of ethnographic research to education has coexisted with social science research psychology and sociology approaches. This theoretical and methodological coexistence stems both from the difficulty in defining education as a distinct area of research and from the complexity of identifying those processes and problems that shape the national educational context. Some of these problems have been exacerbated in the last two decades by the growing crisis in public education—the high percentage of students failing or dropping out of school, the social and economic devaluation of teaching, the growth of marginalized populations requiring specific educational approaches, and the need to implement reforms that allow for political negotiation between the government and sectors of civil society.

Behaviorism and Functionalism

One of the dominant research traditions in the field of educational research during the 1970s and early 1980s in Mexico was the positivistic approach associated with psychology, behaviorism, and psychometric analysis. The emphasis on behaviorism and psychometric analysis in education was primarily translated into pedagogical practice in elementary education. At the same time dominant thinking in sociology maintained a dominant functionalist and systems theory. The traditions of psychology and sociology have left their mark on educational policy and practice, producing an elaborate set of plans and programs of study under the banner of what has come to be called "instrumental rationality." The principles of functionality, means-to-end rationality, scientific management, generalization, homogeneity, and efficiency continue to be dominant.

The curricula in elementary education as well as at all levels of the educational system are influenced through social and educational policies by this dominant tradition of behaviorism. Despite its generic interest in efficiency, behaviorism has contributed to the increase of educational problems. Low levels of educational attainment, high student failure and dropout rates, and the increasing gap between educational policy and social and community needs are but some of the problems that continue to rise. Such increase is criticized as being caused by the emphasis on "psychologism,"[4] efficiency, and instrumental rationality—all characteristics of this period.

Ethnography breaks with these traditions by not upholding the principles of efficiency, normative structures, nor "what ought to be." Instead the role of the ethnographer is to document the particular processes involved in schooling and its daily specificity, and not to supervise what appears to be the homogeneous performance of school activities.

Participatory Research and Marxist Criticism

During the 1970s and 1980s, a series of critical approaches concurrently pointed to the weaknesses of the dominant tradition that were not considered to be qualitative by their supporters. Among these, the most important approach was *action research* or *participatory research*. In Mexico, as in other Latin American countries, this approach arose as a critique of traditional theoretical and practical research, which was characterized by its isolation from the problems and expectations of situational change experienced by marginalized sectors (Tedesco, 1989).

In general, participatory research seeks to vindicate individuals in society, is action and change-oriented, and is carried out by research teams who are aware of the needs of marginalized groups. Though it would be impossible to give a precise date for the emergence of this approach, its presence in Latin America is evident toward the end of the sixties and early seventies. The terms participatory research and action research, even though they represent two distinct lines of thought, are used as synonyms and become integrated under the concept of "participatory action research" (Schmelkes, 1991).

In Latin America this school of thought seeks to explore the causes of social marginalization and, in the process, attempts to generate strategies for change through praxis (research to action). Participatory action research appears under various names and with different modalities, whether in the topical research of Paulo Freire; Colombian action research by Fals Borda (1981); militant research in the work of the Brazilians Miguel Darcy de Oliveira (1982) and Freire (1982) himself; and participatory research as such.[5]

Participatory action research is characterized by the mobilization of a certain political consciousness and the generation of self-governed experiences. The processes it initiates are often, however, interrupted by financial and political factors; hence, participatory research tends to develop short-term goals and small-scale projects.

One of the most highly developed areas of participatory research in Mexico is adult education, which is directed primarily at solving the problem of illiteracy. The major institution involved in adult education is the Centro de Cooperación Regional para la Educación de Adultos de América Latina y el Caribe (CREFAL, Central Cooperation Center for Adult Education in Latin America and the Caribbean), with headquarters in Pátzcuaro in the state of Michoacán. For more than forty years CREFAL's substantive mission has been to train and prepare individuals throughout Latin America and the Caribbean interested in general social well-being, and adult education in particular. CREFAL conducts projects in informal education for adults or indigenous communities (Calvo, 1993) and works with the Organization of American States (OAS) in designing alternative educational programs for culturally differentiated groups.

Nonprofit institutions in Mexico also use participatory action research to link educational activities to community needs. The Centro de Estudios Educativos (CEE, Center for Educational Studies, A.C.) has given the most attention to involving communities in the implementation of specific educational projects mainly geared toward basic education. Their activities include the design of experiments in which parents design curricula and actually teach. The preschool community education project, which is currently under way in the low-income area on the outskirts of Mexico City and was described by Pérez et al. (1986), is an example of CEE's efforts. These efforts emerge from the design and development of curricula based on community participation. Similar projects involving secondary education teachers in rural schools in Tluichihuayan, in the state of San Luis Potosí, are described by Rosas (1987).

In addition to the work being done by CREFAL and CEE, other institutions of higher education are conducting similar projects, namely, the Centro de Investigacion de Servicios Educacionales, Universidad Nacional Autónoma de México (CISE-UNAM, Center for Educational Research and Services at the National Autonomous University of Mexico)(Barabtarlo and Theesz, 1985); the University of Puebla; and the Centro Educativo Ixtliyollotl (CEI, Ixliyollotl Educational Center) (Garduño and Lorandi, 1992).

Unlike ethnographic research, participatory research seeks to involve the entire community in defining and resolving certain problems and in transforming such reality. Ethnographic research, on the other hand, focuses more on the understanding of educational processes, with a possible long-term contribution to change. The two approaches have coexisted in Mexico without convergence or exchange, and dialogue between these two approaches might be initiated, as is currently proposed by critical ethnography in the United States.

Marxist approaches in educational analysis are derived from dialectical and class discourse, borrowed from the ideas of the reproductionist school represented by Althusser (1974), Bourdieu and Passeron (1977), and Bowles and Gintis (1976) as well as the critique of capitalist schooling formulated by Baudelot and Establet (1981) and dependency theory. Ivan Illich has also greatly contributed to this debate.

In contrast to these schools of thought, ethnography does not necessarily emanate from a Marxist or transformative theoretical framework. It does not condemn tradition or argue for innovation prior to examining what actually occurs in schools and classrooms. Ethnographers do not see their role as directly or necessarily being related to "consciousness raising" in communities. However, ethnographers do incorporate the critiques of dominant educational views generated by their discoveries.

Ethnographic studies raise the veil from small fragments of reality, so that the actions and voices of repressed subjects that have been overpowered by the imposition of stereotypes constructed by hegemonic groups can be distinguished. Ethnographers can present their collaborators with an interpretation of the data collected. They can also contribute to the social interpretation of subjects and to the gradual modification of the content or implementation of educational policies.

The Epistemological Antecedents of Ethnographic Research

Just as various inter- and intradisciplinary stances can be found in the analysis of educational problems, educational ethnography in Mexico varies in its explicit acknowledgment or identification of epistemological antecedents. Though all researchers recognize the importance of producing descriptive texts, not all are interested in epistemological matters nor do they recognize the theoretical or methodological positions that have influenced them. It is common for ethnographers to state that their sole methodological reference point is cultural anthropology, insofar as it uses certain techniques and research instruments; but ethnographers usually do not explore the epistemological bases of their thinking, their conceptions of reality, the generation of knowledge, or the construction of meaning in any great detail.

Though not much thought is given to these matters, two epistemological antecedents equally fruitful in Mexican ethnography can be identified. The first antecedent attempts to go beyond the limitations of structural and phenomenological approaches, derived from the Latin American discourse of the state in Gramsci and Heller's theory of everyday life. This perspective describes processes more than symbolic texts and attempts to extend the theoretical scope of construction at the same time as it documents the relationship of local idiosyncrasies to the general framework in which they occur. As a result of this epistemological influence, ethnographic research is thus inserted into a broader context in which dialogue coexists closely with theory from the earliest phases of research. Thus in this process certain categories are pre-defined before fieldwork, and ethnographers continually record the contrasts between such categories and the dimensions, or conditions, that actually intervene in the work of teachers or everyday school life (Rockwell, 1982, 1987; Aguilar, 1986; Mercado, 1985; Sandoval, 1986).

Another epistemological antecedent, from the interpretative sciences, stems mainly from the symbolic interactionism of the Chicago School—the comprehensive sociology of Max Weber (1969); the social phenomenology of Alfred Schütz (1974) and his concept of multiple realities; the hermeneutics of Gadamer (1977) and Ricoeur (1981); and the holistic approach of anthropology. Such an approach seeks to explore the interpretation of socially shared meanings in depth. Of utmost importance is the degree of intentionality, the actors' voices, styles of interaction, patterns of behavior, and the general context within which the specific production of symbolic, communicative, and cultural texts arises (Bertely, 1990). Studies using this approach examine participants' interpretation of social categories and the signifying relationships that are socially constructed through intersubjectivity. In this approach the ethnographer's gradual production of analytic constructs is closely linked to his/her understanding of the participants' patterns of signification. During this construction a continuous and parallel dialogue is established between those analytic constructs and pre-existing theoretical frameworks. Ethnographic studies of this type were pioneered in Mexico by Paradise (1991, 1989, 1987, 1985a, 1985b) and continued by Bertely (1993, 1992a, 1992b), Hernández (1989), and Robles (1993). A variety of current projects subscribe to this type of epistemological framework (Street, 1993).

Analysis of Educational Dimensions

Educational ethnographic research in Mexico can be categorized according to three basic dimensions identified from an extensive literature review on qualitative research conducted by the authors of this chapter: (1) institutional and political dimensions; (2) curricular dimensions; and (3) social dimensions.[6] Each study is identified by its major contributions in each of these dimensions and by its relevance to the political, economic, and social context of Mexico. For the purpose of this chapter such review of ethnographic research is more than just an inventory of studies conducted. It points to some of the major challenges facing educational policy in Mexico and the problems that these studies identify. The categories presented here reflect the relative emphases of the authors. In some cases certain studies could be included in one or more dimensions, depending on their emphasis.

Institutional and Political Dimensions

This category includes research that (a) seeks to interpret and document both the institutional dynamics and processes that intervene in teaching, as well as the daily repercussions of educational policies in schools; and (b) the symbolic construction of alternative consensi among teachers. Most of these studies deal directly with basic education; only a few are concerned with secondary and higher education.

In the studies pertaining to basic education there are interesting analyses of institutional life in Mexican primary schools, derived from what has been conceptualized as the formative dimensions of teaching (Rockwell, 1982). These approaches have helped define an analytic field that incorporates not only the pedagogical aspects of being a teacher but also those related to unions (Sandoval, 1986); the construction of teachers' identity (Castañeda, 1989; Remedi et al., 1989); and the way in which students (Gallegos, 1988; Levinson, 1992) and teachers (Aguilar, 1986; Carvajal, 1988; García, 1986; Medina, 1992) construct their daily experience and social relations within schools. There are also studies that document the role played by communities and parents in institutional life (Mercado, 1985); the "invisible conditions" of teaching (Ezpeleta, 1992); and the role of gender in educational relations (Aguilar and Sandoval, 1991; Salinas, 1988; Delgado Ballesteros, 1991, 1992).

The research on secondary and higher education has studies that analyze and document the relationship between educational policies, institutional dynamics, and pedagogical practices (Bárcena, 1987; Rueda Beltrán and Canales, 1991, 1992); instances of political control over teachers (Calvo, 1984; Mayer, 1982); specific experiences in the symbolic construction of alternative teaching cultures (Street, 1993); and the continuing debate between educational innovation and rationality (Zorrilla, 1989).

In this dimension some of the institutional and political problems affecting the daily experience of the central actors in Mexican schools are clearly made visible: (1) the working conditions of teachers; (2) the ways in which teachers, students, and parents organize, struggle, reach agreements, or conquer spaces within schools; and (3) the existence of educational institutions as political spaces of contest and contradiction. These non-pedagogical issues are of utmost importance in a context characterized by a general economic crisis marked by teachers' income levels, restrictive monetary policies, contestation of hierarchical school organizational forms, and Mexico's democratizing interest in the practice of educational policy.

Curricular Dimensions

In addition to the above-mentioned studies, research that seeks to discern how academic knowledge is constructed in classrooms, particularly through the curriculum, is also found in Mexico. For example, the research of Ruth Paradise (1979) analyzes not only teacher–student interactions in class but also the corresponding function of schooling in socializing children in later years into a productive labor force. Her research adheres to the reproductionist approach of the seventies and conceptually falls within the analysis of the hidden curriculum.

Other research in this dimension analyzes not only the implicit aspects of the school curriculum but its explicit management as well. Explicit management includes the types of knowledge that are constructed in the process of transmitting academic learning and that help to define its topical, operational, and situational character (Edwards, 1986). Research distinguishing between the formal curriculum, consisting of plans and programs of study that emanate from the educational intent of the Secretariat of Education, and the actual curriculum, determined by the specific conditions of the teaching profession, has been conducted (Rockwell, 1982; Avila, 1989).

In addition, research has been conducted that emphasizes the implications of specific curricular models for students' learning processes. From the implementation of educational policy at various academic levels, curricular models emerge where teaching by subject and teaching by areas can be identified, particularly at the middle or secondary level. Quiroz (1991), for example, has studied the relationship between the specialized presentation of academic content and the way students appropriate such content into fragments.

Aside from the purely curricular debate, this dimension also includes studies on pedagogical and didactic classroom interactions. Teaching processes in specific areas such as the natural sciences (Hernández, 1989; Avilés, 1987; Rockwell and Gálvez, 1981; Candela, 1989), and sex education (Stock, 1987) have been documented at the basic elementary level. At the secondary and higher education level, there are studies of history (Lerner, 1991), and of scientific values and content associated with the training of professionals at the college level (Campos et al., 1992; Hernández and López, 1991; Fortes and Lomnitz, 1991).

Other studies in this dimension subscribe to a constructivist theoretical framework. Ethnography is portrayed here as a technique for data collection that complements the methods of critical inquiry. Observations serve as feedback for pre-established concepts that identify the ways in which students construct different levels of cognitive approximations to the object of study. One example is the research on the practice of dictation in first grade based upon the ideas of Jean Piaget (Ferreiro, 1984). Another similar project is a teacher-training project based on teaching the fundamentals of basic education through the teaching of mathematics. This project is influenced by the conceptual framework of the French school represented by Brosseau (1986), Vergnaud (1981), and Freudenthal (1983). Its results have given rise to didactic proposals which have been taken up at the national level (Fuenlabrada et al., 1990). Because this research is directed at the construction of knowledge from within the child's reality, it is mostly found in basic education research.

This attention to school dynamics and the treatment of academic content has given rise to other studies, such as the analysis of the relationship between the use of class time and the teaching of primary school textbook content (Gálvez et al., 1981) or the process of socialization and learning in secondary level classrooms (Cornejo, 1986, 1991). Finally, evaluation and assessment studies as well as systemic analysis of schools have fostered extensive research on the impact of evaluation criteria and the instrumental rationality implicit in educational programs as they apply to student failure, collective organization, and actual school dynamics (Varea, 1983; Escalante and Robert, 1987; Bertely, 1985; Garnica, 1991; Levinson, 1992).

The curricular dimension of ethnographic research has highlighted various educational problems which, unresolved as yet, function within the daily practice of Mexican schools: (1) the scant attention given to the hidden school curriculum; (2) the way in which students are socialized to perform in the workplace; (3) the questioning of a homogeneous, national, and general set of plans and programs of study in a plural society; (4) the obstacles posed by curricular models that present a fragmented appropriation of academic contents; (5) the lack of relevance and meaning of the academic knowledge and content taught; (6) the dominance of pedagogical traditions that hamper the construction of didactic situations, which allow students to generate hypotheses and permanent cognitive constructs; (7) the high rates of failure in Spanish and mathematics; and (8) the arbitrariness of evaluation criteria that determine much of what is done and can be done in Mexican schools.

Social Dimensions

Mexico's reality is characterized by the presence of different economic and cultural groups and by a diversity of historical processes that impede access to a homogeneous national reality. In most cases this diversity denotes the existence of inequality, injustice, segregation, and social exploitation. Education is viewed as one of the ways in which to bridge the gap separating the different sectors of the population.

Many ethnographic studies classified under the social dimension document the ways in which the educational process relates to economically, culturally, or historically differentiated groups. For example, within the educational process socioeconomic characteristics and practices are seen as elements that influence the academic success or failure of students, the types of interaction that arise in classrooms, or the way communities signify the learning of academic contents. Thus certain authors show the impact of these elements on the differential teaching of reading and writing (Rámirez, 1980); pedagogical experimentation (Olivera, 1961); student behavior (Safa, 1992); dropout school problems; (Molina, 1989), and educational interaction (Cornejo, 1988). Other studies analyze the maintenance or transformation of traditional production practices (Campos, 1971; López, 1990). Still another area of research is the social context of schools (Calvo, 1976; Robles, 1988).

Within the social dimension, cultural and linguistic differences are important. Although there is debate as to the use of linguistic criteria in classifying the indigenous population of Mexico and in eliminating the confusion between language, culture, and ethnicity (Díaz Coder, 1990), this criterion is the one most commonly used in the census. It is estimated that the population of Mexico includes fifty-six linguistic groups, totaling eight million indigenous speakers (approximately 9 percent of the country's total population). If those who maintain their cultural practices—albeit without speaking indigenous languages—are included, this figure would increase significantly.

Despite the policies for assimilation, incorporation, or integration that indigenous peoples are subjected to, the sociocultural persistence of indigenous peoples, and the Mexican and Latin American forums, symposia, and conferences of indigenist political or intellectual organizations have generated demands in favor of indigenous peoples. These demands led to the 1978 establishment of the Dirección General de Educación Indígena (DGEI, General Directorate for Indigenous Education) at the Secretariat of Public Education and the recently proposed constitutional reform of Article Four, which, for the first time in Mexico's history, recognizes the pluricultural composition of the Mexican nation.

Interest in indigenous education has developed parallel to the interest generated by the DGEI's bilingual–bicultural curricular model. Both the distribution and the extreme concentration of languages[7] have inspired a number of sociolinguistic studies (Coronado et al., 1981; Hamel, 1983, 1984, 1988; Hamel and Muñoz, 1981, 1982; Muñoz, 1983; Muñoz, 1980). Within this area there are studies that analyze and evaluate the best ways to promote bilingual teaching in schools, to calibrate the gradual use of both languages, and to design textbooks and materials that respond to such bilingual needs. Some sociolinguists have elaborated alphabets in mother tongues like Otomí (Muñoz, 1983).

Other studies under the social dimension focus on the use of communication styles constructed in the daily interactions of indigenous children and their teachers in DGEI schools. Luis analyzes the Zapotec case (1982); Sánchez, the Otomí (1991a, 1991b); and Valentínez, the Purépecha (1982). Though linguistic issues appear as analytic references, these studies seek to interpret their effect on the intersubjective construction of specific school contexts. Ornelas (1991) seeks to document the role of linguistic heterogeneity in the construction of academic content while Valentínez (1982), using an analysis of the persistence of Purépecha language and culture in teacher–student interactions, shows how school learning rests upon material that is culturally familiar to children. Sánchez (1991a, 1991b) documents daily life in the bilingual–bicultural schools of an Otomí community and finds that they are less institutionalized than standard or mainstream schools, allowing for the emergence of mechanisms for cultural resistance, appropriation, and innovation.

Many indigenous students in rural areas attend federal or state schools, which require bilingual services irrespective of whether the schools are linked to the DGEI or not. In the case of the Mazahua Indians, ethnographic studies carried out in two state schools in the State of Mexico reflect the adaptations in learning and teaching that both students and teachers construct through intercultural communication and understanding. In this research the focus is not on schools *for* indigenous people but on indigenous people *in* schools—thus the importance of analyzing socialization processes before interpreting what actually happens in classrooms is highlighted as important (Paradise, 1991, 1989, 1987, 1985a, 1985b; Bertely, 1992a, 1992b, 1992c; and Robles, 1993).

In the foregoing research there are two types of interpretation concerning the relationship between school and indigenous students. In one interpretation the oppressive and arbitrary nature of academic messages is described, along with their role in the Hispanization[8] and cultural assimilation of ethnic minorities (Vargas, 1982; Cisneros, 1990; Rodríguez, 1983; Hernández, 1990). This perspective can also be found in the studies on the training of indigenous teachers (Calvo and Donnadieu, 1982; Moreno and Botho, 1982). In the other interpretation school is seen as a flexible space, adaptable to the sociocultural practices, interests, and expectations of interacting groups and subjects (Paradise, 1991, 1989, 1987, 1985a, 1985b; Bertely, 1992a, 1992b, 1992c; Robles, 1993). Both types of interpretation correspond to the academic areas that deal with culturally different children's experiences (Paradise, 1990).

Since the 1940s indigenous people have migrated to cities; 30 percent of the current population resides in poor urban neighborhoods. Their interest in schooling is different from that found in rural areas. Among indigenous communities that maintain close links to farming there seems to be less expectation for schooling than among established urban groups. A comparison of the Mazahua Indians in the State of Mexico is made with the Yalaltec Indians who have settled in the metropolitan periphery of Mexico City (Bertely, 1992a, 1992b, 1992c, 1993).

There are also differences in the academic success of the various urban cultural groups. Though it is estimated that one out of five indigenous students fails to complete primary school, there are professional associations representing indigenous city-dwellers of Purépecha or Zapotec origin that include members with high levels of schooling. There are also schools where academic success can be associated with students from a specific cultural group (Vargas, 1982; Bertely, 1992a). Since these students attend standard or mainstream schools, their success does not seem to derive from cultural continuity or compatibility between the academic model and their sociocultural backgrounds.

This appears to be one of the reasons for the debate between sociolinguists and John Ogbu (1987) in the United States. The sociolinguists explain the academic performance of minorities by the presence or absence of communicational conflicts (Vogt et al., 1987; Moll and Díaz, 1987), while Ogbu and his followers utilize the concept of "cultural model." Under the concept of cultural model, Ogbu defines the understanding that people have of their universe—social, physical, or both—and that of their behavior within that universe. This understanding stems from historical differences experienced by groups in their initial incorporation into the dominant or majority society, and of the patterns of response they have created, which correspond to the subsequent treatment they have received from that society. This explains why voluntary minority immigrants to the United States are successful in school (Punjabis and Chinese), while non-immigrants introduced involuntarily (American Indians, Mexican Americans, Afro-Americans, and Hawaiians) present low levels of academic performance (Gibson, 1987; Ogbu, 1974). This perspective has not been fully developed in Mexico (Bertely, 1992c, 1993), but it appears to be an important contribution toward understanding the school situation of indigenous migrants who leave the countryside to migrate to the city by identifying the adaptation strategies that indigenous students use (Bertely, 1992a).

There are also studies categorized under the social dimension that document particular historical processes where specific actors introduce

and promote schooling in specific communities. Traditionally, the historical dominant view of education in Mexico has not taken these processes
into account, thus currently giving rise to a developing interest in the
"other history" or "regional history" (Galván, 1982).[9] Thus a number of
research projects have emerged that study the introduction of schooling
and its meaning for subjects, groups, or specific locations, as well as the
ensuing values, practices, and conflicts in a kind of "historical ethnography." Access to local, regional, and national archives is of vital importance
to this research as is the compilation of the life histories of protagonists in
such processes (Bertely, 1992c, 1993; Alfonseca, 1993).

As can be seen, ethnographic research within the social dimension
contributes to the consideration of: (1) the impact of characteristics, socioeconomic practices, and distribution of wealth affecting the academic
success of students; (2) the way in which schooling practices negate, fragment, and stereotype the social experience of students; (3) the importance
of "otherness" and "the different" in the design of educational policies. To
document the plural character of Mexico's national identity is a reflective
contribution to preventing discrimination or the devaluing of Mexico's
indigenous cultures or languages. It invites Mexicans to stop conceiving of
themselves as a "negated civilization" (Bonfil, 1990).

Conclusion

This chapter has pursued two objectives: (1) the description of the state of
the art in Mexican ethnography, and (2) the identification of some of the
challenges facing educational policy in Mexico as well as the limitations
and possibilities of daily social action in schools.

While a considerable amount of research has been cited, many important studies were not included nor covered. These omissions are not
intentional but are the result emanating from the difficulty of establishing
interinstitutional links in Mexico that ensure the diffusion of research results and publications. The overview presented herein also does not present
an evaluation according to orthodox academic criteria, which would make
a distinction between "truly ethnographic" and "non-ethnographic" products. The institutional conditions of production, the variety of topics, and
the different professional training of those who do ethnography in Mexico
have led to a similar variety of theoretical orientations and levels of academic quality in ethnographic production. Diverse though these levels of
quality may be, all research projects make some contribution or contain
some important information. However, with regard to the diversity of

theoretical orientations, it would be worth discussing whether the field of ethnography can be defined as something compact and complete, in terms of orthodox methodology, or as a field in process. The epistemological debate must also be refined so as to identify the common bases of research as well as the differences.

Another interesting question arising from this overview is the variety of data sources for research. Aside from incorporating the classical techniques of observation and interview, there is a growing use of the narrative, life histories, and local and personal archives. Arising from such a variety of data sources are some questions for consideration: Is it possible to diversify the documentation of those voices that intervene in the social action of a subject or group, incorporating different sources of information? Does this variety of sources require that we re-formulate and review some of the methodological criteria now prevalent in ethnographic research?

With regard to the second objective of this study—identifying the challenges facing educational policy in Mexico—each dimension documents a variety of findings that pose countless questions about some of the political, institutional, curricular, and social stereotypes that are imposed on daily school practice as "mandatory" norms. In some cases, especially in reproductionist theory studies dominant in Mexico, protagonists appear to be defined by such stereotypes. However, in most other studies, subjects regain their active roles as the builders of specific intersubjective realities, capable of adapting each situation to their daily social activity.

The organization of production in each of the dimensions points to some of the educational problems and possibilities that appear to require further attention. These are synthesized with the following directives:

1. Review the centralizing approach that has characterized the design of educational policies in Mexico. This implies reinterpreting and legitimizing institutional practices based upon local and regional requirements and characteristics. Research findings show how the various protagonists enter into negotiation within schools and how they appropriate and adapt to their institutional organization in differing degrees.

2. Broaden the prevalent view of teaching, no longer restricting it to its purely pedagogical aspects but incorporating its administrative, political, labor, union, social, and personal dynamics as well. This would lead to new policies for teachers in all of these aspects.

3. Formulate proposals legitimizing the curricular adaptations implemented by teachers and authorities in the various regions, municipalities, or communities of Mexico. This would have results if a degree of independence of these curricular adaptations from national plans and programs of study had been previously established. Research findings point to the existing gap between the curriculum on paper and in reality.
4. Consider students' points of view, behaviors, and expectations in building academic knowledge. Studies show that the processes of cognitive development, the styles, interests, expectations, and social experiences of students determine not only the meaning they give to academic knowledge but also their academic performance.
5. Recognize the urgent need to review the role of schools in a pluricultural society, including minorities, and to salvage the culture, language, and traditions of indigenous communities so that school will be a space that revitalizes students' ethnic identity while giving them the means to establish favorable intercultural relations.

In Mexico many of these demands have been incorporated into recent educational reforms at the level of political discourse, resulting in the Educational Modernization Campaign, the General Law for Education,[10] the new Plans and Programs of Study in Basic Education,[11] and the design of supporting materials like textbooks for students or manuals for teachers. The ethnographic studies reviewed here share many of the concerns and definitions expressed by these current educational policies.

Beyond that discourse, however, research has not found a sufficient connection between the intentions and efforts of academics and those of politicians; most researchers have yet to analyze the measures taken and, especially, the ways in which change is effected. The question remains: Should ethnographers consider taking an "ethical" or legitimizing stance regarding the political use of their findings?

Similar concerns are reflected in the academic debate within the United States. Anthropologist Evelyn Jacob (1993) states that even if our concepts are not related to the wider social context, our actual role within it is not clear. Researchers do not lead the general debate on education, nor do they bring their concepts, perspectives, or interests to bear. However, if they did make this information available to the protagonists, would it not help to change prevailing educational stereotypes?

In Jacob's view we need to promote systematic forms of communication, that is, become involved in the training of teachers, in educational practice, in discussions with policy makers and the media, and in interactions with other groups. Such a perspective would include making linkages with foreign colleagues sharing the same concerns. To borrow from Gibson (1987) and the case of immigrants acting outside their cultural enclaves, the challenge we face is to become acculturated without becoming assimilated. As ethnographic researchers in Mexico, we are defining ethnography as it applies to our contexts, our cultural differences, languages, and socialization patterns within particular political spaces. We embrace the opportunity both to continue learning from our research and experiences and to project the realm of such experiences into the consciousness of other researchers, particularly those interested in the globalization of ethnographic research.

Notes

1. Though there is no unified concept for the meaning of educational ethnography, in its broadest sense it is a form of qualitative research that attempts to describe and interpret in a detailed, profound, and analytical manner a group's activities, shared beliefs, daily educational practices or processes, from the point of view of members of that group or culture, as they occur in their natural milieu, and it also seeks to place the resulting data within a broader cultural, political, and social system.

2. Manuel Gamio (a disciple of Franz Boas), Moisés Saenz (a disciple of Dewey), Julio de la Fuente (who was an assistant to Malinowski during his research in Oaxaca in 1939), Aguirre Beltrán, Guillermo de la Peña, and Patricia Greaves are examples of ethnographic researchers.

3. Other works reviewing ethnographic research in Mexico are Inclán (1992) and Corenstein (1991, 1992).

4. The term *psychologism* refers to the reductionist use of psychological theories in the design of curriculum, program development, teaching and learning objectives, and evaluation strategies. In this reductionist approach, non-psychological processes that intervene in social practices, such as specific political, institutional, social, and cultural policies, are ignored. The theoretical principles of the conductivist or behaviorist approach, based on stimulus–response relationships, clearly coincide with the current educational policy, which is basically interested in defining the parameters needed to measure the efficiency of the national educational system. Such efficiency, while ignoring factors related to quality, emphasizes educational outcomes, the content covered, the objectives attained, and the numbers of students who are serviced and promoted.

    Psychologism as well as efficiency correspond to "instrumental rationality," defined by Max Weber as the expansion of the criteria of rational decision-making in diverse social arenas as instrumental action with a means to an end. Habermas uses this concept in referring to modern societies where legitimacy is based on the capacity to organize subjects (people) in accordance with well-defined final actions.

5. For a more detailed review of this school, see Barquera (1991), De Landsheere (1982), De Schutter and Yopo (1983), Gajardo (1983, 1985), Schmelkes (1991), Yopo (1982) and Zúñiga (1991).

6. In reviewing the types of ethnographic research that exist in Mexico, the foci of research as well as recurrent themes and contrasts in the types of problems and issues were identified. Such identification explains why the authors of this chapter constructed analytic categories broadly defined as "dimensions." These dimensions are defined not only

for their classification schema, but also for their ability to provide information about the educational problems of Mexico, which have been documented. In addition, they also point to the educational levels that have been under study and the degree of attention they have received as ethnographic studies in Mexico. The dimensions are: institutional and political, curricular, and social.

7. At one extreme, Náhuatl is spoken by 1,400,000 inhabitants; at the other, Pápago is spoken by only 236 persons. Five languages encompass 60 percent of all indigenous speakers (Náhuatl, Maya, Zapotec, Mixtec, and Otomí, in degree of use).

8. The term *Hispanization* (*ladinización* in Spanish) refers to a process of assimilation which leads to the negation of indigenous culture in favor of the majority mestizo (combined Indian and European) cultures.

9. The level of exploitation in which the Indians of Mexico find themselves led to the uprising of the Zapatista Army for National Liberation (EZLN) in the state of Chiapas in January 1994. The "armed democracy" as a strategy of struggle attempts to guarantee attention to the historical demands that have not been resolved without aspiring to power. The intent of this movement is to pressure the government of Mexico to make political decisions that favor the indigenous groups within the country. Opening the road to democracy means, from their perspective, opposing the party that has retained power for the past forty years and that has neither heard nor resolved their demands—the Partido Revolucionario Institucional (PRI, National Revolutionary Party). Among the demands of the EZLN is an education of quality for their children, the building of schools, the hiring of teachers, and respect for native languages and cultures. For that reason the state budgets have been designated to include curricular proposals that effectively meet the needs of the indigenous populations of Mexico. Institutions such as the Consejo Nacional de Fomento Educativo (CONAFE, National Council of Educational Promotion), and the Dirección General de Educación Indígena (DGEI, General Bureau of Indian Education), among others, design educational proposals to that end.

    Other government offices, union and private, attempt to favor the correlation of political forces with different alternatives that will modify the state of exploitation in which the Indians of Mexico find themselves. The problem, however, is far from being resolved. The "modernizing" discourse of the current government is being strongly questioned about the existence of such noncomformities. The political vision requires complementing a perspective that is founded in globalization while another attends to the internal demands of the country. These seem to have been subordinated to a myth, and the consequences from this are apparent.

10. Research findings and outcomes in education in Mexico have, without doubt, been important outputs for the recent reforms in educational policies. The following can be identified:

    In 1989 the official program of Educational Modernization was elaborated, which, among many other objectives, sought the modification of the elementary level curriculum. This "modernization" is concretely stipulated in the National Agreement for the Modernization of Basic Education. In it the federal government, the states, and the teachers' union collaborate to obtain the following objectives: (a) the reorganization of the educational system (decentralization of basic education and the creation of organic entities of social participation at different levels of the educational system, including schools themselves); (b) the reformulation of content and educational/instructional materials, which includes the introduction of constructivist tendencies in the teaching of reading, writing, and mathematics as well as the renovation of obligatory and free textbooks for students and teachers; this change basically modifies the prevailing plans and programs of study; and (c) the revaluing of the magisterial or teaching function, through mechanisms that promote teachers and their salaries and provide appropriate training.

    In the General Law for Education (1993) the aforementioned actions of educational policies gained legal standing. Educational federalism is legislated; this allows state governments to define priorities in terms of their budgets as well as adaptations in regional curricula. The participation of society in education is regulated to go beyond local Parent Associations. For the first time in Mexico's educational policies, equity in education is legislated by a series of measures directed toward socially and economically disadvantaged groups and regions lacking education. The State assures the existence of preschool programs and primary and secondary education. As a goal of this type of education, knowledge and democratic practice are included. Teachers are reassessed and valued, and basic education is expected to respond to the linguistic and cultural characteristics of each of the indigenous groups, of the disperse, rural population and the migrant groups by adapting its programmatic delivery.

11. In Mexico the plans and programs of study constitute the educational planning of content and process for all of basic education (preschool, primary, and secondary) throughout all of the national territory. In this manner a child in the state of Yucatán will be learning the same content as a child in Chiapas or Nuevo Leon by using the free textbooks that are distributed throughout the country under the same plans and programs.

References

Aguilar, C. (1986). *El trabajo de los maestros: Una construcción cotidiana.* Unpublished master's thesis, DIE-CINVESTAV-IPN, México, D.F., México.

Aguilar, C. and Sandoval, E. (1991). Ser mujer, ser maestra: Autovaloración profesional y participación sindical. In *Textos y pre-textos: Once estudios sobre la mujer* (pp. 4–21). México, D.F.: El Colegio de México.

Alfonseca, C. (1993). *La Escuela Rural Federal en los distritos de Texcoco y Chalco (1923–1936).* Paper presented at II Simposio de Investigación Educativa: Escuela en la Cultura, Cultura en la Escuela. CIESAS, México, D.F., México.

Althusser, L. (1974). Ideologia y aparatos ideológicos de Estado (apuntes para una investigación). *Revista Mexicana de Ciencia Política*, 78, 5–28.

Avila, M. (1989). *Análisis del curriculum formal y del curriculum vivido de la prueba operativa de Sonora.* (Research monograph). Hermosillo: México: Universidad Pedagógica Nacional.

Avilés, M.V. (1987). *Diagnóstico de la enseñanza de las ciencias naturales en la escuela primaria en el Estado de Michoacán.* (Cuadernos 2). Morelia, México: Centro de Investigación y Desarrollo del Estado de Michoacán.

Barabtarlo, A. and Theesz, M. (1985). La metodología participativa en la formación de profesores. *Perfiles Educativos*, 27, 72–77.

Bárcena, A. (1987). *Ideología y Pedagogía en el Jardín de Niños.* México: Océano.

Barquera, H. (1991). Una revisión sintética de la investigación participativa. In *Investigación participativa: Algunos aspectos críticos y problemáticos* (pp. 37–71). (Cuadernos del CREFAL 18). Pátzcuaro, Michoacán, México: CREFAL.

Baudelot, C. and Establet, R. (1981). *La escuela capitalista.* México, D.F.: Siglo XXI.

Bertely, M. (1985). *La realidad emocional y sensual en la familia y en el Jardín de Niños.* Unpublished master's thesis, DIE-CINVESTAV-IPN, México, D.F., México.

Bertely, M. (1990). *Lectura de significados en la relación educativa desde un enfoque etnográfico.* Paper presented at Coloquio: La relación educativa, varios enfoques, múltiples lecturas. UPN, México, D.F., México.

Bertely, M. (1992a). Adaptaciones escolares en una comunidad mazahua. In M. Rueda Beltrán and M.A. Campos (Eds.), *Investigación etnográfica en educación* (pp. 211–234). México, D.F.: UNAM.

Bertely, M. (1992b). Adaptaciones docentes en una comunidad mazahua. *Nueva Antropología*, 42(12), 101–120.

Bertely, M. (1992c). *Aproximación histórica al estudio etnográfico de la relación indígenas migrantes y procesos escolares: Familias yalaltecas asentadas en la periferia metropolitana.* Paper presented at the Third Inter-American Symposium on Ethnography and the Classroom, Albuquerque, NM.

Bertely, M. (1993). *El uso social de la lengua escrita y la escolarización entre los vecinos "abiertos" de Yalalag, Oaxaca (1939–1948).* Paper presented at II Simposio de Investigación Educativa: Escuela en la cultura, cultura en la escuela. CIESAS, México, D.F., México.

Bonfil, G. (1990). *México Profundo, una civilización negada.* México, D.F.: Grijalbo.

Borda, F. (1981). La ciencia y el pueblo. In *Investigación participativa y praxis rural: Nuevos conceptos en educación y desarrollo comunal* (pp. 19–47). Lima, Peru: Mosca Azul Editores.

Bourdieu, P. and Passeron, J.C. (1977). *La reproducción.* Barcelona: Laia.

Bowles, S. and Gintis, H. (1976). *Schooling in capitalist America: Educational reform and the contradiction of economic life.* New York: Basic Books.

Brousseau, G. (1986). Fundements et methodes de la didactique des matematiques. *Recherches en didactique des matematiques, 7,* 7–12.

Calvo, B. (1976). *El contexto social de un experimento pedagógico en una comunidad urbana.* Unpublished bachelor's thesis, Universidad Iberoamericana, México, D.F., México.

Calvo, B. (1984). *¿Quién es el estudiante normalista? Un caso de control político del Magisterio.* Unpublished master's thesis, Universidad Iberoamericana, México, D.F., México.

Calvo, B. (1993). *Educación no formal en poblaciones indígenas.* Paper presented at Foro de Consulta Popular para la planeación democráctica del sector educativo. CREFAL, Pátzcuaro, Michoacán, México.

Calvo, B. and Donnadieu, L. (1982). *El difícil camino de la escolaridad (el maestro indígena y su proceso de formación).* (Cuadernos de la Casa Chata 55). México, D.F.: CIESAS.

Campos, M.A. (1971). *Escuela y comunidad en un pueblo de Acolhuacan.* Unpublished master's thesis, Universidad Iberoamericana. México, D.F., México.

Campos, M.A., Gaspar, S., and López, C. (1992). Oferta y asimilación de valores científicos en la enseñanza de la biología. In M. Rueda Beltrán and M.A. Campos (Eds.), *Investigación etnográfica en educación* (pp. 181–208). México, D.F.: UNAM.

Candela, M.A. (1989). *La necesidad de entender, explicar y argumentar: Los alumnos de primaria en la actividad experimental.* Unpublished master's thesis, DIE-CINVESTAV-IPN, México, D.F., México.

Carvajal, A. (1988). *El margen de acción y las relaciones sociales de los maestros: Un estudio etnográfico en la escuela primaria.* Unpublished master's thesis, DIE-CINVESTAV-IPN, México, D.F., México.

Castañeda, A. (1989). La identidad de la práctica educativa a nivel medio superior y superior. In M. Rueda Beltrán, G. Delgado Ballesteros, and M.A. Campos (Eds.), *El aula universitaria: Aproximaciones metodológicas* (pp. 299–306). México, D.F.: UNAM.

Cisneros, E. (1990). *El proceso de transmisión cultural y educación formal en las comunidades indígenas mexicanas.* (Cuadernos de Cultura Pedagógica). México, D.F.: Universidad Pedagógica Nacional.

Corenstein, M. (1991). *Qualitative educational research in Mexico.* Paper presented at the Annual Meeting of the American Educational Research Association, San Francisco.

Corenstein, M. (1992). Panorama de la investigación etnográfica en la educación en México: Un primer acercamiento. In M. Rueda Beltrán and M.A. Campos (Eds.), *Investigación etnográfica en educación* (pp. 359–375). México, D.F.: UNAM.

Cornejo, A. (1986). Socialización y aprendizaje en un salón de clase. *Cuadernos del Colegio,* 30, 44–61

Cornejo, A. (1988). *La escuela secundaria de Xoco: Un estudio de caso sobre procedencias socioeconómicas e interacciones educativas en un grupo de alumnos.* Unpublished bachelor's thesis, UNAM, México, D.F., México.

Cornejo, A. (1991). Estudiantes y prácticas educativas en el aula: Análisis de un caso. In M. Rueda Beltrán, G. Delgado Ballesteros, and M.A. Campos (Eds.), *El aula universitaria: Aproximaciones metodológicas* (pp. 59–83). México, D.F.: UNAM.

Coronado, G., Franco, V.M., and Muñoz, H. (1981). *Bilingüismo y Educación en el Valle del Mezquital.* (Cuadernos de la Casa Chata 42). México, D.F.: CIESAS.

Darcy de Oliveira, R. and Darcy de Oliveira, M. (1982). The militant observer: A sociological alternative. In *Creating knowledge: A monopology?* Toronto, Ontario, Canada: International Council for Adult Education.

De Landsheere, G. (1982). *La investigación experimental en educación.* París: UNESCO.

De Schutter, A. and Yopo, B. (1983). Desarrollo y perspectivas de la investigación participativa.

In *La investigación participativa en América Latina*. (Retablo de Papel 10). Pátzcuaro, Michoacán, México: CREFAL.

Delgado Ballesteros, G. (1991). Las relaciones de género en el salón de clases. In M. Rueda Beltrán, G. Delgado Ballesteros, and M.A. Campos (Eds.), *El aula universitaria: Aproximaciones metodológicas* (pp. 139–148). México, D.F.: UNAM.

Delgado Ballesteros, G. (1992). Las diferencias de género en los usos del lenguaje en el aula. In M. Rueda Beltrán and M.A. Campos (Eds.), *Investigación etnográfica en educación*. (pp. 261–287). México, D.F.: UNAM.

Díaz Coder, E. (1990). *Diversidad sociocultural y educación en México*. Seminario de Estudios de la Cultura. México, D.F.: CNCA.

Edwards, V. (1986). *Los sujetos y la construcción social del conocimiento escolar en primaria: Un estudio etnográfico*. (Cuadernos de Investigación Educativa 19). México, D.F.: DIE-CINVESTAV-IPN.

Escalante, I. and Robert, M. (1987). *La evaluación en la Escuela Primaria*. (Colección Cuadernos de Cultura Pedagógica. Serie Investigación Educativa 5). México, D.F.: Universidad Pedagógica Nacional.

Ezpeleta, J. (1992). El trabajo docente y sus condiciones invisibles. *Nueva Antropología, 42* (12), 27–42.

Ferreiro, E. (1984). *La práctica del dictado en el primer año escolar*. (Cuadernos de Investigación Educativa 15). México, D.F.: DIE-CINVESTAV-IPN.

Fortes, J. and Lomnitz, L. (1991). *La formación del científico en México: Adquiriendo una nueva identidad*. México, D.F.: Siglo XXI.

Freire, P. (1982). Creating alternative research methods: Learning to do it by doing it. In *Creating knowledge: A monopoly?* Toronto, Ontario, Canada: International Council for Adult Education.

Freudenthal, H. (1983). *Didactical phenomenology of mathematical structures*. Amsterdam: Reidel.

Fuenlabrada, I. (1990). *Formación de profesores sobre áreas fundamentales de la educación básica*. Final report. DIE-CINVESTAV-IPN, México, D.F., México.

Gadamer, H. (1977). *Verdad y método: Las grandes líneas de una hermenéutica filosófica*. Salamanca: Sígueme.

Gajardo, M. (1983). Investigación participativa: Propuestas y proyectos. *Revista Latinoamericana de Estudios Educativos, 13*(1), 49–85.

Gajardo, M. (1985). Evolución, situación actual y perspectivas de las estrategias de investigación participativa en América Latina. In *Teoría y práctica de la educación popular*. Pátzcuaro, Michoacán, México: CREFAL.

Gajardo, M. and Werthein, J. (1983). Educación participativa: Alternativas metodológicas. *Revista Latinoamericana de Estudios Educativos, 13*(3), 83–104.

Gallegos, A. (1988). *Vida de los adolescentes en la escuela secundaria: Una aproximación desde lo cotidiano*. Unpublished bachelor's thesis, Escuela Normal Superior de México, México, D.F., México.

Galván, L.E. (1982). *La palabra Mazahua (Documentos municipales para la historia de la educación indígena)*. (Cuadernos de Casa Chata 61). México, D.F.: CIESAS

Gálvez, G., Rockwell, E., Paradise, R., and Sobrecasas, S. (1981). *El uso del tiempo y de los libros de texto en primaria*. (Cuadernos de Investigaciones Educativas 1). México, D.F.: DIE-CINVESTAV-IPN.

García, C.M. (1986). *La Escuela DPR 16–0720-5: Crónica de un desentreñamiento*. Unpublished master's thesis, DIE-CINVESTAV-IPN, México, D.F., México.

García Salord, S. and Vanella, S. (1992). *Normas y valores en el salón de clases*. México, D.F.: Siglo XXI.

Garduño, L. and Lorandi, M. (1992). Desarrollo y evaluación del proyecto educativo Ixtliyollotl. *Revista Latinoamericana de Estudios Educativos, 13*(3), 109–121.

Garnica, A.B. (1991). *El papel de la evaluación dentro de las tradiciones escolares*. Unpublished bachelor's thesis, Escuela Normal 2 de Nezahualcóyotl, México, D.F., México.

Geertz, C. (1987). *La interpretación de la cultura*. México, D.F.: Gedisa.

Gibson, M. (1987). The school performance of immigrant minorities: A comparative study. *Anthropology and Education Quarterly,* 18(4), 262–275.

Hamel, R.E. (1983). El contexto sociológico de la enseñanza y adquisición del Español en escuelas indígenas bilingües en el Valle del Mezquital. *Estudios de Lingüística Aplicada,* 20, 37–104.

Hamel, R.E. (1984). Sociocultural conflict and bilingual education: The case of the Otomi Indians in Mexico. *Interaction through Language,* 36(1), 113–128.

Hamel, R.E. (1988). Determinantes sociolingüísticas de la educación indígena bilingüe. In *Signos: Anuario de Humanidades 1988* (pp. 319–376). México, D.F.: Universidad Autónoma Metropolitana.

Hamel, R.E. and Muñoz, H. (1981). Bilingüismo, educación indígena y conciencia lingüística en comunidades otomíes del Valle del Mezquital, México. *Estudios Filológicos,* 16, 127–160.

Hamel, R.E. and Muñoz, H. (Eds). (1982). *El conflicto lingüístico en una zona bilingüe de México.* (Cuadernos de la Casa Chata 65). México, D.F.: CIESAS.

Hernández, J. (1989). *La enseñanza de las ciencias naturales: Entre una re-descripción de la experiencia cotidiana y una resignificación del conocimiento escolar.* Unpublished master's thesis, DIE-CINVESTAV-IPN, México, D.F., México.

Hernández, E. (1990). *Procesos educativos, ladinización y resistencia étnica en la Frontera Sur.* (Research monograph). Tuxtla Gutiérrez, Chiapas, México: Universidad Pedagógica Nacional.

Hernández, J. and López, C. (1991). La enseñanza de las prácticas de laboratorio en la Facultad de Psicología de la UNAM. In M. Rueda Beltrán, G. Delgado Ballesteros, and M.A. Campos (Eds.), *El aula universitaria: Aproximaciones metodológicas* (pp. 197–209). México, D.F.: UNAM.

Illich, I. (1977). *Un mundo sin escuelas.* Mexico, D.F.: Nueva Imagen.

Inclán, C. (1992). *Diagnóstico y perspectivas de la investigación educativa etnográfica en México 1975–1988.* (Cuadernos del CESU 28). México, D.F.: Centro de Estudios Sobre la Universidad, UNAM.

Jacob, E. (1993). Social context: Moving to the mainstream. *AERA-Division G Newsletter,* 20, 1–5.

Latapí, P. (1991). Algunas observaciones sobre la investigación participativa. In *Investigación participativa: Algunos aspectos críticos y problemáticos.* (Cuadernos del CREFAL 18). Pátzcuaro, Michoacán, México: CREFAL.

Lerner, V. (1991). La enseñanza de la historia en el salón de clases: Información versus formación. In M. Rueda Beltrán, G. Delgado Ballesteros, and M.A. Campos (Eds.), *El aula universitaria: Aproximaciones metodológicas* (pp. 149–166). México, D.F.: UNAM.

Levinson, B. (1992). *Contra toda la diferencia: Producción de una cultura de la igualdad en una escuela secundaria mexicana.* Paper presented at Third Inter-American Symposium on Ethnography and the Classroom, Albuquerque, NM.

López, A. (1990). *Relación escuela-comunidad: Estudio de un caso.* Unpublished bachelor's thesis, Colegio de Pedagogía, UNAM, México, D.F., México.

Luis O.F. (1982). *Los niños monolingües zapotecas ante la educación primaria.* Unpublished bachelor's thesis, CIESAS, México, D.F., México.

Mayer, E. (1982). Los alcances de una política de educación bicultural y bilingüe. *América Indígena,* 42(2), 269–280.

Mayer, L.L. (1982). *Centros de poder en una facultad de la UNAM.* Unpublished bachelor's thesis, Universidad Iberoamericana, México, D.F., México.

Medina, P. (1992). *Ser maestro, estar en la escuela: La apropiación cotidiana del trabajo escolar en las relaciones entre maestros.* (Informe de Investigación 4). México, D.F.: Universidad Pedagógica Nacional.

Mercado, R. (1985). *La escuela primaria gratuita, una lucha popular cotidiana.* (Cuadernos de Investigación Educativa 17). México, D.F.: DIE-CINVESTAV-IPN.

Molina, A. (1989). *Estudio exploratorio de los aspectos cualitativos de la deserción del sujeto escolar a nivel primaria: Dos estudios de caso en el ámbito familiar y escolar en la zona sur del D.F. (Pedregal de Santo Domingo).* Unpublished bachelor's thesis, Colegio de Pedagogía, UNAM, México, D.F., México.

Moll, L. and Díaz, S. (1987). Chance as the goal of educational research. *Anthropology and Education Quarterly*, 18(4), 300–311.

Moreno, G. and Botho, A. (1982). *¿Qué somos los maestros bilingües en el Valle del Mezquital?* Unpublished bachelor's thesis, CIESAS, México, D.F., México.

Muñoz, H. (1980). Castellanización y conflicto linguïstico. *Boletín de Antropología Americana*, 2, 129–146.

Muñoz, H. (1983). *La escuela otomí: Entre la castellanización y el bilingüismo.* (Cuadernos de la Casa Chata 78). México, D.F.: CIESAS.

Ogbu, J. (1974). *The next generation: An ethnography of education in an urban neighborhood.* New York: Academic Press.

Ogbu, J. (1987). Variability in minority school performance: A problem in search of an explanation. *Anthropology and Education Quarterly*, 18(4), 312–334.

Olivera, M. (1961). *Las condiciones socioeconómicas de los educandos en la experimentación pedagógica.* Unpublished bachelor's thesis, Escuela Nacional de Antropología e Historia, México, D.F., México.

Ornelas, A. (1991). La heterogeneidad lingüística y sus efectos en la construcción del conocimiento escolar en el aula. In M. Rueda Beltrán, G. Delgado Ballesteros, and M.A. Campos (Eds.), *El aula universitaria: Aproximaciones metodológicas* (pp. 169–179). México, D.F.: UNAM.

Paradise, R. (1979). *Socialización para el trabajo: La interacción maestro-alumnos en la escuela primaria.* (Cuadernos de Investigación Educativa 5). México, D.F.: DIE-CINVESTAV-IPN.

Paradise, R. (1985a). *Una resistencia efectiva frente a las presiones de la urbanización: El caso de los migrantes mazahuas a la Merced.* Paper presented at Primer Encuentro de Estudios sobre la Región Mazahua, México, D.F., México.

Paradise, R. (1985b). Un análisis psicosocial de la motivación y participación emocional en un caso de aprendizaje individual. *Revista Latinoamericana de Estudios Educativos*, 15(1), 83–93.

Paradise, R. (1987). *Learning through social interaction: The experience and development of Mazahua self in the context of the market.* Unpublished doctoral dissertation, University of Pennsylvania, Philadelphia.

Paradise, R. (1989). *Cultural meaningfulness in nonverbal interaction: Mazahua children learning how to be separate-but-together.* (Research monograph). México, D.F.: DIE-CINVESTAV-IPN.

Paradise, R. (1990). *Pasos hacia la comunicación intercultural: Las adaptaciones de niños mazahuas y sus maestros en la práctica dentro del aula.* Paper presented at Seminario para la Cultura, Consejo Nacional para la Cultura y la Artes, México, D.F., México.

Paradise, R. (1991). El conocimiento cultural en el aula: Niños indígenas y su orientación hacia la observación. *Infancia y Aprendizaje*, 55, 83–85.

Pérez, J., Abiega, L., Zarco, M., and Schugurensky, D. (1986). *Nezahualpilli: Educación Preescolar Comunitaria.* México, D.F.: CEE.

Pineda, J. and Zamora, M. (1992). *Disciplina, procesos sociales e institución escolar.* (Informe de Investigación 1). México, D.F.: Universidad Pedagógica Nacional.

Quiroz, R. (1991). Obstáculos para la apropiación de los contenidos académicos de la escuela secundaria. *Infancia y Aprendizaje*, 55, 45–58.

Ramírez, B. (1980). *La enseñanza diferencial de la lecto-escritura y su relación con factores socieconómicos.* (Cuadernos de la Casa Chata 30). México, D.F.: CIESAS.

Remedi, E., Aristi, P., Castañeda, A., and Landesman, M. (1989). *Maestros, entrevistas e identidad.* (Research monograph). México, D.F.: DIE-CINVESTAV-IPN.

Ricoeur, P. (1981). *Hermeneutics and the human sciences. Essays on language, action and interpretation.* Cambridge, England: Cambridge University Press.

Robles, A. (1988). *Los preescolares: ¿Páginas en blanco o sujetos con historia?* Unpublished bachelor's thesis, Universidad Pedagógica Nacional, México, D.F., México.

Robles, A. (1993). *Tiempo muerto o tiempo vivo: Niños Mazahuas en una escuela rural.* Paper presented at IV Simposio Interamericano de Investigación Etnográfica en Educación, CISE-UNAM, México, D.F., México.

Rockwell, E. (1982). *De huellas, bardas y veredas: Una historia cotidiana en la escuela.* (Cuadernos de Investigación Educativa 4). México, D.F.: DIE-CINVESTAV-IPN.

Rockwell, E. (1987). *Reflexiones sobre el proceso etnográfico (1982–1985)*. (Research monograph). México, D.F.: DIE-CINVESTAV-IPN.

Rockwell, E. and Galvez, G. (1981). *La enseñanza de las ciencias naturales en cuatro grupos de primaria*. (Research monograph). México, D.F.: DIE-CINVESTAV-IPN.

Rodríguez, M. (1983). *Los mazahuas de San Felipe del Progreso, Estado de México. Educación e ideología en las escuelas albergue*. Unpublished master's thesis, Universidad Iberoamericana, México, D.F., México.

Rosas, L., (1987). Una experiencia de innovación educativa. *Cero en Conducta*, 2(9), 10–15.

Rueda Beltrán, M., Delgado Ballesteros, G., and Campos, M.A. (Eds.). (1991). *El aula universitaria: Aproximaciones metodológicas*. México, D.F.: UNAM.

Rueda Beltrán, M. and Campos, M.A. (Eds.). (1992). *Investigación etnográfica en educación*. México, D.F.: UNAM.

Rueda Beltrán, M. and Canales, A. (1991). La relación educativa universitaria: Análisis de casos. In M. Rueda Beltrán, G. Delgado Ballesteros, and M.A. Campos (Eds.), *El aula universitaria: Aproximaciones metodológicas* (pp. 101–124). México, D.F.: UNAM.

Rueda Beltrán, M. and Canales, A. (1992). La educación universitaria: La función de la clase. In M. Rueda Beltrán and M.A. Campos (Eds.), *Investigación etnográfica en educación* (pp. 235–248). México, D.F.: UNAM.

Safa, P. (1992). *¿Por qué enviamos a nuestros hijos a la escuela? Socialización infantil e identidad popular*. México, D.F.: Grijalbo.

Salinas, G. (1988). *Las maestras de primaria: Una visión antropológica de su vida cotidiana y su trabajo docente*. Unpublished bachelor's thesis, Escuela Nacional de Antropología e Historia, México, D.F., México.

Sánchez, M. (1991a). *Santa Catalina, una realidad inadvertida*. Paper presented at Encuentro Nacional para el Desarrollo de la Educación Indígena, UPN, México, D.F., México.

Sánchez, M. (1991b). *El proceso de apropiación de la lecto-escritura en los primeros grados de las escuelas primarias de una localidad otomí*. (Research monograph). Instituto Superior de Ciencias de la Educación del Estado de México, Toluca, México.

Sandoval, E. (1986). *Los maestros y su sindicato: Relaciones y procesos cotidianos*. (Cuadernos de Investigaciones Educativas 18). México, D.F.: DIE-CINVESTAV-IPN.

Schmelkes, S. (1991). Fundamentos teóricos de la investigación participativa. In *Investigación participativa: Algunos aspectos críticos y problemáticos* (pp. 73–87). (Cuadernos del CREFAL 18). Pátzcuaro, Michoacán, México: CREFAL.

Schmelkes, S. and Lavin, S. (1988). El CEE y la investigación acción en educación. *Revista Latinoamericana de Estudios Educativos*, 17(3–4), 129–143.

Schütz, A. (1974). *El problema de la realidad social*. Buenos Aires: Amorrortu.

Stock, E. (1987). *Los libros de texto gratuitos en México y su contexto en materia de educación sexual: Un estudio aplicando el método etnográfico*. Unpublished bachelor's thesis, Colegio de Pedagogía, UNAM, México, D.F., México.

Street, S. (1993). *Un renacer cultural para el magisterio: Maestros de base en el movimiento democrático chiapaneco*. Paper presented at Simposio de Investigación Educativa: Escuela en la cultura, cultura en la escuela. CIESAS, México, D.F., México.

Tedesco, J.C. (1989). Los paradigmas de la investigación educativa. *Universidad Futura*, 1(2), 2–16.

Valentínez, M. (1982). *La persistencia de la lengua y la cultura purépecha frente a la educación escolar*. (Colección Etnolingüística 24). México, D.F.: Instituto Nacional Indigenista.

Varea, A. (1983). *El fracaso escolar y la Escuela Nueva: Un estudio metodológico*. Unpublished master's thesis, DIE-CINVESTAV-IPN, México, D.F., México.

Vargas, M.E. (1982). *Educación y cultura: La educación bilingüe y bicultural en comunidades purépechas*. México, D.F.: Instituto Nacional Indigenista

Vergnaud, G. (1981). Queques orientations theoriques et methodologiques des recherches francaises en didactic des matematiques. *Recherches en didactique des matematiques*, 22, 12–30.

Vogt, L., Jordan, C., and Tharp, R. (1987). Explaining school failure, producing school success: Two cases. *Anthropology and Education Quarterly*, 18(4), 276–286.

Weber, M. (1969). *Economia y sociedad: Esbozo de sociología comprensiva.* Mexico, D.F.: Fondo de Cultura.

Yopo, B. (1982). *Metodología de la investigación participativa.* (Cuadernos del CREFAL 16). Pátzcuaro, Michoacán, México: CREFAL.

Zorrilla, J. (1985). La educación en el aula. In L. Luna (Ed.). *Los estudiantes: Trabajos de historia y sociología.* México, D.F.: CESU-UNAM.

Zorrilla, J. (1989). *Innovación y racionalidad educativa: El caso del CCH en la UNAM.* Unpublished master's thesis, UNAM, México, D.F., México.

Zorrilla, J. (1990). *Impacto familiar en la situación escolar.* (Research monograph). México, D.F.: CESU-UNAM.

Zúñiga, L. (1991). La investigación participativa: Antecedentes para una consideración crítica. In *Investigación participativa: Algunos aspectos críticos y problemáticos* (pp. 89–125). (Cuadernos del CREFAL 18). Pátzcuaro, Michoacán, México: CREFAL.

Section II

Qualitative Studies of Social, Educational, and Institutional Change

The previous chapters provided an overview of educational ethnographic research in Latin America. Most of the authors of these chapters were trained as ethnographers and have a background in social and cultural anthropology. The following chapters describe qualitative studies that appropriate ethnographic methods. The authors in this section are primarily trained in qualitative sociology and are interested in documenting social, educational, and institutional change. Chapters Four, Five, and Six range from studies of popular education implemented in non-formal educational settings (Stromquist) to broad-based social movements that impact schools and families (Schmukler), to formal educational settings attempting to implement institutional and pedagogical innovations (Zorrilla).

The three authors are documenting social processes with which they feel varying degrees of identification and solidarity. Although their studies were not "participatory research" in the Freireian sense of co-constructing knowledge through transformative action with participants, the authors were in one way or another involved in the settings under study in the sense of lending moral and, in some cases, technical support to the projects. This positionality of being in solidarity with the groups under study challenges many of the tenets of traditional ethnographic research, which has been criticized by many feminist and critical theorists as neo-positivist.

Roman (1992), for example, argued that traditional ethnography (and some critical ethnographies) are part of a positivist project that "affirms a social world that is meant to be gazed upon but not challenged or transformed" (p. 573). Much of the political and epistemological debate that takes place within qualitative research in North America has not been informed by the thirty-year experience in Latin America with participatory research, which views the generation of knowledge and emancipatory social action as intimately linked. This blurring of the distinction between research and action is more clearly exemplified in Barabtarlo y Zedansky and Theesz Poschner's chapter in the last section of the book.

This lack of awareness on the part of North American researchers is, in part, due to the fact that documentation of Latin American popular education projects has seldom been translated and published in North American journals. (For exceptions see Magendzo, 1990 and Vaccaro, 1990.) Furthermore, many of those engaged in participatory projects were more dedicated to doing their work than writing about it. Thus many of the participatory projects of the last thirty years in Latin America have at best resulted in local reports that have not been widely disseminated or at worst have gone completely unrecorded. Perhaps the most complete documentation of this work is contained in a series of publications of the CREFAL (Centro Regional de Educación Participativa en América Latina) in Pátzcuaro, México. (For excellent overviews of this work in Spanish, see Gajardo, 1985 and Vejerano, 1983.)

Therefore, while the level of actual researcher participation in the projects under study was minimal, their commitment to the documentation of these projects is clear. Both Stromquist and Schmukler have been strongly influenced by Latin American feminist theory and a concern—borne of experience with totalitarian governments—with institutional and social democratization movements. Zorrilla has been employed by the same institution Universidad Nacional Autónoma de México (UNAM) that developed and implemented the innovative secondary schools that he studied.

Interestingly, both Stromquist and Zorrilla end up raising serious questions about the pedagogical effectiveness of the projects they studied. While Stromquist found some positive unanticipated social and affective effects of the project she studied, Zorrilla found that the laudable premises of the innovation he studied were so distorted by political maneuver that their pedagogical intent was totally subverted.

Nelly Stromquist describes in Chapter Four the impact on poor Brazilian women of a literacy program (MOVA; Movimento de Alfabetizacao de Jovens e Adultos) in São Paulo, a program with the intellectual and political support of Paulo Freire, who was the city's secretary of education during the program's first two years. Stromquist identifies through her study the failure of many of the program's emancipatory objectives, while at the same time describing some unanticipated benefits of these programs for poor women. She concludes by suggesting ways in which the political socialization of women must be rethought in ways that take into account how literacy needs fit into the hierarchy of survival needs poor women encounter in everyday life.

Beatriz Schmukler, author of Chapter Five, has been studying the role of women in the democratization of social institutions for two decades. Their experience with military dictatorships has created an intense interest among Argentinian, Chilean, Paraguayan, and Uruguayan educational researchers in the role of schools in authoritarian societies. (In this regard, see especially the work of Juan Carlos Tedesco and José Joaquín Brunner.)

Schmukler documents the shift that women have made from the private to the public sphere and women's impact on schools and other social institutions. An early symbol of this shift is the ever present image in Schmukler's work of the Mothers of the Plaza de Mayo, who marched to protest the abduction of their children by the military and who encompassed the image of housewives taking the public space of the central plaza as their own. At a more micro level of analysis her work documents the daily gendered negotiations that occur within the family and between the home and the school. In her work Schmukler captures the synergistic relationship between the democratization of families and the democratization of schools.

In Chapter Six, qualitative sociologist Juan Fidel Zorrilla describes a study that explores some of the latent functions of a progressive educational innovation in Mexico City. In 1970 the Mexican government supported the creation of a series of innovative high schools (Colegios de Ciencias y Humanidades—CCH) under the auspices of Mexico's National University in Mexico City. These schools were supposed to reflect state-of-the-art pedagogy and developmental theory. Zorrilla, along with numerous other qualitative researchers (Cornejo, 1992; Bartolucci and Rodriguez, 1983) have engaged in longitudinal qualitative studies of these schools. Zorrilla found that there was a disturbing gap between the intentions of the reformers and the realities of school and classroom life. He describes how Mexican teachers' material work conditions and the less structured, avant-garde approaches to pedagogy in these schools left many students with an anomic education. Drawing on Durkheim's notion of anomie, he describes a nearly normless culture of seemingly arbitrary grading and idiosyncratic instruction. His findings, reflected through a series of case studies, in some ways echo those of Delpit (1988) and others who argue that when pedagogies do not make explicit the rules of the "culture of power," students without strong, middle-class supports in the home do less well. Zorrilla links his thesis of anomie to the institutional structures, the curriculum, and the very pedagogy students are exposed to.

References

Bartolucci, J. and Rodriguez, R. (1983). *El colegio de ciencias y humanidades (1971–1980): Una experiencia de innovación universitaria*. México, D.F.: ANUIES.

Cornejo, A. (1992). Estratégias de supervivencia de los estudiantes en el salón de clases. In M. Beltrán Rueda and M.A. Campos (Eds.), *Investigación etnográfica en educación*. México, D.F.: Universidad Nacional Autónoma de México.

Delpit, L. (1988). The silenced dialogue: Power and pedagogy in educating other people's children. *Harvard Educational Review*, 58(3), 119–139.

Gajardo, M. (1985). *Teoría y práctica de la educación popular*. Pátzcuaro, Michoacán, México: CREFAL.

Magendzo, S. (1990). Popular education in nongovernmental organizations: Education for social mobilization? *Harvard Educational Review*, 60, 49–61.

Roman, L. (1992). The political significance of other ways of narrating ethnography: A feminist materialist approach. In M. LeCompte, W. Millroy, and J. Goetz (Eds.), *The Handbook of qualitative research in education*. San Diego, CA: Academic Press.

Vaccaro, L. (1990). Transference and appropriation in popular education interventions: A framework for analysis. *Harvard Educational Review*, 60, 62–78.

Vejerano, G. (1983). *La investigación participativa en América Latina*. Pátzcuaro, Michoacán, México: CREFAL.

Chapter Four
The Political Resocialization of Women in a Brazilian Literacy Program (MOVA)

Nelly P. Stromquist

Many adult literacy programs today, particularly those of a nationwide scope, emphasize the provision of coding and decoding skills. Only in cases of exceptional political regime change do literacy programs contemplate the creation of new citizenship values by combining the teaching of literacy with themes and discussions that link the process of reading and writing to the socioeconomic and cultural problems that have led to the previous failure of individuals to achieve literacy. The prevailing apolitical literacy programs make the assumption that as literacy skills develop there will be a relatively automatic ascent toward increased awareness of the need for becoming an active participant in one's community and country, and that involvement in problems and matters with collective impact will inevitably ensue.

While a "political engagement" is avoided by governmental programs as something that distracts from pedagogical concerns, and challenges vested interests, there are few literacy programs outside revolutionary changes that genuinely address the need for resocialization of participants. Literacy programs that call for resocialization are usually termed "emancipatory literacy" and are based on Paulo Freire's principle of consciousness raising or critical reflection (Freire, 1972), by which, in the process of learning literacy, individuals are enabled to understand their world and to act upon it. Literacy programs conducted by non-governmental groups have often been explicit in their objectives of transforming citizen values; yet these programs have been very limited in coverage, usually serving numbers that represent a microscopic proportion of those in need. Moreover, these programs have rarely been the subject of research at the classroom level (Lind and Johnston, 1990).

In aiming at the resocialization of the individual, it is assumed that the adults attend literacy programs primarily to receive new information and that these individuals will welcome political information. By political,

I mean information that addresses personal and collective problems from a perspective that identifies who does and does not benefit from current social arrangements, and discusses how these problems may be addressed.

There are few studies that consider the characteristics of nonliterates and are at the same time sensitive to the roles that literacy development and practice play in the context of their lives (Fingeret, 1991; Merriam and Caffarella, 1991). These studies inform us that literacy acquisition by adults is dependent on changes in the life cycle and that gender attributes, particularly being a woman, substantially affect the meanings and uses of literacy (Rockhill, 1987). Women are vulnerable to the life cycle because their existence usually centers on the "other," whose demands for time and attention at the household level influence and shape the time and space resources of women. These demands vary with the age of the children, and as children grow older their demands on the mother and on other women in the family diminish. Over time domineering husbands are contested by their wives or simply die, thus releasing women from their control.

Against the preceding background, an experience worth exploring is a city-wide literacy program in São Paulo, Brazil, called MOVA (Movimento de Alfabetizacao de Jovens e Adultos). This undertaking offers real promise for the understanding of literacy programs for adults because of the following features: (a) its large-scale nature, affecting the entire city of São Paulo—a rather unusual feature for literacy programs conducted under non-revolutionary conditions; (b) the active role of grass-roots organizations in the design and implementation of the program, making MOVA an instance of change with uncommonly strong and diverse forms of community participation; (c) substantial financial and technical support by the government (in this case the local municipality); and (d) a relatively sustained effort, as the program lasted three years.

Particularly suitable to the consideration of political resocialization in literacy programs was MOVA's stated main goal of creating new citizens for the "construction of a democratic and popular alternative, the radical transformation of political structures and social organization."[1] MOVA thus pursued emancipatory objectives beyond providing reading and writing skills. The program also had the intellectual and political support of Freire, the renowned educator who brought us the concepts of *concientizacao*,[2] cultural action, dialogical education, and generative themes. Freire served as the city's secretary of education during the first two years of the program.

MOVA was initiated and sponsored by the Workers' Party (Partido dos Trabalhadores; PT), a new political force that seeks to bring greater social justice to Brazilian society (Torres, 1990; Keck, 1992). The creation of MOVA and the nature of its objectives were fully consonant with the PT's philosophy of expressing the interests of the workers and the poor at the political level (Keck, 1992, p. 239). Initial numerical targets of MOVA were to make 60,000 persons literate per year and thus produce 180,000 new readers by the end of the PT administration in December 1992. Freire, MOVA's official leader, saw literacy as essential to democratizing the municipal government. Specifically, MOVA sought to educate those who would become the new militants of the social movements.

The Context

São Paulo represents the industrial and financial heart of Brazil. With a population of 10 million (1992 census), it is one of the largest and most impressive urban centers in the world. The city, large as it is, receives 300,000 new inhabitants per year, many of them from the Northeast, dislodged from the countryside by the expansion of agroindustries and their insatiable claim for land.[3] While getting a factory job is increasingly difficult in São Paulo, those who do are paid wages considerably higher than those of other workers. The illusion and distant promise of a good job make São Paulo a particularly strong magnet.

Educationally, the city is extremely diverse. It has a highly educated population and some of the best universities in the country. At the same time, it also has an estimated 1.3 to 2 million illiterates, or about 15 percent of the city's inhabitants. Most of the illiterates are *nordestinos* (people from the Northeast), although they have typically lived in the city for more than twenty years. Today approximately 300,000 of São Paulo's children do not go to school. The problem of illiteracy is not limited to those who have never been to school. Many of those who have attended public school for a few years may be as poor readers as those without schooling. On the other hand, some unschooled people have nevertheless managed to make sense of a few printed signs in their everyday lives. Persons especially likely to become trapped in conditions of illiteracy are those who must work intensively to survive economically; not surprisingly, women are overrepresented in this group.

MOVA in São Paulo

MOVA's literacy program was conceived as a very decentralized operation. It was to be run and implemented by grass-roots organizations existing at the neighborhood level. The municipal government was to provide salaries for literacy monitors (called *monitores*, and referred to as "monitors" throughout the rest of this chapter), and funds for educational materials and basic services such as light and water. There would be no centrally imposed curriculum, but by providing ongoing training for the literacy monitors and their supervisors, the municipal government ensured some similarity of methods of instruction and program objectives. Each grassroots group would deliver the literacy program through classrooms (called *nucleos*), each of which needed a minimum of 15 students to be recognized and supported.

MOVA was publicly launched on October 29, 1989. By April 1991 there were approximately 557 *nucleos* run by 45 grass-roots groups[4] with diverse literacy qualifications, ranging from a four-year experience in running literacy programs to organizations with no previous educational activities. Persons who became *monitores* and supervisors were trained for 34 hours. Supervisors provided constant monitoring of the classes and ensured that educational materials were available.

Focus of the Study

Because São Paulo is immense, the study zeroed in on one area of the city, the Eastern Zone (Zona Leste). This area has 3 million inhabitants; it also has more than 100 *favelas*, where 12 percent of its population lives. According to studies by local groups, Zona Leste has a population estimated to be about 35 percent illiterate and 55 percent semi-literate.

In analyzing MOVA literacy programs, this paper focuses on the classroom experience from the perspective of the women who attended the literacy classes. It asks how the women lived their participation in literacy classes and to what extent this experience, through social interaction and discussion of topics, fostered the creation of new citizens, as intended by MOVA objectives. To what extent did the monitors succeed in this objective? How did women participants react to debates about political issues?

Since a common feature among the literacy programs run within MOVA is the objective of creating citizens who can be active in their communities and in societal issues, monitors were told to discuss political themes and in several cases were assigned political themes to raise the awareness of the literacy students regarding their conditions of oppression and subordination. Following the principles proposed by Freire for critical reflection:

. . . critical and liberating dialogue, which presupposes action, must be carried on with the oppressed at whatever the stage of their struggle for liberation. The content of that dialogue can and should vary in accordance with historical conditions and the level at which the oppressed perceived reality (Freire, 1972, p. 52).

This study focuses on 20 women in six *nucleos*. While all these women defined themselves as having a need for literacy skills, their levels of education were extremely varied, ranging from those who never went to school to one who had completed sixth grade—a phenomenon increasingly common among adult literacy learners.

Data derive from semi-structured interviews with these 20 women, each interview lasting between one and two hours.[5] The women were interviewed three times over the course of three years (from 1991 to 1993). Class observations and informal conversations with monitors were also conducted during that time to examine and understand the dynamics between monitors and students and among students.

One striking feature of participants in adult literacy programs was also their heterogeneity in terms of age. The 20 adult literacy students in this study tend to fall into a skewed distribution, with those older than 30 years more represented than younger women, despite the fact that several of those interviewed were women attending early afternoon classes, a time at which younger married women enjoy more freedom of movement in Brazilian culture and also a time that is less disruptive of domestic life. Those who participated tended to be women with children that could take care of themselves (i.e., seven years or older) or older women who lived alone. The average age of the adult women was 44. There was an overrepresentation of widows relative to the general population; they composed 15 percent of the participants. There were only four in ages 20 to 30; among those in that age group, two were single and the two others had children whose grandparents could babysit.

The Meanings of the Literacy Class
The MOVA classes were open to women and men alike; however, more women were present in the classes I observed. Being a minority, men tended to sit together or toward the back of the classroom. Men did not participate in ways substantially different from women, and their presence did not seem to inhibit the women students.

Before examining the influence of the literacy classes on the political resocialization of women, it is necessary to understand the meanings participation in literacy classes had for them. From the women's perspective, the literacy classes constitute very desirable social spaces. The classroom emerges as a setting that is socially approved for women and which can offer services that are not available elsewhere. Three meanings of social space can be detected.

A Site for Social Distraction

The classroom is generally described by the students as a place where women may have a good time away from home, feel at ease, and enjoy some laughter and amusement. The women participants often portray the literacy classroom as one in which "very good conviviality" reigns. The existence of entertaining peers, amusing stories, good talk, and good laughter persistently characterize the classroom. Jovenira indicated that she felt happier and more talkative after attending class: "It is different from staying only at home working. Before my classes, I stayed home alone, crying. I felt overwhelmed by many problems." Alicia, who was having marital problems, indicated that she took the classes to have a good time: "I don't have much dialogue with my husband; the situation is tense at home."

Noting the limited possibility for social recreation among older women, Margarida, one of the senior participants and one who reported all kinds of health problems, said: "I find life difficult. It is difficult to live with little money. Because of this we do not eat well, we eat meat once a month, we do not dress well, we go to the doctor and [afterward] don't have money to buy medicines." She continued: "The monitor gives us much encouragement to read. It is a super place. Everybody has a good time, talks, laughs. Now we have a coffee break; there are cookies, cakes. It is very pleasant. This is the only place where I go and have a good time."

By the time of my second visit, June 1992, program designers had learned to maximize the congenial nature of the classroom by establishing a coffee break. This interlude, which often took a full half hour, was characterized by intense dialogue on social and personal issues. The fact that everyone took turns in preparing the coffee and bringing cookies, crackers, or popcorn made this break more intimate as it allowed the students to learn more about each person through what she brought or prepared for the coffee break.

The importance of the literacy classroom as a site for social distraction for women must be seen in the context of Brazilian culture. In a society where women face restricted physical mobility, they do not have the same access to many settings for social interaction beyond that provided by the family, the market, and the church. Unlike men, women do not have access to the ubiquitous neighborhood bars where hours may be spent with friends while drinking and talking. Most women, especially those with small children, are relegated to their homes, and their outings are carefully, if informally, monitored. The attendance at literacy programs provides women with a socially sanctioned setting, as in the classroom they will be under the tutelage of a monitor and devote themselves to learning. The literacy program also provides them with a socially acceptable reason for putting aside domestic work, for it is generally expected that literacy will improve, certainly not worsen, the women's ability to cope with family responsibilities.

A Self-Help Group

Most of the married adult women who participate have a supportive husband who allows them to attend literacy classes and to shuffle domestic routines for a while. The presence of a supportive husband appears to play an essential role in the participation of women in educational programs. However, many of these women have significant problems at home. Marital violence was not reported in the interviews, but problems linked to the stress of economic survival, arguments with the husband, and worries about the children's welfare and safety are part of the low-income women's everyday scheme of things.

Alicia, a woman with a sixth-grade education and thus the most highly educated of the group, had indicated originally that she participated in the literacy program to update her literacy skills. But later she confided that she participated in the program because her husband was seeing another woman and that she had serious problems with him at home. In her words, "Seeing that I am not the only one with problems, that other people had problems, helped me."

Maria Aparecida, a woman who continued to attend MOVA classes even after she passed the exam that would allow her to move into fourth-grade classes, stated:

We help each other, we calm each other down. [We discuss] many things that our husbands say and we have to forgive. . . Problems with children. . . I also talk with other students so that they don't lose hope.

According to Maria Terezinha, a young mother of four:

We spoke [in the classes] a bit about our lives. Thus people would see how the life of each of us really is. Thus we learned about one another. There is no one who doesn't have problems. There are people who suffer even more than we do. The main problems were the domestic fights, the fights with the husband. One learned to live by seeing we all have problems.

Other comments made by the women also reflected the therapeutic nature of the MOVA classes:

We talk about each other's problems. We give ourselves advice. We learn how to live better.
In class I have a good time; I don't worry as much.
At home when I am nervous I break things. Here I relax.

Informal assistance networks are also developed through the literacy classes. The women often indicated that "If someone is looking for a job, she asks the others for help. We help each other."

The Informal Social Club

For women with limited opportunities to develop and visit friends, the literacy class soon becomes a place where friendships can be made, renewed, and deepened. The social setting in which low-income people live is more than simply a context; it acts as a physical boundary and terrain for people's actions and events. Far from being passive, such a setting affects the everyday lives of people in multiple and powerful ways. The neighborhood for many of these women is perceived as dangerous. The women's physical mobility through the community is limited. Due to their domestic responsibilities and the often threatening conditions of the neighborhood, women do not have the opportunity to develop friendships with other women.

Most of the good will is directed toward the literacy monitors. The participants become strongly identified with their monitor, to whom they refer by first name—denoting a rather unusual monitor–student relationship in the Brazilian context, where there is traditionally a distance between them. Most of the monitors are praised for their patience, caring qualities, and ability to listen. In fact the identification is so strong that in several cases women stopped attending the literacy program when they lost their monitors (as happened when one monitor left because she got married and subsequently moved to another city).

"She is super," "She is great," "I like her very much," are frequent comments. A student expounded, "Neide is engraved in my heart. She taught everything correctly. Many people there didn't even know how to write an 'o'!" A woman, considerably older than her monitor, stated, "Ana is a second mother to me. She is very patient. If you don't know and ask, she will come to you and explain." Several students reported making a point to talk to the monitor outside the classroom and one said she would come to class half an hour earlier to be able to speak to her monitor alone. Affection for the monitor is not predicated exclusively on her caring and sympathetic traits. The women also detect in the monitor practices that are conducive to learning, as in the statements, "She is great with us. If you don't understand, she will explain again," and "When we ask her to repeat, explain, check if we are right, she explains; if we ask her not to mark the notebook with red, she complies."

The women also had positive views of their peers in the classroom. "I met people, I made good friends," said one. "I like everybody. If I leave, I will miss them a lot," said another. The women not only meet women in similar economic circumstances but realize that others have made significant accomplishments within their reading/writing limitations. One woman participant asserted, "I got to meet other people, people with responsibility, mature people."

The literacy space as an informal social club is not incompatible with learning. In one of the literacy activities, a group of women was shown a map of Brazil and then asked to cut and color the state from which they came. As they were looking at the map and handling the scissors and the paper with the shape of their state, one could not help but notice their tremendous excitement in seeing themselves represented through the paper cutouts on this large poster with the shape of Brazil. There was a great amount of talking and laughing over the shapes they cut, when they wrote on them the name of their state, colored the paper cutout, and later pinned them on the map. The whole activity took about one hour and was accompanied by much questioning of each other regarding letters and sounds, and personal history of how it was when they lived elsewhere. The most frequent statement made during this learning activity was "This is fun."

Unintentionally, the literacy classroom offers the non-reading women the opportunity to meet other women with similar constraints and, often, similar experiences of poverty and subordination. For many women it is the first time they can see on a collective scale that their personal situation is far from unique. In this new setting friendships develop quickly. These friendships are not ones in which the women will visit each other at home or be in constant touch through the telephone (as is the case for middle-class women) or even at the marketplace, but ones that are normally limited to the class meetings. Thus the expectation of seeing the other students becomes a strong incentive to attend the literacy lessons.

In all, the literacy classes fulfill several important functions for the participants. The classroom emerges as a desirable social space where the pains and concerns that accompany a life of poverty are temporarily forgotten and where friendly exchanges about life and personal problems can be entertained. It has the therapeutic effect of a self-help group. The learning function of the literacy program is not forgotten, but the learning process becomes expanded to cover life in its multiple manifestations and not just the ability to read and write a few words and phrases.

The Political Message of the Classroom

From the perspective of MOVA program designers, the literacy classes should address themes and issues that enable students to become aware of the causes of exploitation in society and how these various forces operate in their lives. This awareness is to be promoted through class discussions on topics such as housing, health, political elections, transportation, and work.

Yet this official objective, when juxtaposed with the other meanings that literacy classes have for women, encounters strong tensions and conflicts. While women and men who attend literacy classes over time enjoy talking about their concrete problems with each other, they nevertheless develop a reluctance to deal with unhappy, unpleasant issues. Illustrative of this reluctance is the following incident. One night, while I was going to observe a literacy class near a *favela*, a young man approached the supervisor who was accompanying me to request the use of her van to take a wounded man to the hospital. After a brief exchange, it seemed that the man was indeed in need of emergency attention and he was transported to the hospital. Upon returning, the supervisor explained that the man had been badly wounded. His intestines had been perforated and he had undergone surgery to save his life. As the supervisor reported this to the monitors and me, everyone could hear. However, I did not observe any reaction on the part of the students. I mentioned this to the supervisor, who in turn asked the monitor. The monitor then, in an attempt to get some discussion going, wrote on the blackboard two sentences: "The man was knifed" and "The man was taken to the hospital." These sentences were read out loud and then the students copied them, without discussion. I again asked the supervisor why no discussion was taking place. She conveyed this to the monitor, who again interpreted my question as a request for action. As she asked the students directly what they thought about the knifing incident, the students gradually, one by one, told of their own encounters with violence. "I have been shot here," said one boy showing his arm. "They shot me in the leg just in front of my house," said another. "I have been knifed twice," said another man. An older woman said, "There is a dead body every weekend in the lot over there." Violence emerged as part of their everyday life: an unpleasant occurrence; nothing that deserved or inspired special discussion.

MOVA was supposed to have an explicit political component. There were indications that such an effort was occurring, but it seemed to be infrequent compared to the more academic content of classes. Most of the political component took place through the elaboration of the "collective text." This strategy, based on the ideas of Freire, begins with a group discussion around a certain pressing issue or problem. Following this discussion the group members contribute their ideas and comments to produce a single story that is then put in written form. From interviews with the monitors and judging from some of the words and sentences used in class, "collective texts" had been written on such issues as the situation of street children, inflation, and transportation.

During my classroom observations of six teachers in June 1991 no instance of collective text writing emerged; likewise, no Freirean-type dialogue could be observed. In classes held by four monitors no political content could be observed; in the case of two other monitors, both exercises and words derived from previous collective texts with a political content. When the collective text was being used, it usually served merely to identify verbs or nouns for the creation of new sentences, this time devoid of political character and reflection.

During my observations in June 1992 and July 1993 I noted stronger efforts to develop a dialogue between monitor and students. I also realized that I had been looking for a dialogue from the perspective of my own experience in university seminars, in which the pace and participation is quick and intensive. In a literacy class there is a congruence between the pace of writing and the pace of expressing ideas. Indeed, many literacy students define themselves not as illiterate persons but persons who cannot speak well and are afraid to speak incorrectly. This being the case, women venture their opinions in shy, hesitant, single-phrase interventions. The monitor does end up talking much more than the students—a situation that emerges as silence expands and has to be cut short.

In their own reconstruction of what goes on in class several women see themselves as active participants, presenting opinions on the various matters the monitor brings up for discussion. Oftentimes the women report giving their opinion on several issues and liking this experience. Several report having been asked "questions about which I never thought before." Other women, however, describe themselves as mostly listeners because they are too "quiet" and "shy" to talk. The themes that they can remember discussing deal with health, cholera, problems at home, AIDS, religion, the government, and the forthcoming municipal elections and their candidates.

Some monitors succeed in fostering analytical comment from their students in subjects that seem at first glance devoid of political content. Such an instance is provided by a classroom exercise in figuring out the student's family budget, an activity developed around a collective text. This exercise, conducted by a less skillful monitor, became a simple adding operation. In contrast, with an effective monitor such as Ademilda the exercise became a springboard for several political discussions. In the hands of Ademilda, each of the budget categories was examined. Particular attention was given to the item "leisure," which for several students was not a regular concept in their everyday life. Ademilda explained the students' right to have some good time in their lives and asked them to identify what activities these would be. The students gradually identified events such as going to the snack bar, seeing a movie, buying a pizza, and taking a trip to the beach. The assignment was to determine what would be a reasonable salary to cover the subsistence and leisure expenses of the students and their families. Gradually, and only after three class sessions, did the students come to the realization that their incomes were woefully small and that they did not cover even the "basic necessities" of life. There was surprise in many eyes. Their comments, though brief, expressed shock and disbelief. Ademilda effectively linked the issue of their salaries to conditions of workers and the state of the economy. In many students, there seemed to dawn a new light.

Discussions about health issues such as cholera and AIDS were welcomed by the students. In narrating their learning experience, many showed the enthusiasm of those who come across a topic for the first time in their lives. Without intending to demean the response of illiterate adults to new knowledge, many reacted in a fashion similar to those of kindergarteners after an interesting story, opening their eyes, showing emotion in their voices. Notice the following accounts about subjects learned in class:

We talked about cholera. How you get it, what to do if you have it, the symp-
toms, how it starts. I knew it existed but now I know how it happens and
what to do!
A doctor came and gave us a chat on how babies are delivered! I didn't know I
was pregnant until a friend told me. I didn't know where babies came
from until my child was ready to be born.
A doctor spoke about the nervous system, high pressure, low pressure.

While knowledge on health issues was often given and accepted, discussions about gender conditions were less frequent. These discussions had helped some women but others had found them distressing. From among the former was this observation:

I found very interesting a class discussion about women who don't go out of the
house, where the husband controls. Before, women were little fools, now they
are well-informed.

But for others,

We spoke about the fact that a woman should have as much command as a
man. But in our [social] class it is not so. The man should not command
equally as a woman. When a woman wants to command, people says she's
talking like a man and he [the spouse] becomes demoralized. When I go out I
tell my husband I am going out, but I have friends who go out without telling
him or must have their husband's permission to leave.

Discussions about formal politics—i.e., the performance of the government, voting rights, the role of representatives—are the least favorably received. This is not surprising in light of women's socialization to be concerned mostly with the private sphere and the widespread belief that politics is a man's world. At the time of my June 1992 visit preparations were in progress for the municipal elections in November. The elections were very important because the Workers' Party—the sponsors of the literacy program—was up for reelection. Their failure to win might mean—as it did— the end of MOVA. Candidates had come forward and their platforms were beginning to shape up. Several women, however, did not want to discuss the candidates because they found the topic "uninteresting." Others had learned more about the political process but this awareness, rather than bringing them in as political actors, had served to make them more cynical and skeptical about the political process. One participant who had come to understand something about politics stated, "There are a lot of political discussions in class to vote for what the candidate will do, not because of his looks." But others, referring to a similar discussion, asserted, "I learned who steals more than others. They are all thieves," and "I know that the winner will do nothing. I will vote for whoever I like" [i.e., is "good looking"]. Corruption was a topic closely associated with politics, especially in those days, when then President Collor was being accused of bribing several industrialists to contribute to his campaign. At times it seemed that the political message of the classroom promoted estrangement from politics by constantly highlighting the untrustworthy nature of politicians and political institutions.

Several monitors reported having a difficult time combining the political and pedagogical objectives of the program. They observed that the students shared a common motivation: having to work and survive as persons in an urban center led them to accept the political message when it concerned a concrete problem in their lives. But political discussions in the abstract or in a more distant mode were not always easy. A young, innovative, and quite popular monitor observed:

The people do not believe in organized struggle. Their lives are too individualized; they fight all the time to survive. I try to involve myself in their lives— talking to the husbands, visiting their homes, seeking causes [for problems] in their lives. But they don't like to talk about the government, the strikes. They make faces; they tell me they do not like it; they become quiet. Then I have to change the subject. . . . I am more successful discussing personal affairs, names of family members, names of buses they take.

The resistance of participants to political themes was corroborated by several participants, particularly older women, one of whom noted, "That talk is good for younger people. At my age that doesn't interest me." But a younger student also echoed this feeling:

The monitors used to talk about politics. Sometimes everyone would participate. Students would mostly listen. The students did not understand what they were talking about. How could we understand if the politicians themselves don't?

The Challenges of Political Resocialization

In referring to changes in one's political understanding and perspectives, two terms may be used. For those who prefer a more contemporary language, the process could be called "transformative" or "emancipatory" learning. I prefer to use the term *political resocialization* for two reasons: (a) to emphasize that this learning is very encompassing and continual, thus part of a process of cultural induction; and (b) to highlight its precise focus, i.e., the understanding of power relations in society and how these relate to institutions, the state, and the self.

The literature on adult motivation for participation in education asserts that while for children the basic motivation for literacy is compliance with authority [of parents], for adults the basic motivation is the "enabling capacity of literacy" or the need to perform better as parents or workers (Beder, 1991, p. 48). While these reasons may be at work, the evidence from MOVA shows that motivations involve the pleasure of the process rather than merely its outcome. Two persistent characteristics of the women participating in the MOVA literacy program are that they live nearby and that they are at a point in their life cycle at which it is possible to rearrange domestic responsibilities, as demands by "others" on their time and attention have decreased. Once in the classroom setting the women discover some unanticipated benefits from the class experience, such as finding a place of great conviviality, seeking refuge from an otherwise difficult existence, and making new friends.

The women's point in the life cycle also affects their openness to political messages. Among the older women the personal project regarding literacy is quite limited: learning to read concrete messages and signs in everyday life—names and price of products, street names, bus routes. The younger mothers seek literacy often to help their children; they tend to be more receptive to political discussions, perhaps because they see the need to solve problems their children face in the community. Among the youngest participants (primarily unmarried and without children), their literacy objectives are to move to higher levels of education to be more competitive in the labor market. How can an "emancipatory literacy" project take account of different personal agendas? How may common claims and desires be established? How can women be incorporated into the macro-political arena without enabling them first to be in control of their own lives? These are questions seldom entertained in "emancipatory literacy" efforts.

In the social exchanges that ensue, women develop a greater sense of confidence and learn to express their opinions. Topics close to their everyday life such as health provoke their interest and participation. Topics that challenge received notions of masculinity and femininity such as those concerning women's areas of decisionmaking and politics are less well received. This behavior—the reluctance to deal with explicit or formal "political issues"—finds some explanation in the sociocultural analysis of literacy conducted by Heath (1983). She observed that "the place of language in the cultural lives of each social group is interdependent with the habits and values of behaving shared among members of that group" (p. 11). She noted that each community has its own way of taking meaning from print and oral language. Through the use of a concept she terms "literacy event"—the occasion when talk revolves around a piece of reading or writing—Heath found that the experience of talking about a text is intimately connected with the facility of reading the same text. Her conclusion was that both oral and written language uses must be considered in understanding literacy events in a social group. In the case of the MOVA women, there was a substantial disjunction between efforts to make them discuss political issues in the classroom and the type of political discourse they engaged in their daily life—which was practically nil at the abstract level. The attempt by the monitors to incorporate political written and oral texts where there were no oral parallels was then a difficult task.

The discussion of formal politics was not only avoided by the women but also deemphasized by the monitors, many of whom did not feel competent or at ease discussing political topics. In part this is due to the fact that many of the literacy monitors are women who, like their students, still subscribe to social norms of women as apolitical actors.

Factors such as the skills necessary for resocializing others also enter the picture. Although commonly taken for granted in political consciousness-raising methods, it is difficult to engage in dialogue with persons who live under subordinate and oppressive conditions. It is also difficult to move from coding/decoding skills into a critical understanding of reality. The difficulty emerges because the translation of a theme (expressed in sentences) into sustained dialogue requires skills monitors do not always have. These skills call for linking micro-level problems felt at the personal level, such as garbage on one's street, poor transportation, or lack of medical attention in the community health post, to greater issues concerning governmental attention to the plight and needs of the poorer social segments of society. The creation of participatory, dialogical interactions is possible but requires monitors' skills in body language, understanding people's experiences and hopes, and smoothing moments of uncertainty and threat.

The failure to obtain a sustained dialogue obliged the monitors to emphasize monitor-initiated activities. Unwittingly, the learning process gradually loses its dialogical nature. In consequence, even though MOVA intended to have both a pedagogical and a political component, the latter became relatively weak.

An additional factor that may weaken attempts at political resocialization obtains in cases where no significant political changes are occurring in the rest of society. A powerful source of the desire for adult resocialization is social change itself (Beder, 1991). These concomitant changes provide the support and context under which new norms may become established. In São Paulo, MOVA operated as an important but modest effort of social change. Its key protector, the Partido dos Trabalhadores, existed itself under fragile conditions. Moreover, the municipal elections in November 1992 returned the political power to conservative elements, who lost no time in terminating the MOVA program.

Drawing Lessons from MOVA
Wikelund et al. (1992) observe that,

Adult participation in literacy education is a complex and multifaceted phenomenon, influenced by numerous interrelated forces in individuals' personal makeup, their families, their lives, and the environment and society in which they grow, learn, work, and live (p. 24).

In the case of low-income women, their social marginality (poverty) combines with their powerlessness (being subject to men's gatekeeping and social definitions of mother and wife) to make the acquisition of literacy a distant dream.

The women's meanings of literacy, in which their social environment and domestic positionality appear as a strong common denominator, compete with the development of politically empowered individuals. A sustained political dialogue around new literacy words and phrases may not emerge simply because of the pedagogical limitations of monitors (their low skill levels for what is a complex task). Important obstacles derive from the women's personal situations. In cases where the political dialogue addresses painful aspects of the women's everyday life—marital violence, inflation, unemployment, transportation problems—women may avoid these topics. This behavior should not be equated with one of apathy on the part of the women but, on the contrary, should be understood in the context of a life that offers limited satisfaction. Literacy classes have an appeal as friendly and carefree settings that women wish to protect.

Program designers must become aware of the substantial disjuncture that emerges between the objectives of those offering a literacy program and those coming to avail themselves of its services. Literacy in adult life comes accompanied by many of the adult responsibilities and constraints. Program designers must increase their understanding of how literacy needs fit into the hierarchy of survival needs women encounter in everyday life. Education is but one small sphere in the existence of the poor adult. As Beder notes, "adult literacy education must focus on meeting learners' goals, for as long as participation is voluntary society can reap its benefits only if learners are able to reap their own" (1991, p. 161). The challenge to literacy program designers here is to satisfy these desires for social conviviality while instilling a sense of critical awareness that will be necessarily painful to the participants. An additional challenge for program implementors will be to tie micro literacy skills to cumulative and coherent knowledge and to collective concerns on the part of the women participants. To attain this objective, it is clear that there is a need for developing a professional workforce for adult literacy education, which cannot continue to rely on part-time monitors or volunteers with little background in education (Lytle et al., 1992). Monitor training emerges as a crucial component in successful literacy programs (see also Lind and Johnston, 1990). Elements in literacy monitor training, in addition to crucial skills to promote reading and writing abilities and practices in adults, will have to include competence in small group instruction and management, personal counseling, and social science research skills to develop and use personal and social profiles of their students. The political resocialization of women is a difficult enterprise that needs much greater understanding to be effectively implemented.

Notes

All translations of data were done by author, Nelly Stromquist.

1.   Secretaria Municipal de Educacao, April 1990, p. 6. See also Secretaria Municipal de Educacao, January 1991.

2.   It should be observed that the feminist movement in the United States has used "consciousness-raising" techniques (using group discussions to reveal personal experiences and to find collective problems and solutions) since the late 1960s. This technique preceded Freire's *conscientization* and thus was an independent development.

3.   Land tenure patterns are extreme in Brazil. According to 1985 data, two percent of rural properties with more than 1,000 acres composed 57 percent of the agricultural land; in contrast, 30 percent of farms smaller than ten hectares accounted for one percent of the farmland. Data for the 1970–1980 decade indicate that the poorest half of the rural

population's share of total rural income fell from 22 to 15 percent. Increasingly unable to survive in the countryside, peasants often see urban life as the only alternative.

4. These statistics tend to oscillate within MOVA and the grass-roots groups. I am citing here those reported in the Relatorio Mensal de Convenios, MOVA-SP, March–April 1991. Coordenacao de Projeto MOVA-SP, c. May 1991.

5. The interviews were conducted by two persons, the author and her research assistant, a native Brazilian with knowledge of interviewing techniques. The responses were not taped because the procedure was feared to cause discomfort to the women. Instead both interviewers took detailed notes and compared their impressions. The first set of interviews took place in the *nucleos*, the second and third in the women's homes.

Classes took place Mondays through Thursdays. Participants could select either an afternoon (usually 2:00 to 5:00 P.M.) or an evening shift (7:00 to 9:30 P.M.).

References

Beder, H. (1991). *Adult literacy: Issues for policy and practice.* Malabar, FL: Krieger Publishing Co.

Fingeret, H. (1991). Meaning, experience, and literacy. *Adult Basic Education,* (1), 45–61.

Freire, P. (1972). *Pedagogy of the oppressed.* New York: Penguin.

Heath, S.B. (1983). *Ways with words: Language, life, and work in communities and classrooms.* Cambridge, UK: Cambridge University Press.

Keck, M. (1992). *The workers' party and democratization in Brazil.* New Haven, CT: Yale University Press.

Lind, A. and Johnston, J. (1990). *Adult literacy in the Third World.* Stockholm: Swedish International Development Authority, 1990.

Lytle, S., Balzer, A., and Reaumann, R. (1992). *Developing the professional workforce for adult literacy education.* Policy Brief PB92–2. Philadelphia: National Center on Adult Literacy.

Merriam, S. and Caffarella, R. (1991). *Learning in adulthood: A comprehensive guide.* San Francisco: Jossey-Bass.

Rockhill, K. (1987). Gender, language, and the politics of literacy. *British Journal of Sociology of Education,* 8(2), 123–148.

Secretaria Municipal de Educacao/Prefeitura do Municipio de São Paulo. (1990). *Principios Politico-Pedagogicos do MOVA-SP.* São Paulo: Movimento de Alfabetizacao de Jovens e Adultos, Secretaria Municipal de Educacao/Prefeitura do Municipio de São Paulo, April.

Secretaria Municipal de Educacao/Prefeitura do Municipio de São Paulo. (1991). *Quatro Prioridades da Secretaria Municipal de Educacao de São Paulo. Construindo a Educacao Publica Popular.* São Paulo: Secretaria Municipal de Educacao, Prefeitura do Municipio de São Paulo, January.

Torres, C. (1990). *The movement of literacy training in São Paulo, Brazil: Between a rock and a hard place.* Paper presented at the CIES Western regional meeting, Santa Barbara, CA, November.

Wikelund, K., Reder, S., and Hart-Landsberg, S. (1992). *Expanding theories of adult literacy participation: A literature review.* Philadelphia: National Center on Adult Literacy.

Chapter Five
The Role of Women in the Democratization of Schools and Families in Argentina

Beatriz Schmukler

This chapter[1] reports data from research done in Argentina from 1985 to 1992 in an attempt to understand whether the new democratic government that came to power in 1983 created the conditions for micro-democratic spaces in daily life, and if so, what influence women had in creating those spaces. Specifically, I was interested in understanding the "democratic potential of mothering." Mothers had played a successful oppositional role against the military regime during the 1970s, as symbolized by the Mothers of the Plaza de Mayo, who marched in protest for their disappeared children. By the 1980s women were leading programs in poor communities that opposed the new austerity measures that accompanied Argentina's economic restructuring. During both the authoritarian and democratic periods, women were confronting the state and creating community organizations outside the formal political system. These were to become new types of organizations, which used participatory methods of decision-making in response to women's dissatisfaction with formal politics.

The data reported in this chapter are part of a larger study that focused on the role of mothers in this broad process of democratization. The data reported here will be limited to vignettes from larger case studies, which focused on the new roles that working class and poor mothers developed within their families and within the public sphere—for example, community organizations or their children's schools.

The study drew on participant observation and interviews among working-class and poor families. Democratization of the families was analyzed by observing changing patterns in gender, authority, and power relationships. These data reported here were taken from a study which focused on family–school interactions with elementary schools and followed a previous study that concentrated on parents with children in secondary schools (Schmukler, 1992a).

A central question of this study was whether democracy was broadly possible without the dissolution of the profound authoritarian roots that permeated social institutions. I wanted to understand whether the new democracy in the political realm created the conditions for individuals to begin a struggle for personal rights and duties at the local level. Institutions in Argentina have traditionally been authoritarian, with a strong and uncritical commitment to hierarchical leadership. Through processes of marginalization, authoritarian systems have repeatedly thwarted the actions of individual actors within institutions. Authoritarian socialization has not been simply a matter of values but of a network of relationships. The family and the school have been the major agents for training individuals in authoritarian values and practices, reinforcing each other's role.

This study focused on mothers because they were the intermediaries between the family and public institutions such as schools. This meant that their anger and assertion of their rights had immediate repercussions within both private and public institutions. The actions of mothers in this transitional period, in which democracy had to be defined and redefined, were part of a process of institutional democratization which paralleled the broader democratic opening in Argentine society. My hypothesis in this study was that the actions of mothers in social organizations outside the home, including their children's schools, would influence the democratization of poor families and promote increased understanding between families and schools, one in which women would demand a voice. As we will see, the first part of this hypothesis was, at least partially, borne out; significant changes in gender roles were negotiated within families. Less progress was seen in the ability of mothers to extend these more egalitarian relations to schools. Some reasons for this resistance on the part of schools is discussed in the final section.

Origins of Women's Movements in Argentina

The first autonomous women's movements, with goals and strategies defined by women, began to emerge during the authoritarian regime of 1976–1982. During this period women were, for the first time, the main protagonists of an anti-authoritarian struggle against the repression of the military regime. As the mothers of the victims (who were largely poor and working class) of this repression, they found themselves leading the struggle against the dictatorship. This struggle led to a redefinition of the concept of motherhood that in turn resulted in changes in notions of femininity. The Mothers of the Plaza de Mayo were generally women without any political experience who engaged in the anti-repressive struggle as they searched for their disappeared children in the waiting rooms of the military headquarters (Navarro, 1989; Fisher, 1989).

Through their actions women-as-mothers were rejecting the call of the military to be the guardians of conservative family life, and they were reconstructing the concept of female altruism that is imbedded in the concept of the sacred mother in Catholic Argentina. Motherhood was no longer a symbol of privacy and isolation within segmented and disarticulated family groups. Instead motherhood encompassed the image of housewives taking the public space of the central civic plaza as their own. Mothers were challenging the image of madness that the military, the media, and representatives of public culture were perpetuating in their labels of the mothers as the "madwomen of the Plaza de Mayo."

Through these social movements led by mothers, women have shown that their understanding of political issues starts from their own personal and emotional experience. Rene S. de Epelbaum, one of the Mothers of the Plaza de Mayo, stated in an interview:

Because, you know at the beginning, we only wanted our children. But, as time passed, we came to a different understanding of what was going on in the world. Today I was listening to the radio and there was somebody who sings very well who was singing about children, about babies starving. This is also a violation of human rights (Navarro, 1989, p. 124).

Thus what begins as a domestic issue of mothers seeking their disappeared children turns into a social movement with implications at other levels.

In 1983 Argentina entered a democratic stage when Raúl Alfonsín became the newly elected president. During the first stages of the Alfonsín government democracy meant the reopening of the electoral process as well as the freedom to start new associations. It led to an increase in social participation because increased numbers of citizens were engaging in political activities and because a transformation of hierarchical and authoritarian relationships within private institutions was taking place. Along with the restoration of political parties, parliament, constitutional law, and the proliferation of non-governmental organizations, the Alfonsín government reestablished a discourse of equal access to social, economic and political institutions (Cavarozzi, 1991)

With the establishment of a democratic government, the profound roots of authoritarianism in the institutions of Argentine society that per-

meated political and daily life became increasingly evident. The liberalization of institutions that were basic to the socialization of new generations,
such as the school and the family, led to a deepening of democracy. Under
the military regime these institutions had played an important role in the
legitimation of authoritarian values and oppressive relations in the society.
Now the traditional role of mothers was increasingly becoming open to
question.

The Renegotiation of Gender Roles
within the Family and in the Community

According to Robertson and Burkart (1979), individual identities are constructed contextually in group or institutional settings. In each group to
which the individual belongs there are social codes that get negotiated
within the group and serve to identify group members. These identifying
codes are composed of several dimensions of sex, age, occupation, status,
degree of solidarity with the group's goals, or other affiliation. These codes
are also determined by the external connections individuals hold with other
groups and the role individuals play as economic or emotional support,
which helps to maintain the boundaries of the group. The negotiation of
identifying codes in each group takes place within an authority system in
which some individuals play the role of authorizing figures.

A result of this new articulation of women's contextual identities was
that identification codes were shifting in the families as women were more
actively recognized as authority figures (Di Marco and Schmukler, 1991).
This initiated a series of changes as women defended their own goals and
desires. Negotiations among women and the rest of the family made their
personal goals more legitimate, more clearly recognized and no longer
merely dismissed out of hand. This, in turn, resulted in an expansion of
women's legitimate spheres of activity and a growth in women's self-
esteem and voice.

Our study found differences between participant (PWH) and non-
participant (NPWH) women households regarding the degree of changes
in gender practices made by family members. Participant women are
those who are members of community organizations, trade unions, or
political parties. We found that within participant women households
negotiations take a new form when, in their community associations,
women begin to articulate ideas about their own subordination. Many
of their former individual strategies represented forms of resistance, which
helped to achieve some personal goals but did not change either the sex-

based division of labor or their own gender identity. New negotiations affected both, as women began speaking in a language of rights. In particular, women's domestic negotiations to overcome personal subordination became increasingly translated into a more general anti-authoritarian discourse that included experiences inside and outside the family. As they saw themselves struggling to recognize their own goals, they recognized other forms of authoritarianism in the family, in their children's schools, and in the public organizations in which they participated. They increasingly understood the reasons for their withdrawal from participation in male political organizations, where they experienced marginalization reminiscent of their feelings of subordination at home (Di Marco and Schmukler, 1991).

In Participant Women Households, mothers who were going through female identity changes were also initiating gender and authority negotiations in their homes. At first, partners of participant women resisted as the latter became increasingly involved outside the home. Husbands pushed their wives to stay at home more in order to carry out their household responsibilities and to spend more time with their husbands and children. The change in their spouses compelled men to confront not only their own loneliness and isolation but also the importance of their wives as companions. At the beginning of the negotiations women expected the approval of their partners, and intended to maintain the sexual division of labor while working in community associations. Participation, then, became a new burden, and the double work day for women became triple. After some period of domestic crisis, disorder, and eventual new agreements about rules, husbands in these households accepted the public participation of wives. As a consequence they integrated themselves more fully into domestic chores and child rearing. Moreover, some of them expressed ideological changes, admitting the benefits of public participation of women and recognizing that their relationships with their wives became more stimulating once women started to participate in community actions. These changing practices and values of men, in response to women's changes and negotiations, played an important role in women's attainment of positions of authority within the family.

Social Motherhood

As women's social action outside the home increased—through such activities as developing social services for the poor, including community kitchens and health and day care centers—they began using a language of personal rights outside of as well as within the family sphere. Women's previous social movements had never challenged their subordinate position in the private and public spheres. On the contrary, the Peronist Party feminine movement emphasized subordination to male leaders. The political opposition to the military regime had considered female questions as second-order problems that tended to divide their democratic movement.

Now, for the first time in the history of Argentina, poor and working-class women were discussing personal goals and consciously defending their right to initiate activities in the community. Thus they were exchanging a private maternal altruism resulting in a form of "social motherhood." Social motherhood had many implications for the redefinition of everyday life in poor neighborhoods in terms of increasing the prestige of women both as organizers and as strugglers for human rights when traditional political organizations were silenced (Schmukler, 1992b).

This newly attained public consciousness and ability to produce results at the community and political level contributed to women's more prestigious position in society. In turn, social motherhood gave women the courage to start negotiations within the family to change the division of labor and to change repressive patterns of interpersonal relations.

The renegotiation of gender roles within families and the community also created a link between a developing critique of authoritarian child-rearing practices in the home and the authoritarian ways that schools treated students. Women went through a period of self-examination wherein their own tendencies to authoritarianism became evident, particularly with regard to their authoritarian child-rearing practices. Consequently, mothers also began to criticize teachers' disciplinary practices with their children. In response fathers also became more critical of the schools' disciplinary actions (Perelman de Solarz, 1992). Schools then became another arena of struggle over changing roles and a challenge for women's new sense of social motherhood.

Families in Process of Democratization and Their Relationships to Their Children's School

In a previous study of secondary schools, we discovered the intention of some mothers to become more actively involved in school issues (Schmukler, 1992a). We supposed that mothers' interests in elementary school issues would be stronger compared to mothers with children in secondary schools. We also presumed that mothers who underwent gender identity changes and who were influential in the democratization of their families would be more active in protesting, organizing, or proposing concrete solutions to pedagogic or other school issues, in contrast to their previous participation in which they were viewed as an extension of their children.

In our study of mother's participation in secondary schools, we found that women's autonomy increased mothers' opposition to teachers' ill-treatment of adolescents, and in some cases they developed rudimentary modes of organization to prevent school failure. However, the study also showed little interest among school administrators and teachers in collaborating with parents, particularly with mothers. We supposed that in elementary schools teachers would have a greater interest in integrating mothers in school concerns since the children are younger and their mothers tend to be more involved.

Unfortunately this was not the case. In the opinion of teachers and administrators, mothers could collaborate in "domestic" arrangements for events like school festivals while fathers were to participate in *cooperativas*, official parent associations which tended to work according to principals' and teachers' goals, i.e., to collect funds for school materials and infrastructure. Fathers were also called on for disciplinary issues.

Moreover, a deficit view of parents by teachers and administrators was prevalent. The following are representative examples of comments made in interviews:

Parents are not interested.
They come with their demands when it's already too late. They don't take charge. They don't go through the learning process with their children.
There are too many unorganized families; the parents are divorced.
There are also families where the parents didn't finish high school, and they don't understand, and for that reason can't help.
There are families that hide what the children do. They lie to us. . . . There are also families in which the mother works outside the home. . . and families in poor socioeconomic situations. . . . There is also the experience of isolation many families felt during the military dictatorship. . . . The children then fail and leave school.

The following vignettes from our case study data show the difficulty that women have in confronting the rigidity of schools' perceptions of mothers' social roles.

Noemí and Lina: Mothers Confront Schools

In the following example taken from our data, Noemí is reflecting on her old patterns of child rearing and, together with her husband, begins to protest the way their child is treated at school. Noemí became engaged in community organizing with other women through an effort to develop a health center. As she got more involved in the group, she increasingly believed in the efficacy of women's actions and helped her husband to accept her activities. Soon she analyzed her own authoritarian modes of educating her children. She became more self-critical with regard to her own child-rearing practices. As she explains in an interview:

I tended to think I had to transfer my own experiences in my parents' home directly to my children. I had a very strict upbringing. If I had realized before how repressive my parents were, I would have avoided many fights with my children. Now, I am critical of myself. Before, I thought I was always right, that I had the absolute truth. . . . My changes are good for the children because before I was overly repressive, demanding very strict limits and time schedules. Without being conscious of it, I was transmitting to the children all these methods I learned from my parents. Since I began to get involved [in the women's community group], I have changed.

Both Noemí and her husband protested teachers' ill-treatment of their children and expressed concerns about their excessive preoccupation with order.

Some teachers are very superficial. They worry about how clean and proper my child is. And I wanted her to talk about how he performs. She treated the children poorly, screaming at them, grabbing a child by the ear and taking him to his chair. I think the teacher should know how to earn respect. My husband was very critical of the way she taught history. He would say, "She should not wash children's minds. Children should think independently."

Since Noemí began participating in the community group, she also pushed her husband to help their children with their homework. Before, Carlos was the typical distant father who only went to school on very special occasions. Noemí says:

I used to go to all the school–parent meetings, and Carlos only looked at the children's exercise books on Sundays. He used to say that children should be left alone, that I should not be controlling them all the time. Now he is the one who visits the school regularly to discuss disciplinary issues. He is more concerned about the children's treatment at school, and he thinks that they should protest when the teacher is unfair.

Although participant mothers are being empowered in the home and the community, they often find resistance among teachers to a more egalitarian relationship between the school and the home. Teachers and administrators tend to feel that they are the ones in control at the school. For example, Lina, another informant, had two children who were viewed as behavior problems at school. The administrator asked her to move her daughter to another school, but said that her son could remain since he was close to finishing his degree. Lina, who was a community leader at the time, had to accept the director's decision to relocate her daughter. On a different occasion, when her son was going to be expelled, Lina fought the decision and it was revoked.

According to Di Marco (1992), there is strong evidence to suggest that gender assumptions may lie behind the decision to expel her daughter. Iris, Lina's daughter, was outspoken and did not adjust to usual expectations regarding girls' behavior. Lina admits that it was impossible for her to defend Iris since she did not behave like a "model" girl. At home, however, Iris feels encouraged by her parents to be outspoken so that, according to her father, she will not be in a position of subordination. This suggests that, as gender behaviors shift within the family, conflicts arise between families and schools. The school transmits expectations that children should conform to gender stereotypes and that parents should more strictly comply with traditional models. While families accept unconventional gender behavior from their children, they come to expect negative sanctions from school (Di Marco, 1992).

Despite their developing critique, poor and working-class parents like Noemí and Lina still idealize the school as an abstract and superior entity that deals in academic knowledge. These mothers view the professionals in schools as superior authorities. Teachers and administrators reinforce this feeling by not allowing parents to have a say in issues relating to teaching. Teachers demand that mothers make sure children do their homework, but they do not see mothers as partners who are able to provide relevant information about the children. The term used by teachers to involve parents is *collaboration*; however, there is little possibility of collaboration between unequal partners. Teachers and administrators assume parents are ignorant, don't care about their children, and fail to support their children's development. The failure of children to perform is usually considered the parents' failure. The prevailing belief is that families who do not have a traditional structure are "abnormal," and this abnormality is mainly responsible for children's lack of success. "Mothers do not control children and fathers do not assume enough of their authority," said one of the school principals.

Thus parents regard the school as sacred, but at the same time they do not trust the system to prepare children for future occupational skills. In addition, school administrators do not accept parents' real participation. "School administrators, who establish boundaries of normality in the family and reserve the right to judge it on that basis, set up parameters that contribute to the fragmentation of parent groups" (Schmukler, 1992a, p. 251). School professionals and parents find themselves unable to communicate with each other, let alone together develop proposals to the State.

Gender and Authority in the Elementary School

Research in Argentine primary schools in the 1980s shows that social interactions reproduce the institutional, hierarchical gender structure (Ackelsberg and Shanley, 1991). Gender-biased values permeate the relationships among teachers, administrators, and parents, the content of textbooks, and the discourse and practice of teachers. Teachers are unable to accept the new modes of motherhood and family structures which represent gender transformations. They seem prejudiced against female-headed households or against any family structure in which mothers are working or absent during the day and fathers are not the real authorities. Male teachers often see themselves as a replacement for the authority of the father, which they view as gradually diminishing in families.

Textbooks also reinforce traditional family values. They portray the "normal" nuclear family structure, and negative sanctions result when families do not conform to this ideal. Wainerman and Raijman (1987) have demonstrated that portrayals of families in textbooks have not changed significantly during this century. Gender differences are portrayed as biological differences. Women are regarded as weak, nurturing, destined to serve others, and dependent upon others' opinions. Men are portrayed as intelligent, creative, and active, and destined to become leaders in the public sphere. Only relatively recently has a new editorial group made some inroads into altering the sexual division of labor. Books by Cukier, Rey, and Tornadu (1979a, 1979b, 1980) show healthy and happy families where fathers take care of babies and mothers work in factories. Families are not portrayed with authoritarian and hierarchical patterns, and the idea of companionship instead of hierarchical authority prevails. Nevertheless, the family is always a father/mother/children unit, leaving the ideal of the "intact" and heterosexual family the norm.

The Female Teacher: An Obstacle to Achieving Gender Equity in Schools?

All of this may seem surprising, since most Argentine teachers are female and one might expect that they would be influenced by women's changing social identities. It is less surprising when we examine the gender structure of the elementary school system during the period in which the study was done. Morgade (1990) reveals that men are only 10 percent of elementary school teachers in the Municipality of Buenos Aires. However, men are over-represented among supervisors (57 percent), directors (31 percent) and teachers who are not in the classroom (26 percent). Over-representation of men in better-paid jobs is due to an explicit labor policy destined to "de-feminize" teaching jobs in elementary schools. According to the promotion policy of the Municipality of Buenos Aires, one male teacher is to be chosen for every three female teachers, regardless of performance, when covering the positions of teachers on a leave of absence. Since 1986, recalls Morgade (1990), male teachers have been favored with more rapid ascension in their professional careers. In order to be promoted, female teachers are required to attend hundreds of superfluous courses to gain enough points for an advanced job category, adding an additional burden to their workload.

Moreover, the Argentine research projects of Bonder (1992), De Rendo and Perelman de Solarz (1988), and Achilli (1988) have demonstrated the difficulty female teachers have in changing their values and practices regarding gender. Bonder mentions teachers' fears that the increasing political participation of women is the cause of loneliness and rejection by men. Achilli (1988), who has analyzed female teacher experiences, found that as the female teachers transmit socially constructed knowledge in the educational system, they are unable to include their own feelings and thoughts. This distance, along with the tendency of female teachers to adapt to formal school discourse, inhibits personal involvement in building knowledge together with the children in the classroom. Palermo (1993), in a qualitative study of female teachers, argues that they reproduce traditional gender values. Girls are viewed as less intelligent, although able to compensate for this weakness with hard work. Boys are seen as having a higher interest in learning, as being more rational and naturally disposed for public affairs. Only a small group of female teachers, who are widows or female heads of household and whose different experiences allowed them to reevaluate the concept of "normal" family life, have a more progressive view of gender (Palermo, 1993).

De Rendo and Perelman de Solarz (1988) studied teachers' practices through the analysis of students' report cards. The report card is the medium through which teachers consolidate their authority over parents, judging the students' performance and the success or failure of parents. The report card is an element of social control that prevents an equal dialogue with the student or the parents. The teacher sends messages and judgments, which are not arguable. Through report cards De Rendo and Perelman de Solarz (1988) see the female teachers as initiating children in a series of rituals leading to conformity to social rules.

In her research with teachers, Palermo (1993) described some transformations in the concept of gender. A small group of teachers in her sample thought that gender was a cultural construction and developed practices which tended to change traditional expectations for boys and girls. When children are spontaneous, according to these teachers, they often choose non-traditional gender-identified activities. It is important to note that these teachers are located in schools where the directors are committed to innovative gender practices, particularly those designed to overcome segregation between girls and boys. This coincides with Achilli's (1988) finding that teachers are essentially transmitters, rather than creators, of knowledge and do not autonomously initiate new practices within the classroom. Palermo also cites Coelho y Gallart's (1986) recommendation regarding the need to involve administrators if we want to obtain long-lasting changes in schools.

Batallán and García (1988), who interviewed teachers about their own experiences, also found that teaching practices in elementary schools were not characterized by the active construction of knowledge in the classroom, but rather that teachers administered knowledge previously organized by the school system. They found that teachers are not able to elaborate on their own practices, to recognize their needs or those of their students, or to be innovative in the classroom (Batallán and García, 1988). They do, however, play an important role in the control of children. As intermediaries between the parents and the state, they are authorized to

establish rules for parents and children. The dilemma is that while teachers have the power to judge the lives of families, they themselves are judged
and evaluated by their superiors in the educational hierarchy, and, at the
same time, feel criticized and judged by parents (Batallán and García, 1988).

Research developed in Argentina at the end of the 1980s and beginning of the 1990s shows that the interactions between the primary school
and the family have generally not been an effective context in which to
positively transform gender stereotypes. The experience of mothers becoming more actively involved in community affairs and influential in the
democratization of families has not helped their voices to be heard in their
children's schools. In their interaction with the schools, they found obstacles to participation and barriers to gaining influence with their children's
teachers. In addition, female teachers have not found the school to be a
favorable setting to question gender identity, and they themselves tend to
transmit traditional concepts of gender.

However, teachers in some public schools attempt to comply with the
policies of the Municipality of Buenos Aires, which, based on the research
of Wainerman and Raijman (1987) discussed above, has recently passed
new policies to promote gender equity in schools. Many of these schools
also use books that show more democratic images of the family. These
changes, however, still have had limited impact on daily gender practices
in the classroom and on the perspectives and practices of school administrators. The Municipality's new policies have not yet become part of a
daily routine. Nor have teachers had a chance to analyze their own gender
transformations and to translate them into a new pedagogical practice
that would challenge current practices.

The democratization of families is a new phenomenon and still in its
early stages. Participant mothers who are experiencing identity changes
have not yet been able to establish more egalitarian relationships with teachers and school administrators. Policies designed to reinforce the democratization of family–school relationships should provide mechanisms for collaboration among mothers, teachers, and administrators toward promoting
a deliberate examination of gender stereotypes in teachers' practices, in
administrators' perspectives, and in family–school interactions.

It is important to remember that democratization requires that both
families and schools should be prepared to initiate more egalitarian relationships. And, as Stromquist makes clear "these settings must be targeted
spaces for the ongoing creation and maintenance of democratic norms"
(Stromquist, 1992).

Implications for the Empowerment of Women
and the Transformation of Social Institutions

While political conditions in Argentina were created that allowed citizens to struggle for "new" collective arrangements, these new citizens had to be constructed through the development of new social identities (O'Donnell and Schmitter, 1986). The hope was that these newly constructed identities would create new values and interpersonal practices aimed at greater integration of marginalized groups into institutions.

In the case of women, however, their transitional gender identities did not automatically confer on them a more central role in private or public institutions. Feminine concerns, as addressed by female neighborhood organizations and renegotiated family roles, have not helped women to become powerful in the community power structure, a structure that is male-oriented and mainly concerned with macronational political and economic questions. As we have seen, social institutions such as schools remain resistant to giving women a larger voice.

It appears, then, that women should consider changing their public approach. The danger of such change lies in the necessity of concealing or weakening women's unique approach to politics, one that reflects their daily experience as women. This dilemma, however, is based on an uncritical assumption about the superiority of male political experience. One might argue that some feminists in Latin America, by emphasizing the need of women to assume male political behavior, "undervalue women's experience and accept the patriarchal reading of the significance of women's lives it claimed to be criticizing" (Elshtain, 1982).

Furthermore, women in neighborhoods tend to label their activity as social rather than political, which seems to be a way of differentiating their activities from male political behavior. These social activities are defined by: (1) the high level of interpersonal solidarity and cooperation prevailing in women's organizations, a reflection of their response to subordination in the private and public spheres; (2) collective survival strategies developed in response to the deepening of the ongoing economic crisis; (3) women's negotiations within the family that promote more egalitarian patterns of sexual relations and act upon the family authority structure as well as representations of masculinity and femininity in the family; and (4) women's struggles against authoritarian regimes during the 1970s and part of the 1980s that articulated modes of resistance developed from their maternal role.

The need to build a constructive politics based on finding solutions to increasing poverty, enforcing a new social policy, and struggling for individual and collective rights in institutions led to a different direction for the political action of women in Argentina. Even if formal political integration is ultimately necessary for women to become competitive in the political system, autonomous organizations have allowed women to construct new identities on the basis of diverse social-class experiences and on the common ground of gender history. This common experience in turn has led them to seek greater influence in those private and public institutions, like families and schools, that reproduce discrimination (Valenzuela, 1992).

I have defined democratization in Argentina as an expansion of social equality and a liberalization of social institutions. Such liberalization implies the struggle of marginal members of society to negotiate rules that will increase their equality, power, and leadership. In particular it takes into account the impact that women's new gender identities might have on the institutions' authority systems, particularly in reproductive institutions (the family and the school) where women have had historical influence but have not achieved positions of leadership. Continued research on groups struggling to open up democratic spaces within schools and other social institutions will provide directions for women as they seek to become new legitimate social and political actors.

Notes

All translations of data were done by the author, Beatriz Schmukler.

1. This chapter was the result of research carried out among families in elementary schools and, in previous projects, in secondary schools. I thank CONICET for supporting this research and Graciela Di Marco, Flora Perelman de Solarz, and Alicia Palermo for their support in this research.

References

Achilli, E.L. (1988). Práctica docente: Una interpretación desde los saberes del maestro. *Cuadernos de Antropología Social*, 1(2), 1–28.

Ackelsberg M. and Shanley, M.L. (1991) *From resistance to reconstruction? Madres de Plaza de Mayo, maternalism and the transition to democracy in Argentina*. Paper presented at the International Congress of Political Science, Buenos Aires.

Batallán, G. and García, J.F. (1988). *Trabajo docente, democratización y crecimiento del niño y el aprendizaje escolar: Su incidencia en la reformulación del rol docente*. Buenos Aires: FLACSO.

Bonder, G. (1992). Altering sexual stereotypes through teacher training. In N. Stromquist (Ed.), *Women and education in Latin America*. Boulder, CO: Lynne Rienner Publishers.

Cavarozzi, M. (1991). Beyond transitions to democracy in Latin America. *Journal of Latin American Studies*, 24, 665–684.

Coelho y Gallart, M.A. (1986). *La imbricación entre el poder y la tarea como límite a la innovación*. Buenos Aires: CENEP.

Cukier, Z., Rey, R., and Tornadu, B. (1979a). *Páginas para mí, Primer Grado*. Buenos Aires: Grupo Aique.

Cukier, Z., Rey, R., and Tornadu, B. (1979b). *Páginas para mí, Tercer Grado*. Buenos Aires: Grupo Aique.

Cukier, Z., Rey, R., and Tornadu, B. (1980). *Páginas para mí, Segundo Grado*. Buenos Aires: Grupo Aique.

De Rendo, A. and Perelman de Solarz, F. (1988). El cuaderno de clase y su autor. *Lectura y Vida*, 2(2), 25–47.

Di Marco, G. (1992). *Las mujeres y la política en la Argentina de los noventa*. Research Report: CONICET. Buenos Aires.

Di Marco, G. and Schmukler, B. (1991). *Cambios en los modelos de Género entre madres e hijos de familias de sectores populares en Buenos Aires, Argentina*. Research Report presented to International Development Research Centre, Ottawa, Ontario, Canada.

Elshtain, J. (1982). *Public men, public women*. Princeton, NJ: Princeton University Press.

Fisher, J. (1989). *Mothers of the disappeared*. Boston: South End Press.

Morgade, G. (1990). *El determinante de Género en el trabajo docente de la escuela primaria*. Unpublished master's thesis, Facultad Latinoamericana de Ciencias Sociales (FLACSO). Buenos Aires, Argentina.

Navarro, M. (1989). The mothers of the Plaza de Mayo in Argentina. In S. Eckstein (Ed.), *Power and popular protest: Latin American social movements* (pp. 124–143). Berkeley: University of California Press.

O'Donnell, G. and Schmitter, P. (1986). *Transitions from authoritarian rule*. Baltimore: Johns Hopkins University Press.

Palermo, A. (1993). *Las Maestras y la Reproducción de valores en el Aula*. Unpublished master's thesis. FLACSO, Buenos Aires, Argentina.

Perelman de Solarz, F. (1992). *Analysis of interviews*. Research Report. Buenos Aires: CONICET.

Robertson, R. and Burkart H. (Eds.). (1979). *Identity and authority*. New York: St. Martin's Press.

Schmukler, B. (1992a). Women and the micro-social democratization of everyday life. In N. Stromquist (Ed.), *Women and education in Latin America* (pp. 246–263). Boulder, CO: Lynne Rienner Publishers.

Schmukler, B. (1992b). The invisibility of mothers in the democratic transition of Argentina. In M. Agosin (Ed.), *Women, children and human rights in Latin America* (pp. 123–144). New York: HarperCollins.

Stromquist, N. (1992). *Micro and macro-democracies: Toward a theory of convergence*. Paper presented at the Conference on Education and Development Revisited, Institute of International Education, Stockholm University, Stockholm, Sweden.

Valenzuela, M.E. (1992). *Women and the democratization process in Chile*. Paper presented at the Conference on Women and the Transition from Authoritarian Rule in Latin America and Eastern Europe, Berkeley, CA.

Wainerman, C. and Raijman, R.B. (1987). *Sexismo en los libros de lectura de la escuela primaria*. México, D.F.: Ediciones del IDES.

Chapter Six
Anomie and Education
The Politics of Innovation in a Mexican High School

Juan Fidel Zorrilla

The Mexican system of higher education (which includes preparatory high schools) has been characterized by high growth in student enrollments for several decades. Enrollments grew continuously from 1961 until 1981.[1] During the 1970s the annual rate of growth peaked at 13.2 percent (ANUIES, 1971, 1972, 1981, 1982, 1991, 1993). This accelerated growth was promoted and financed by the federal government under the administration, first, of President Luis Echeverría, 1970–1976, as a crucial part of its political agenda; then from 1976–1982 the administration of President José López Portillo, who continued to endorse the same "populist" policies vis-à-vis higher education.

By the beginning of the 1980s the Mexican higher education system had reached a stage of rapid massification (Guevara, 1981) that provided increased educational opportunities, particularly for some social groups and individuals. This trend changed dramatically, however, in 1982, as Mexico, along with the rest of Latin America, entered a devastating economic crisis. "La crisis" as it has commonly become known, was triggered by an inability of the federal government to service a mounting foreign debt. This resulted in a smaller economic role for the government and a tremendous decrease in the proportion of public expenditures available to education (Kent and de Vries, 1994). For example, at the end of the 1980s the annual rate of growth in enrollment was a mere 1.34 percent, whereas the annual rates of demographic growth in the 1960s and 1970s—when those students were born—were 3.4 percent and 2.7 percent respectively (Kent and de Vries, 1994).

In Mexico these new policies are part of a larger "neo-liberal" project. The net result has been a series of attempts on the part of succeeding federal administrations to balance the budget while also channeling a high proportion of the budget to service the foreign debt (Banco Interamericano de Desarrollo, 1991; Cardoso and Helwege, 1990).

At present the growth within the higher education system has become stagnant. The sudden massive growth of the higher education system and its equally abrupt stagnation pose a number of theoretical problems concerning the social, political, and economic functions of public education policy. The role of the federal government's political agenda in effectively changing the overall internal and external context of higher education stands out as a main factor. However, the impact of governmental educational policy on institutions of higher education, especially during the years of expansion, was not as strong as had been foreseen by policy documents at the time (Bartolucci and Rodríguez, 1983; Castrejón, 1976; Latapí, 1976; C.F. Pérez, 1980; Péreznieto, 1980; Zorrilla, 1988). Furthermore, despite the reversal of the expansive orientation of education policy in 1982, the impact of expansion upon the organization of the academic system continued to be felt, as throughout the 1980s institutions with shrinking budgets in real terms had to make do for the rest of the decade (Kent, 1990; Kent and de Vries, 1994). By December 1994 another financial crisis of major proportions was made public in Mexico, creating new unforeseen circumstances for the operation of public services, which promises to have dramatic effects on the educational system.

These radical financial and educational changes deeply affect individuals and institutions and create a need for documentation of how these changes are experienced at the individual and institutional level. It is in this role that researchers are called upon to identify and document the nexus between structural processes and the lived experiences of different social actors.

This chapter draws attention to the significance of qualitative research in uncovering specific types of linkages between individuals and institutions in a Mexican public school created in the wake of the massive growth process at the beginning of the 1970s. First, the institutional milieu of higher education is analyzed in its evolution from traditional higher education to more recent innovative approaches, followed by an examination of the interrelationship between personal and institutional conditions through a series of individual cases drawn from in-depth student interviews. These cases are taken from part of the fieldwork that the author undertook during the 1985/1986 school year. They are analyzed using Durkheim's classical sociological concept of anomie in *Suicide* (1971), which has been adapted for the purpose of this paper. The following sections cover the evolution from traditional to current patterns of higher education in Mexico; the tension between political goals and academic values;

the socio-political context of the study (the politics and academic life of the Colegio de Ciencias y Humanidades [CCH] of the Universidad Nacional Autónoma de México [UNAM]); a discussion of student strategies using the concept of anomie from Durkheim's theory; and finally a brief analysis of two individual cases.

The Evolution of the Present System of Higher Education in Mexico

Mexican public high schools, known as *bachilleratos*, were created during the second half of the nineteenth century and were modeled after the French *baccalaureat*. They are part of the public and private higher education system in Mexico and date back to 1910, when what is now the National Autonomous University of Mexico (UNAM) was founded.[2] As a result the bylaws that govern the overall academic conditions of the *bachillerato*, undergraduate, and graduate levels are similar. This situation prevails in almost all public and private institutions of higher education.

The relative size of enrollment in the *bachillerato* within institutions of higher education can be quite considerable. Thus 47 percent of the total enrollment at UNAM in 1992 corresponded to the *bachillerato*. There are extreme cases, as in the case of the University of Guadalajara or the Autonomous University of Guerrero, where there is a higher percentage of students in *bachillerato* than in undergraduate and graduate degree programs.

Until 1968 Mexican higher education had very clear social functions: (1) to train the professional, managerial, political, scientific, and cultural elites of the country; and (2) to promote upward social mobility. Publicly funded institutions of higher education cover well over 80 percent of current enrollment.

Higher education was organized in terms of different *carreras,* or careers—that is, undergraduate programs of study for each of the liberal professions plus a few natural science, social science, and humanities programs. Each *carrera* was rigidly separated from all others, in terms of both curriculum and tracking options for students. At the end of an undergraduate degree program a *licenciatura* (bachelor's degree) is obtained. This degree "licenses" a student to work professionally in certain areas which, by law, require such a degree (hence the term *licenciatura*). At this point each licensed professional can then become a *maestro de asignatura* (part-time teacher) at the university. At present almost all undergraduate degree courses are taught by *licenciados* (people with undergraduate degrees) in each profession who moonlight by teaching one or two four-hour courses a week. The few existing full-time posts are designated for distinguished professors. A clear and rigid separation of teaching and research is evident. Research takes place in centers and institutes endowed with full-time research posts. Graduate programs represent less than 2 percent of total enrollment today.

New Trends in Mexican Higher Education

In 1968 a student protest at UNAM against police brutality grew into a movement demanding political reforms. The movement was bloodily suppressed by the federal government, which in turn eroded the government's legitimacy. In an effort to win back legitimacy, the administration of President Echeverría (1970–1976) channeled huge financial resources into a rapid and major expansion of enrollment in higher education and into the creation of new educational institutions. Existing hiring procedures for new faculty were overwhelmed, and faculty were hired without much attention to academic standing or ability. Screening mechanisms for student admission were similarly lax. Public institutions of higher education became far more attentive to internal political stability than to the academic achievement of students or faculty. At the same time the federal government placed more value on the impact of this massive growth of higher education on its own legitimacy than on academic efficiency or scientific output.

Academic life changed dramatically. With a growing student population and ever bigger subsidies from the federal government, the number of full-time tenured posts increased considerably in public institutions. However, because there was no tradition of supervision for individualized study, with few institutional exceptions the notion of providing tutorials or counseling simply did not take hold. The effective workload of these new full-time posts was modeled on the activities of the old part-time teacher. In fact, full-time posts rarely involved more than eight or ten hours of teaching per week. For the remaining thirty or so hours per week full-time academic staff were free to engage in personal projects or supplement their income by working elsewhere. However, most teaching continued to be undertaken by part-time teachers, who depended more and more on juggling several part-time teaching jobs in different institutions. The number of teachers hired to service the rapidly expanding undergraduate student population increased fivefold in ten years. These new improvised faculty members themselves had at best a *licenciatura* degree.

With this increase came an upsurge of teacher unions, which rapidly grew into enormously powerful organizations in public universities. These unions became quite crucial in maintaining or upsetting the political stability of institutions of higher education. At the peak of their influence unions managed to impose a single national pay standard for each of the six academic categories in all higher education institutions in the country (*homologación*), which, some argued, acted as a disincentive for quality academic teaching and research since output and quality became irrelevant for earnings.

Universities launched various strategies for upgrading their full-time faculty by increasing the proportion of teachers and researchers with master's degrees and doctorates. A new and sizeable elite of highly qualified academics consolidated their positions in large public universities and research centers. This scientific elite pushed hard for a new academic income policy based on evaluation. In 1984 the National System of Academics was set up to effectively challenge the homogeneous system of incomes for faculty and the political hold of unions on institutions.

Such diverse trends gave rise to a great heterogeneity in the quality of teaching, research, and education. Internal and external efficiency varied greatly from one program to another, with some programs and institutions achieving high academic quality while others remained veritable academic backwaters. Nonetheless, quality in academic performance became less consistent, and the prestige of public education was negatively affected. Despite attempts at curricular change and an increase in the number of undergraduate programs of study, most programs remained rigid. Adding to the problem, at some public institutions enrollments reached enormous proportions, making institutional governance more complex.

The Growing Conflict between Political Goals and Academic Values

As a response to meeting the demands of the overall growth in student enrollments, new schools were opened in Mexico during the 1970s and 1980s, most of which tended to reproduce the existing institutions. However, a few "modern, innovative" types of institutions appeared at the same time that "old, traditional" institutions continued to exist. The creation of most of these new institutions at the time was justified by an expressed need for innovation in higher education and a naive belief that these institutions were synonymous with progress (Zorrilla, 1989; Bartolucci and Rodríguez, 1983).

Some of these institutions, including the institution where I did fieldwork, the Colegio de Ciencias y Humanidades (CCH) of the UNAM, proclaimed themselves to be radical innovations. In fact, they were neither radical innovations nor conservative changes (Kent, 1990), but rather the result of public debates on the nature, aims, content, scope, fairness, function, and finances of the public educational system. The decision to create new institutions and the guidelines for change were arbitrarily made by the Mexican authoritarian political system based upon the notion that educational expansion was needed (Brunner, 1990; Zorrilla, 1989a; Kent, 1990).

The creation of such institutions and the changes that ensued were not questioned because they were justified by the presumed inadequacy of the existing institutions. Research indicates that these justifications were not based on any sort of diagnosis of the system. In fact the existing literature on higher education in the educational journals of the 1970s indicates that the main topics under discussion were the likely demand for higher education, policy making, and its planning implications. The literature does not provide any models of how the system might work better. Instead what was apparent during the 1970s was the explicit assumption that public higher educational institutions were created mainly in order to appear to be different from existing ones, with the implicit assumption that such difference was itself a guarantee of progress (Zorrilla, 1989a). Furthermore, it was never made clear whether the issue at stake was to change educational processes while keeping the same goals or to establish different goals (Zorrilla, 1989a). The highly centralized and authoritarian nature of Mexican political life resulted in a process of quick, arbitrary, and nonreflective decision making. Some of these decisions had positive outcomes, others did not.

To understand the impact of this relationship between the political regime and the public educational system, several facts are essential. First, the federal government entirely funded the enormous expansion and differentiation of the public higher education system in the 1970s. Mexican presidents have such political clout that they have both de jure and de facto decision-making powers, freeing them from the complex negotiations with Congress that are part of the political system in the United States. Second, 90 percent of the budget of the National Autonomous University of Mexico is funded by direct subsidies from the federal government. None of the educational expansion that took place, including that of UNAM, could have been undertaken without the direct participation of the Mexican president.

In some cases the speed with which these presidential decisions took place was extraordinary, as in the creation of the CCH in early 1971. A total of one hundred days elapsed between the moment the president of Mexico called the president of UNAM to announce the decision to fund the new institution and the opening of three different campus buildings to receive more than 15,000 students (Zorrilla, 1986; Bartolucci and Rodríguez, 1983). Those one hundred days included the conceptualization of the new institution and its curriculum. When the university's administrators were summoned by the Mexican president, they had no idea what to expect. Between the beginning of January and mid-April 1971, the following events took place: (1) The Mexican president decided to fund a project for a new type of high school; (2) UNAM's administrators located the places where the three different campuses were going to be built and acquired the property; (3) architects designed the buildings; (4) administrators obtained the funds, and classrooms and laboratories were built; (5) the curricula of all the subjects were conceptualized; (6) teachers were hired; (7) the administration of the different campuses was organized; and (8) the new schools opened.

The emphasis was so focused on building and organizing the campuses that the educational process itself was overlooked. There were no attempts made to observe, analyze, describe, and compare the actual development of the new system with desired performance outcomes. Both the general public and specialists in education were overwhelmed by the incredible speed with which this promising new institution was set up. Lost in the midst of such commotion was the importance of sound planning and the development of a well-organized curriculum.

Politically, the growth of student enrollment in higher education became a major source of political authenticity for the federal administration. The political benefits were viewed as outweighing the educational problems that resulted from hasty improvisation. Higher education institutions were presumably quite content to see their budgets continuously expand, and in this light educational problems were viewed as the necessary cost of such an expansion.

Its effect was so strong that even critics fell prey to its attraction. Most of the literature written until the mid-eighties that deals with this period has emphasized the overall socioeconomic logic involved in the government's actions (R.M. Pérez, 1983; C.F. Pérez, 1980; Bernal, 1979; Latapí, 1976; Jiménez, 1987; Castrejón, 1976; Péreznieto, 1980). None of the literature mentioned the effects of the conditions of massive education, nor was there observation, analysis, or interpretation of the educational outcomes. The government's action was generally viewed as commendable by most authors.

It should be noted that, although not all higher education institutions created during this decade followed the same pattern of hasty improvisation, the fact remains that universities and technological institutes sprouted up all over Mexico, supported with immense publicity and no documentation of the actual educational processes. Such impressive political effectiveness, however, did not preclude a series of unintended consequences for the governance of institutions of higher education and their academic quality.

Politics and Academic Life in the CCH

The opening of the Colegio de Ciencias y Humanidades (CCH) was greeted with enthusiasm by specialists, the intelligentsia, sectors of the press, and the political left because it seemed to provide a good opportunity to steer a new institution in the direction of a widely felt need for change in Mexican society. The subsequent academic direction of the CCH became shaped by the university's political situation. From 1968 to 1982, the UNAM was subject to severe internal political pressure from radical students and teacher groups who had participated in the legitimate 1968 protest movement, for which many had even spent time in prison (Zermeño, 1978). This pressure was all the more difficult to respond to since there were no outlets for it in the wider Mexican political system, given the system's total resistance to democratization at the time. The UNAM was cornered historically into managing within its own confines, a problem stemming from the rigidity of the national political system. Such pressure turned inward and led to frequent stoppages, student strikes, and increased violence on the campuses. From UNAM's perspective, the government's decision to generously fund the expansion of higher education, including the *bachillerato*, provided an ideal opportunity for channeling such pressure. For UNAM's authorities, the creation of the CCH became a crucial asset in formulating a political answer to radicalized internal pressure.

Within the political context of the university, the success of UNAM's response to political pressure depended on reaching internal political stability throughout the institution, which meant reaching implicit compromises with all internally active political groups. Because this pressure was not equally exerted on all schools, faculties, centers, and institutes of the university, each compromise between academic values and political goals was negotiated differently. Yet not all academic values and practices were equally embedded in all of the institutions. Because the CCH was formally developed against the grain of academic tradition, at CCH traditional academic values suffered considerably. UNAM's administrators quickly made the maintenance of internal stability a priority, demanding little or no regulation of the educational performance of teachers and students. Thus the CCH became an arena for the pursuit of political goals by teacher and student groups and UNAM's administrators.[3] This convergence of interests created political stability, but sometimes at the expense of educational goals.

The CCH campuses became the bases from which partisan movements were supported and launched. Actions intended to strengthen the educational requirements and discipline of students tended to be branded as politically motivated actions infringing on academic autonomy or union rights. Under these conditions, educational goals often languished.

Elsewhere I have argued that the design of the CCH curriculum was so hastily developed that several contradictions occurred that could not be ignored (Zorrilla, 1988). The education at CCH was supposed to cater to the learning needs of students by emphasizing reading and writing as opposed to traditional rote learning. By decreeing that all teaching should be "active, critical, and interdisciplinary," the search for new methods in many cases became the end rather than the means of instruction (UNAM, 1971; Colegio de Ciencias y Humanidades, 1979). Some teachers could justify virtually any action, even neglect, by appealing to innovative, active, interdisciplinary education, since academic values and discipline had been disqualified. At the same time the traditional liberal academic structure continued and continues to this day to guarantee freedom in teaching (*libertad de cátedra*), which guarantees the unhindered pursuit of academic activities. In such a climate, each teacher literally became accountable only to him/herself.

Within this context new methodologies and techniques were partially applied or applied with little expertise. However, there were some teachers who displayed an enormous zeal in their educational commitment, and they motivated their students to undertake more creative tasks. At the same time, other teachers rarely showed up to teach their classes. These disparate behaviors occurred with the tacit approval of the school's administration, which had become overwhelmed by constant pressure from political groups.

The Lived Experiences of Students at CCH

CCH students normally take an average of five courses in the first semester: Reading I, Writing I, Physics, History I, and Mathematics I. By the second semester they take advanced versions of the same subjects except for Physics which is replaced by Chemistry. When students talked in interviews about their teachers, they talked about their personal styles of teaching. Such assessments covered a wide variety of experiences that varied from student to student. By and large, out of every four classes, one was reported by students as being good, another as being average, and two as displaying unsatisfactory teaching. The criteria students used to judge and describe teacher performance tended to focus on teacher absenteeism, inconsistency in grading, and a perceived lack of quality education in the classroom.

Some typical unsatisfactory experiences are described by students in the following manner:

Reading I:

The teacher rarely came to class. As for grading, she gave some examinations and supposedly she also took into account participation in class dynamics, but as she was frequently absent, there was little chance of participating. When she was not absent, she asked a few questions and that counted as participation.

The teacher was very punctual and never failed to attend class. From the very beginning she told us how she evaluated. But in actual fact she just talked and talked.

In this subject I did not really have a teacher in either semester. He would come at the beginning and would ask for a report, and would then disappear until the end of the semester when he would collect it.

Mathematics I and II:

He was really a very bad teacher and he was frequently absent. He was a bit irresponsible, as he taught without any interest, and you could not ask any questions because it made things much worse. Most students failed; only three out of forty passed. The next semester we had him again. At the end of the course he announced that everybody had copied and only a few passed again.

He was an average teacher. He dictated his lesson and gave homework, but he was absent a lot.

I really thought for a time that he was a good teacher, and I did not realize until afterward that he was not very good, as he did not explain fully. He belabored just a few basic points while other teachers were covering a lot of ground. He was rarely, if ever absent, and most students failed that course.

Physics:

The teacher did not fulfill his obligations. After being absent for a week, he would come just once, and then he would be absent for another week, returning once again only to announce an examination.

He would not even enter the classroom. He was absent most of the time. He would give the highest marks to those who spoke a lot; if you only participated a few times, you got a C. The whole course was covered in a couple of lessons.

In Physics we had a female teacher who suddenly stopped attending class. Halfway through the semester, a replacement arrived. He was a wonderful teacher, but heaven knows how he evaluated.

Writing I:

The teacher gave away good grades to just anybody. If you had prepared a presentation in class, you would get an A, but if you did not do anything, you would simply go to the student commissioned by the teacher to keep a record of all grades and ask him to mark you with an A, and you would get an A.

Writing II:

Throughout the first and the second semesters she only came six or seven times, and I am not exaggerating. But in the end, only very few failed to pass.

Chemistry:

The very same teacher that abruptly stopped attending class came back during the following semester. She was o.k., we all had a great time in class, a lot of jokes and she was frequently absent. Who knows how she evaluated our work. Some guys who hardly ever came to class got Bs; it was highly arbitrary and some people benefited from it.

At the beginning of the semester we had the same teacher who had given us Physics the previous semester. After a while we did not have anybody, finally a replacement came and he did not attend much either, but I passed.

History I and II:

The teacher would talk and talk for two hours at a time. At the end, he asked for an open essay. I got a C with a long essay 20 pages long, some others received an A for three pages.

With this teacher, 60 percent of all students failed. If you gave a good oral presentation you would be exempt from having to sit for an examination. All those who took the exam failed it.

He had a lot of problems with the school, and apparently he was thrown out. He only came to the classroom five times. He would stay less than half an hour for an hour and a half class. We went to see the principal to complain about him and the reading teacher. Even though the history teacher lost his job, I still see him around.

Coping with Ambiguities: Student Strategies

Students openly admitted that passing their subjects depended on two factors: (1) guessing what the logic of grading was all about; and (2) complying with the teacher's demands no matter how absurd they appeared to be. The institution had very little control over what content was taught, how it was taught, grading procedures, and teacher attendance. In order to pass a subject, students faced a teaching situation in which most of the rules of the game were set by the teacher rather than the institution.

Faced with unpredictable and idiosyncratic demands from their different teachers, students learned that the key to success lay in understanding what the teacher wanted them to do, rather than learning the curriculum. Not surprisingly, student success in such a system was seen by students as depending to an enormous extent on understanding the will of the teachers, a knowledge requiring specific skills that did not necessarily coincide with academic skills. This situation seemed to generate an inordinate number of docile students who were not motivated to study. Most of the time students seem to accept existing conditions while at the same time critiquing them. However, immersed as they were in these conditions, their main goal appeared to be to survive as a student.

One of the few institutional resources collectively available to students was group complaints directed at the administration. In only one of the cases observed did student complaints successfully work to get a teacher fired, and in another case the teacher who was reported took it seriously and responded positively to the complaints, changing his/her class behavior. Complaints become more frequent in cases of teacher absenteeism and strict grading practices. They were far less likely when absenteeism was linked to lax grading on the part of faculty. In fact a pattern of subtle trade-offs was observed, in which students who refrained from complaining to the administration about teacher absenteeism often found themselves receiving inflated grades from the teacher. For example, a teacher observed during field work in another class argued with students who formally complained about her absenteeism that school authorities were persecuting her on political grounds. When the teacher offered to be more "considerate," they did not follow up their complaint, and all of these students passed with high grades.

This general academic situation is one in which student and teacher actions are taken in a context of ambiguous or inexistent norms. However, norms in the school are very clear in some arenas, such as the allocation and distribution of classrooms to groups, groups to teachers, wages to teachers, and general scheduling practices. In other words, CCH appears to function far better in the area of school administration than in its actual educational delivery, which is in itself an important indicator of the operative values of the school system.

Durkheimian Anomie

To understand the complex nature of relationships between students and teachers, the concept of anomie from Durkheim's *Suicide* provides a conceptual framework for understanding the CCH. Durkheim explains the rise in number of suicides by pointing to the consequences that occur when large numbers of people are thrown into unexpected and ambiguous situations that throw them off balance. Durkheim's analysis is not relevant merely to elements of order and balance between individuals; it extends further to the elements of order and balance in individual personality. This means that norms, values, and rules are an important social component of each individual personality, and that when they are lacking the probability of major changes in behavior increases significantly (Parsons, 1968).

This argument led Durkheim to debate the problem of the social regulation of individual behavior. It is here that one can find a theoretical approach that explicitly addresses the relationship between the structural and the individual dimensions of society. Durkheim states that there is nothing in the psychological constitution of humans that can establish limits on the pursuit of goals. Human beings alone among all creatures are capable of setting up unattainable goals. Such pursuits necessarily result in condemning oneself to perpetual frustration and misery. In the absence of instinct, nothing in human nature can limit such tendencies; hence the need for an acceptable external force to impose limits. Such a power cannot but be moral. Only society, either directly or through one of its institutions, is in the position to assume the role of a regulator, because it is the only moral power superior to and accepted by the individual. But such regulation can be useful only if those subjected to it consider it fair and legitimate. However, when society is disturbed by sudden change—a painful crisis or a rapid transformation—it is unable to exercise its regulatory action. In the absence of such regulations, new types of behavior can arise.

For example, the collapse of a traditional pre-modern order brought with it the end of social ruling over economic activity. As economic progress became an end in itself, profit, instead of being considered the means servicing an end beyond itself, became the supreme end of individuals and societies (Durkheim, 1971). As a result of unlimited expectations and the possibility of continuous growth, economic activity becomes anomic. Unrestrained by any other consideration, economic life is subject to constant turmoil and crisis. The "passion for the infinite" reigns supreme (Durkheim, 1971, p. 204).

In this chapter I have argued that the specific conditions under which the CCH was created can be used to explain the emergence of an institution in which personal and political goals could be pursued without hindrance while at the same time effectively distorting the liberal academic tradition, resulting in an anomic academic context. In many cases new patterns of academic behavior previously negatively sanctioned became acceptable. Student assessment of such an academic context indicated that the system promoted opportunistic strategies on the part of students.

While success under such a system might be thought to be easier than in a more traditional one, one has to keep in mind that CCH graduates a mere 50 percent of its students. This graduation rate suggests major difficulties in adapting to such a system. A major question arises as to the type of social resources that become necessary for success. In order to examine the link between this type of structure and the individual strategies of students, two different patterns of student adjustment are examined in the cases that follow below.

These two students are quite different in terms of social origin and academic backgrounds. One student is middle-class, while the other comes from a poorer background. The middle-class student has a good academic record but the poorer student has struggled throughout his academic career. Yet the "good" student is failing at CCH while the other student manages to survive. Family structure and anomie appear to be significant factors in understanding these outcomes.

According to Durkheim's theory of anomie, the unrestrained pursuit of personal and group goals creates a state of personal disorientation that has important consequences for behavior. Students are puzzled by teachers' behavior because of the ambiguity of demands that appear to them to be arbitrary. In the absence of traditional patterns of academic authority, students overcome this disorientation by considering education as merely a useful credential, which can justify coping with an anomic context. To view education in this way fits into the anomic structure, insofar as it stands for the pursuit of non-academic goals, in this case family and personal goals, even at the price of becoming an accomplice to dubious academic practices. At the same time the pursuit of such a strategy teaching that success goes hand-in-hand with adjustment to authoritarian practices can often be academically meaningless. It also teaches that formal rules and regulations are not as important as real power vested in authority. Opportunistic acceptance of authority and disregard for formal rules are traditional traits of Mexican political life. Such correspondence suggests a paradoxical nexus between an educational anomic structure and authoritarian political values. This is all the more surprising in view of the explicitly democratic nature of work at the CCH.

Once the likelihood of such a nexus has been established, the mechanics of the interrelationship between personal strategies, family situations, and school dynamics can be closely examined. The following two cases depict the students mentioned above.

Alvaro: A "Good" Student Drops Out

Alvaro was 16 years old at the time of fieldwork. He was born in the state of Vera Cruz, and his parents, who were native to Vera Cruz, married and divorced young. His father studied economics for a few semesters at UNAM but dropped out to start his own business. His mother had one year of high school. They divorced when Alvaro was 6, at which time his father bought an apartment where Alvaro lives with his mother. After the divorce Alvaro's mother took a job filing archives at the university.

Alvaro had a 13-year-old brother who lived with him and his mother until six months before this study. His brother moved in with his grandparents in Vera Cruz because he was doing poorly in school. With his brother gone, Alvaro spent a great deal of time with friends or fellow students. At school he often missed class and stayed on the school grounds, where he played the guitar with two other boys.

In one of his interviews, Alvaro pointed to the futility of attending class if he could get good grades simply by studying on his own. He was far more interested in relating to other boys who shared his fondness for music. The school did not make any strong demands to attend regularly or to study harder. Alvaro found challenges elsewhere, such as buying a song book and practicing his guitar. At home he and a friend, who lived in a neighboring apartment and liked *boleros*, played the guitar and sang in their spare time.

On weekends his mother left Alvaro on his own. He observed that, "She also has the right to have a good time." Alvaro would then invite large groups of friends to the apartment, where they talked and sang until three or four in the morning. Alvaro claimed, "Our parents know we are quiet and well behaved. Only very occasionally do we buy a bottle, and we all have just one drink."

During the years when Alvaro's mother and brother lived together his school performance was good or excellent. When his brother moved to Vera Cruz, he was left facing lonely weekends and a very loose family relationship with his mother. His interest in peer ties and pastimes gave him the opportunity to create a social group that placed very specific expectations on him—to provide a place to meet every week. School, on the contrary, exerted no pressure, not even the mechanisms for detecting his absence from class. His ability to cope, for a time, with all of his subjects without studying or attending class led him to get involved with a group of peers for playing music.

Academically Alvaro had been, up to that moment, a very good student. His grades in primary school were straight A's. In middle school he got 9.3 out of 10. When he entered CCH he got 8 out of 10, which is only fair (6 out of 10 being the lowest passing grade). At the beginning of his third semester at CCH, at the time I began fieldwork, and a few months after his brother left for Vera Cruz, he stopped attending class regularly. Nonetheless he passed four out of five subjects, which by CCH standards is not bad. Even though he hardly went to class, his fellow students considered him to be quite brilliant since he didn't seem to need to study, even in mathematics. Despite his absence from class, he studied an average of five to six hours a week. During the fourth semester he stopped attending class altogether, even though he still went to school to hang out with his friends and play guitar on the school grounds. By the end of the semester he had failed all of his subjects.

Alvaro's case is used to illustrate how, paradoxically, an anomic education does not make it easier for everyone to pass. Alvaro's case also illustrates the importance of emotionally strong peer ties vis-à-vis weakened ties in the family; hence the involvement of Alvaro with a group of peers where he had an important position. With anomic conditions in the family and at school, his academic performance quickly deteriorated, even though he was one of the ablest in his class. His brother, after failing, made the decision to go and live with his grandparents, which represented a non-anomic family setting. Until that moment Alvaro's relationship with his brother provided him with a minimal family tie. When his brother moved out he was completely derailed, and Alvaro faced on his own an extremely weak family and school social environment. His involvement with his peers represented an effort to create a strong social reference group. Throughout all these events the school remained unaware and uninterested in what was happening, even though Alvaro was an excellent candidate for higher education. Alvaro drifted out of school but not off the school grounds, where he continued to play guitar with his friends.

Benito: Working the System

Benito, who attended the same classes as Alvaro, was an academically poor student who succeeded in remaining in school despite his limited achievement. He failed first and third grades in primary school, finishing with an average grade of 7.5, which in Mexico is a mediocre performance. In middle school he failed seventh grade and had to go to night school. When he finished night school he tried to enter a teacher training school but did not pass the entrance examination. He then went to a commercial school for a semester but didn't continue because it was too expensive, after which he applied to the UNAM school system and was placed in CCH.

At the end of his first semester Benito failed mathematics. He took another examination with a teacher well known for passing students easily. Benito acknowledged, "in truth, I studied very little for this exam," and that passing in this case was a function of "finding the right person to pass with." Benito also failed physics, but at the next round of examinations he obtained the lowest passing mark. In other subjects he had an average just above the minimum. During the second semester he failed writing workshop, and in a later exam passed it with the minimum. It should be mentioned that the teacher in charge of the writing workshop rarely went to class, and another teacher ended up giving the exam.

At the end of the third semester he got good grades in Mexican history but the minimum in all others. In fourth semester he failed one subject, got the minimum grade in math and science, and a high grade in history. Since groups have the same teachers in the third and fourth semesters, most students improve their marks from one semester to the next. Benito's average improved continuously, which is the opposite of what happened to Alvaro. In Benito's case, his performance depended to a great extent, though not entirely, on the opportunities provided by the workings of an anomic system.

Conclusion

In summary, this chapter has examined how relations among public educational policy, an emergent, innovative school system, and individual school careers for two students are intertwined. Insights have been framed using Durkheim's concept of anomie, which sheds new light on educational innovation, political ideology, authoritarian relationships, and students' differentiated school career paths. The educational system appears to be neglecting valuable types of students while tolerating poor scholastic performance on the part of teachers and students. The examination of anomie in school life suggests that current academic practices are probably promoting the wrong type of academic performance on the part of students and, at the same time, reproducing traditional authoritarian values. My intent is not to suggest a return to some mythical golden age of "traditional education." Such education has tended to be rigid and memoristic and clearly in need of change. However, more than two decades of experimentation with innovation suggest that many educational policies, as they confront political realities at the school level, have unintended consequences that favor those students who either have other social resources outside of school or become adept at cynically manipulating the system.

Of all students entering UNAM's system of *bachillerato* of which CCH is a part, only half graduate. The other half drop out, fail, or simply leave courses unfinished (Rodríguez, 1986). As they enter secondary school, this cohort represents the top 40 percent of their generation, since the other 60 percent did not attend beyond middle school. Thus, since CCH draws its student body from the top 40 percent of Mexican students, this failure rate requires explanation. This study is a beginning and an invitation to continue this explanatory project.

Notes

Translations of data were done by the author, Juan Fidel Zorrilla.

1. Annual rates of growth by decade of university enrolment: 1961–1971 (5.4%), 1971–1981 (12%), 1981–1990 (3.6%) (ANUIES, 1993).
2. The Mexican system can be confusing for North Americans, since the Mexican *bachillerato* (corresponding to the level of the North American comprehensive high school) has a college prep curriculum and is incorporated into the Mexican system of higher education.
3. Nearly 70 percent of CCH teachers were born between 1940 and 1949 and belong to the same political generation of the UNAM that experienced the political movements of the late 1960s. Thus for many the CCH is a very important reference point in their political and working lives.

References

ANUIES. (1971). *Anuario Estadístico 1971*. México, D.F.: ANUIES.

ANUIES. (1972). *Anuario Estadístico 1972*. México, D.F.: ANUIES.

ANUIES. (1981). *Anuario Estadístico 1981*. México, D.F.: ANUIES.

ANUIES. (1982). *Anuario Estadístico 1982*. México, D.F.: ANUIES.

ANUIES. (1991). *Anuario Estadístico 1990*. México, D.F.: ANUIES.

ANUIES. (1993). *Anuario Estadístico 1993*. México, D.F.: ANUIES.

Banco Interamericano de Desarrollo. (1991). *Progreso Económico y Social en América Latina: Informe 1991*. Washington, D.C: Banco Interamericano de Desarrollo.

Bartolucci, J. (1989). *Posición social, trayectoria escolar y elección de carrera: Seguimiento de una generación de estudiantes universitarios: UNAM 1976–1985*. Unpublished master's thesis, Facultad de Ciencias Políticas y Sociales, Universidad Nacional Autónoma de México (UNAM), México, D.F., México.

Bartolucci, J. and Rodríguez, R. (1983). *El Colegio de Ciencias y Humanidades (1971–1980), una experiencia de innovación universitaria*. México, D.F.: ANUIES.

Bernal, S.A. (1979). *CCH: Un sistema educativo diferente*. México, D.F.: ANUIES.

Brunner, J.J. (1990). *Educación superior en América Latina: Cambios y desafíos*. México, D.F.: Fondo de Cultura Económica.

Cardoso, E. and Helwege, A. (1990). Below the line: Poverty in Latin America. *World Development*, 20, 23–44.

Castrejón, D.J. (1976). *La educación superior en México*. México, D.F.: Secretaría de Educación Pública (SEP).

Centro de Estudios Educativos. (1972). *Revista de Centro de Estudios Educativos, II*, 125–165.

Colegio de Ciencias y Humanidades. (1979). *Documento 1*. México, D.F.: UNAM.

Colegio de Ciencias y Humanidades. (1986). *Editos e inéditos del CCH*. México, D.F.: UNAM.

Durkheim, E. (1967). *De la división del trabajo social*. Buenos Aires: Schapire Editor.

Durkheim, E. (1971). *El suicidio: Estudio de sociología*. Buenos Aires: Schapire Editor.

Guevara, N.G. (Ed.). (1981). *La crisis de la educación superior*. México, D.F.: Nueva Imagen.

Instituto Nacional de Estadística. (1991). *Agenda Estadística 1990*. Aguascalientes, México: Instituto Nacional de Estadística.

Jiménez, M.F. (1987). *El autoritarismo en el gobierno de la UNAM*. México, D.F.: Ediciones de Cultura Popular.

Kent, R. (1990). *Modernización conservadora crisis académica en la UNAM*. México, D.F.: Nueva Imagen.

Kent, R. and de Vries, W. (1994). Evaluation and funding policies in Mexican higher education. *The Review of Higher Education*, 43, 12–30.

Latapí, P. (1976). *Comentarios a la reforma educativa*. México, D.F.: Prospectiva Universitaria.

Parsons, T. (1968). *The structure of social action. A study in social theory with special reference to a group of recent European writers*. New York: Free Press.

Pérez, C.F. (1980). *La universidad del futuro*. México, D.F.: UNAM-CESU.

Pérez, R.M. (1983). *Educación y desarrollo: La ideología del estado*. México, D.F.: Editorial Línea.

Péreznieto, L. (1980). *Algunas consideraciones acerca de la reforma universitaria en la Universidad Nacional Autónoma de México*. México, D.F.: UNAM.

Rodríguez, G.R. (1986). La pirámide escolar en el bachillerato (análisis de la eficiencia terminal en el CCH). In J.F. Zorrilla (Ed.), *Los universitarios: La élite y la masa* (pp. 29–52). México, D.F.: Cuadernos del CESU-UNAM.

Rodríguez, G.R. (1991). *Series históricas de la matrícula escolar*. México, D.F.: CESU-UNAM.

UNAM. (1971). Tercera época. *Gaceta UNAM*, 2, 21–34.

Zermeño, S. (1978). *México: Una democracia utópica: El movimiento estudiantil de 68*. México, D.F.: Siglo XXI.

Zorrilla, J.F. (1986). El proyecto educativo del CCH y los maestros. In J.F. Zorrilla (Ed.), *Los universitarios: La élite y la masa* (pp. 79–90). México, D.F.: CESU-UNAM.

Zorrilla, J.F. (1988). La educación en el aula. In L. Luna (Ed.), *Los estudiantes: Trabajos de historia y sociología*. México, D.F.: UNAM.

Zorrilla, J.F. (1989a). *Innovación y racionalidad educativa: El caso del Colegio de Ciencias y Humanidades de la UNAM*. Unpublished master's thesis, Facultad de Ciencias Políticas y Sociales, UNAM, México, D.F., México.

Zorrilla, J.F. (1989b). El prestigio de las ideas. In J.F. Zorrilla (Ed.), *Nuevas perspectivas críticas sobre la UNAM: Cinco estudios* (pp. 31–48). México, D.F.: CESU-UNAM.

Zorrilla, J.F. (1992). *The function of qualitative analysis in Mexico: Perspective from an escuela normal*. Washington, D.C.: ERIC.

Section III

Qualitative Action Research for Teacher Development and Improved Classroom Practices

Drawing on action research and collaborative research traditions within Latin America, the chapters in Section III attempt to have a direct impact on schooling through their link to teacher development and curricular change. While most qualitative research in North America attempts to add to our understanding of schooling from a sociocultural perspective, some qualitative research programs also attempt to have a more immediate impact on educational practice. One type of qualitative research that is achieving increased legitimacy in North America is research done by school practioners (Anderson, Herr, and Nihlen, 1994). Another type of research is done by collaborative, interdisciplinary teams, like those led by Luis Moll at the University of Arizona, who have studied the "funds of knowledge" of local communities and worked with teachers and schools to find ways to build on these funds through curricular and instructional strategies (Moll, 1992). These collaborative action research strategies have developed in Latin and North America largely independently of each other.

In Chapter Seven, Elvira Souza Lima provides an overview of the emergence of qualitative research in Brazil, the exodus of intelligentsia during the military coup of 1964, and the subsequent reemergence of qualitative research both from researchers in exile and from those within Brazil. She describes her attempt to teach an in-service course in the Brazilian state of Matto Grosso while simultaneously engaging in action research. This case study describes the transformation that takes place for the teacher of the course as well as for the students. The basis for such transformation is her ability to adapt instruction to the local context rather than expecting students to adapt.

One of the consequences of this adaptation was the eruption of spontaneous singing by the students during class time, where the lyrics embodied their sense of entitlement and rights, their criticism of social injustices, and their closeness to nature. Another consequence was the use of silence as constructed meaning and the use of time and space, which often was extended by the students' interest in learning. Finally, Souza Lima explains that, by reflecting on the use of language for teaching and for learning, both the teacher and the students in this course reconstructed the nature of their interactions.

Rather than study teachers, Anita Barabtarlo y Zedansky and Margarita Theesz Poschner work collaboratively with teachers who are investigating their own professional development. Barabtarlo and Theesz, the authors of Chapter Eight, have taken a participatory stance inspired by the work of Paulo Freire (1971) and the group process approach elaborated by Pichón Riviere (1983) and applied these approaches to teacher development. They insist on breaking down the usual dichotomy between research and practice, and have created through years of work with teachers a participatory action research model that challenges teachers to reflect critically on their classroom practices. Their chapter exemplifies qualitative research as social praxis in which the boundaries between research and practice are blurred.

In Chapter Nine, Margarita Brenes, Natalia Campos, Nidia Garcia, Marta Rojas, and Emilia Campos describe a collaborative qualitative research project in Costa Rica which, like the University of Arizona studies referred to above, generates new knowledge about classrooms, schools, and communities, while at the same time, through collaboration with teachers, attempts to modify educational practices that are based on faulty assumptions about the nature of poor communities. This initial study began with a three-year descriptive ethnographic study with several low-income urban schools and teachers, and evolved into a longer longitudinal study that expanded upon the learning of this initial research to consider the changes in teacher training that would be needed to transform the teaching and understanding of teachers. The second stage of this study used the categories of time and space, content and process, as well as classroom behaviors to capture the use of language and control within classrooms. Teachers became part of the research team and reflected collectively with the other researchers about their own teaching. Hence the teacher as subject becomes subject as teacher, and in so doing creates a set of training modules for other teachers to use for their own transformation.

References

Anderson, G.L., Herr, K., and Nihlen, A.S. (1994). *Studying your own school: An educator's guide to qualitative practitioner research*. Thousand Oaks, CA: Corwin Press.

Freire, P. (1971). *Pedagogy of the oppressed*. New York: Herder and Herder.

Moll, L.C. (1992). Bilingual classroom studies and community analysis: Some recent trends. *Educational Researcher, 21*(4), 20–24.

Pichón Riviere, E. (1983). *El proceso grupal: Del psicoanálisis a la psicología social*. Buenos Aires: Nueva Visión.

Chapter Seven
Teachers As Learners
The Dialectics of Improving Pedagogical Practice in Brazil

Elvira Souza Lima

Qualitative research is not new in Brazil. In fact it is a methodology that emerges from the history of Brazilian education of the 1960s. Authors such as Pereira (1960) and Fernandes (1966) were pioneers in the field and contributed to the understanding of this type of research at a time when Brazil was undergoing tremendous political and economic change. Qualitative methodologies were used widely for the documentation of community field projects and studies, and were the methodologies of choice for many of the popular education initiatives in literacy.[1] With the military coup of 1964, the growing popularity of qualitative methods came to an end. The interest academicians had in qualitative research declined during the military dictatorship from 1964 to 1984 as positivist paradigms espoused by the new regime became widely supported.

It has only been in the last decade, once political amnesty was granted and democracy was reinstated in Brazil, that qualitative research has regained its standing in academic circles, particularly in education. Today qualitative research in Brazil has taken on its own character, little influenced by the current educational trends from industrialized countries where qualitative methodologies have become increasingly popular in the last two decades. It is helping to shape innovative educational experiences that foster the understanding of working class and minority education. While many of these new experimental programs are rooted in the Brazilian tradition of popular education, they also have benefited from the development of ethnographic studies. Ethnography of schooling in Brazil is viewed as a powerful tool to be used for constructing knowledge not only about school dynamics but also about teaching and learning processes.

In this chapter I present a brief historical background of ethnography in Brazilian education and illustrate its impact by describing a recent innovative public school intervention in which I participated as a teacher—the *Projeto Inajá*. I will focus on my teaching experience in a different cultural context and discuss the fact that diverse cultural experiences constitute a complex phenomenon that may challenge the pedagogical knowledge of teachers. To understand cultural diversity an accurate analysis of classroom interactions is necessary. I point to the use of ethnography as a helpful source of knowledge for teachers and as a tool that mediates the construction of knowledge in such situations.

The Development of Qualitative Research in Brazil

Qualitative studies became accepted in Brazil, in large part, due to a broad cultural environment that welcomes and embraces many different ways of expression and production of knowledge. In the 1950s important developments in the humanities and the social sciences were evident in the works of historians Sergio Buarque de Hollanda (1974) and Caio Prado Junior (1953). By the beginning of the 1960s a number of distinguished scholars such as Darcy Ribeiro (1975) in anthropology, Florestan Fernandes (1966) in sociology, and Celso Furtado (1964) in economics were publishing a consistent body of work committed to the rigorous analysis of Brazilian reality as a contribution to the political, economic, and cultural development of Brazilian society.

Brazilian society witnessed two major events in education at that time, a debate over the state of education in the country and the mobilization for popular education.[1] The national education debate commanded significant attention from unions, student organizations, state officials, scholars and university professors, the Catholic Church, and other religious organizations. There were two main conflicting trends of thought, one that argued in favor of public lay education and the other in favor of private education, usually provided by religious groups. A great number of social scientists came forward to defend what they thought was of crucial importance to the development of Brazil as a nation—that is, free, public nonreligious education for all children.

The second major event was a widespread movement for popular education and culture[2] that reached all sectors of Brazilian society. The arts, theater, and music, perhaps the most powerful forces, saw the emergence of a generation of composers and playwrights. An impressive number of plays was produced, and theater was made accessible to members of the working class through performances in working neighborhoods and shantytowns.

One of the main goals of popular education was the promotion of literacy, in particular the eradication of adult illiteracy. A number of programs were developed in different parts of the country. The one in the state of Pernambuco later became internationally known through Paulo Freire's writings. In Friere's method, the literacy process started with the introduction of word/themes that represented meaningful facts, events, and objects from the student's immediate experience. An important principle of this method was respect for the students' knowledge. Sensitivity to class-based cultural differences was also considered necessary for improving the level of education of Brazilians.

The public versus private school debate in education and the movement for popular education and culture represented a national effort by progressive sectors of Brazilian society to push for social reforms. This was a threat not easily accepted by conservative groups, who succeeded in thwarting these educational, political, and cultural movements through the coup d'etat of 1964 and the four years of political oppression that followed. By 1968 the political situation was worse; repression increased to the point where a great number of the most prominent Brazilian scholars and scientists were forced into exile. The dictatorship affected all fields of knowledge and research in Brazil. The most impressive loss was the large number of experts and activists from the fields of education, the social sciences, and the humanities who fled the country, since expression of their intellectual and political ideas represented a threat to their and their families' lives.

The students of those scholars, however, remained in Brazil, and they were able to play a very important role in the history of Brazilian education. It is partially due to the survival of this generation that the losses in Brazilian scholarship were not absolute. Following the social and political changes of the late 1960s, areas such as anthropology, sociology, and philosophy all but disappeared from many of the schools' curricula. Professionally, each of these disciplines did not achieve the standing in careers that it previously had. Psychology, which was a fairly recent field in Brazilian academia, continued to develop, but it was completely dominated by influences of behaviorism and psychometrics.

The school system underwent an educational reform that affected all levels of education. This reform brought the North American model to the Brazilian educational system, dramatically changing some of the basic principles that had always oriented education in the country. One of them was the shift from the emphasis on collective learning to individual achievement.

At the beginning of the dictatorship a positivist approach to teaching and learning was favored. This situation gradually changed as sociology of education and philosophy of education began to develop as important disciplines when sociologists and philosophers turned to education as the only area in which they could act. As a result, when the dictatorship ended there was a mature group of education professionals with interdisciplinary educational backgrounds who had already produced an important body of work. While other fields had to reorganize themselves and find their new place in academic life, education was well-established and able to move forward.

The political opening also made accessible sources of knowledge that had vanished during the dictatorship, such as the works of exiled Brazilian social scientists, of Marxist thinkers, and of the European sociology of education. By the end of the 1970s an interest in action research and participatory research, which had developed in Europe through the influence of Freire was also beginning to be observed in Brazil (Brandao, 1982, 1984; Minayo, 1992). This methodology was gradually applied to educational research. The works of Bakhtin (1986) and Vygotsky (1984, 1987) also became available, contributing to the important shift from positivism to a dialectical approach to education, transforming once more the theoretical background for pedagogical action inside schools.

The development of macro and sociological analyses of institutions brought to light the need and importance of unpacking the mechanisms that led to social selection in schools; that is, a selection based on social class as the determinant factor of an individual's success or failure in the formal educational process, which contradicts the school system's ideology of individual selection based on merit and personal development and reveals social inequality as a basis of the formal educational process. Popular education in Brazil had already revealed that there were significant differences between mainstream and working-class behaviors and values that affected the process of learning. It also revealed the learning potential of marginalized populations, a fact that questioned the stereotype of economically deprived populations as culturally deprived, a theory popularized by compensatory education in the United States. This population's successful performance in the popular education programs suggested that inadequacies might also exist within the school system itself rather than solely in the individuals who were failing.

These analyses strengthened the need to explore the mechanisms by which students were marginalized within schools. Classrooms became viewed as complex micro-communities that demanded new methodologies. Researchers began to turn to methodologies that would allow them to explore those issues in depth. The use of qualitative methodologies, especially ethnography, gradually became the most important tool for constructing knowledge about schooling and teaching/learning processes.

Today an important trend in Brazil is the exploration of interdisciplinary approaches to educational research. The researcher's aim is not to look at one given situation from different perspectives, but rather to integrate the perspectives of different areas of knowledge when investigating a given phenomenon. In so doing researchers are dealing with questions in which single events are acknowledged as a function of epistemological significance in which factors do not exist independently and in isolation. To understand this fully, multiple methodological approaches are required.

Ethnography is not a new approach to the study of schooling and children's learning processes in Brazil since it had already been used in the 1950s at the Department of Education of the University of São Paulo (Pereira, 1960). Its reemergence in the 1980s can be regarded as a natural development of the popular culture and popular education traditions. Its widespread use today (Gazetta, 1989) confirms that researchers believe that ethnography contributes to the understanding of the interaction among the multiple factors constituting the educational phenomenon that creates situations in which learning does or does not occur. These researchers also believe that the knowledge produced by ethnographic studies is valuable in the formulation of new educational policies and practices that promote learning and the development of all students. Consequently these policies will contribute to the reduction of school failure, in particular during the first years of school (Souza Lima and Gazetta, 1994). Educational administrators are becoming increasingly interested in applying the results of qualitative research in general, and ethnography in particular, to design and evaluate innovative programs that may effect structural changes in the public school system (Pereira, 1960; Pereira and Foracchi, 1969). The following description and analysis of the *Projeto Inajá* will illustrate how ethnography can capture uniqueness aspects of an educational innovation.

The *Projeto Inajá*

O Inajá não é brincadeira não,
organizado pela turma do sertão,
tudo isso para melhorar
nosso povo e a educação.

Projecto Inajá is not a joke,
It was organized by the people of sertão,

All this was done to improve the life and education of our people.
(Song and lyrics by the Students/Teachers)

Projeto Inajá[3] was developed in the region of the Araguaia River in the central Brazilian state of Mato Grosso, just south of the Amazon rain forest. This region is known as an important focus of resistance to migrant settlements. Acute disputes over land have led to serious confrontations between natives and farm settlers. The social movement in defense of the natives has been supported by the Catholic Church through the work of Don Pedro Casaldaliga.

In Mato Grosso's public system of education, many educators work under difficult conditions. Teachers often are required to travel long distances every day on dirt roads or by river boats. Some have to deal with the cultural differences between the children from the *sertão* and the children from Indian tribes. Salaries are low; yet teachers share a feeling that education is important and are committed to their jobs.

Popular movements and organizations have demanded better conditions for education in consonance with education officials' concerns about improving schools through improvement of teacher education. In fact, a major concern of the state of Mato Grosso is the large number of un-trained teachers, the so-called lay teachers, who have limited schooling, sometimes no more than three years of elementary school. In order to make up the years of schooling they missed, lay teachers are required to give up their teaching jobs and move to urban centers hundreds of miles away. The *Projeto Inajá* offered to bring teachers back to school to attend *Magisterio*, the official course required for teaching at the elementary level in Brazil.

The *Projeto Inajá* was an experimental teacher education program especially designed to respond to the particular needs of a group of 120 lay teachers who were working in communities around the Araguaia River. The project was developed through a joint effort between local community leaders, educators from the Office of Education of Mato Grosso, and professors from the Universidade de Campinas (State of São Paulo). It was conceived as a three-year program (1987 to 1990) attempting to link pedagogical theory and practice.

Teachers remained at their normal teaching job during the school year and had full-time classes (eight hours a day) during summer and winter vacations (a total of six sessions) taught by professors from São Paulo. While at their jobs teachers were assisted by a staff consisting of educationally minded members of the community, who were also in charge of collecting data in order to verify whether, and to what extent, the concepts taught at the *Projeto Inajá* courses were effectively applied in their classrooms. A more general objective of the project was to evaluate the impact of student/teacher participation in everyday practices of the classroom.

Ethnographic research data were used at different stages: (1) to establish the content of curriculum and pedagogical practices; (2) to monitor teachers in their performance in their classrooms; and (3) to evaluate teacher learning through a qualitative evaluation based on portfolio assessment and actual teaching performance at the end of three years.

At graduation all teachers received an official diploma from the Office of Education that enabled them to teach in the formal educational system anywhere in the country. In order to obtain a tenured position later, teachers were able to take state exams.[4] All but one of *Projeto Inajá*'s graduates succeeded in getting tenure.

The project questioned the formal system of education because it proposed to adapt itself to students' lives rather than have students adapt to the system's needs. It proposed an approach to teacher education in which the cultural experiences of the students were respected and taken into account in the curriculum and in pedagogical action. In this respect the strength of popular education in Brazil played a major role. It contributed to the changes *Projeto Inajá* brought to the system by making acceptable a design that represents a true effort to incorporate cultural experience in the teaching–learning process of formal education. Further, the project also earned recognition for qualitative evaluation as a valid method for assessment of learning. Although professionals may share the belief that teaching–learning situations need to take the knowledge and culture of the students into account, applying this belief to actual teaching situations seldom produces the desired results. To work in a context where one's culturally determined behaviors are not dominant is a particular challenge to educators.

I was invited to join *Projeto Inajá* to teach the psychology unit. In what follows I describe the context in which I worked, the basic teaching ideas that guided my pedagogical action, and the transformations that took place in my teaching through interaction with the students/teachers. As I acted to transform the participants' perceptions of children as subjects of teaching and learning, I was simultaneously being transformed by my joint reflections about learning. I became the subject of my own teaching as I worked with the students/teachers in the analysis of their teaching and learning experiences during the three years of *Projeto Inajá*.

The Community

The town of Santa Terezinha do Araguaia was the site of the last segment (July 1990) of the project. Located in a semirural area with difficult access, Santa Terezinha sits beside the Araguaia River. There is a great sense of space because of the flatness of the land. One could say that the people are almost surrounded by the sky. This peculiar situation is complemented by extraordinary bright lights that seem to come not only from an always-shining sun but also from the deep tones of red in the soil.

Social events in the town include dancing, political meetings, and soccer and volleyball games with teams from nearby towns. Electric power, recently installed in the town, made it possible to have access to other parts of the country through television. To watch television, however, is a collective activity, with people gathering in homes to watch soap operas. Narratives of people's lives are constantly interwoven with those of soap opera scenes. Comments and long conversations are motivated by themes and events shown on the screen.

Community life seems to be very important for people in Santa Terezinha. Doors are kept open most of the time; thus the limits between inside and outside, private and public spaces are very tenuous. People gather together frequently, sitting in small groups in front of their homes. They do not necessarily talk much; periods of silence are very common and seemingly "part of the conversation."

There is little presence of written language in Santa Terezinha. Newspapers and magazines are rare. Few signs are seen around the city. News spreads mouth-to-mouth, and occasionally communications are provided by a truck with sound equipment. While oral language plays a more dominant role than written language in the everyday life of the community, literacy is accorded great importance.

There are no banks; therefore, all financial transactions are done with paper money. Everybody seems able to deal comfortably with mathematical operations required to work on such a basis, including the *indios*, native Brazilians, who come to the village to sell their artifacts.

There is no medical care available, and medicines can be bought at poorly stocked drugstores. People frequently resort to what is called popular medicine and to homeopathy. Since resources are scarce, there is a lack of instructional materials and supplies in the local schools.

The Content of the Course

The objective for the child development psychology course I taught in

Santa Terezinha was to promote the construction of formal knowledge using a cultural–historical–theoretical framework. The basic theoretical principles were taken from Henri Wallon (1941, 1942), L.S. Vygotsky, (1929, 1934), and from the Russian school of psychology and pedagogy (Elkonin, 1978; Leontiev, 1972; Davidov, 1988, among others). Wallon and Vygotsky opened the path to understanding human development from a historical perspective for psychology.[5]

Building on such theoretical background, I planned to discuss with the students/teachers the process of development considering the biological and social nature of human beings. Culture and the role of culture in learning processes would be presented considering the students' own milieu and the children they taught. In order to illustrate children's behaviors, learning strategies, interactional processes, and language uses, I planned to videotape local children. As complementary material, I took a collection of video segments from children in different cultures and from different parts of Brazil so that I could show diversity and at the same time point out the similarities human beings share across cultures in their learning and developmental processes. Selected texts, some of which I extracted from previous ethnographic studies of classrooms, were used as supporting material in the classroom. In the discussion of learning processes, I used recollection and storytelling about the participants' own experiences as students, during their previous formal school training, the three years at *Projeto Inajá*, and in their roles as teachers.

The Concept of Teaching

Any teaching action relies on a theoretical framework that accounts for the teacher's concept of teaching. The construction of formal knowledge is based upon everyday concepts. Formal knowledge can be appropriated by individuals through the conjoint action with individuals who have already appropriated it. In order to transform and construct new concepts, human beings depend upon interactions directly with teachers, mentors, and masters or, indirectly, through books, scientific and artistic production, and artifacts. The objective of doing so is to construct new categories of analysis that will transform the perception of and action upon reality. Thus individual knowledge has to be continuously transformed by the act of learning.

As teachers we have an institutionally constructed knowledge about the act of teaching and expectations of students' behavior. We assume that culturally constructed behaviors meaningful for both teachers and students in the institution provide the basis for teaching. Patterns of interaction within the institution are historically constituted. Thus students internalize the institution's conception of the roles of teacher and of student. Developing a teaching role depends on factors such as having constructed these concepts as a student, the necessary transformation of role as one becomes a teacher, the specific posture assumed while connecting dialogues with the many voices participating in the construction, and the appropriation of formal knowledge. Further, the role of teaching is a consequence of social image. Representations about knowledge and about more experienced individuals, as well as the emotions these representations provoke, are also part of one's conception of self as a teacher.

One of the fundamental transformations necessary to further the appropriation of knowledge by the student is to modify the power relationships inside the institution. Knowledge can only be appropriated if there is cultural consonance between teacher and students. The notion of consonance implies that people are aware that culturally constructed behaviors are the basis for human interaction and that cultural diversity does not prevent learning from occurring. Consonance means finding compatibilities, the common ground for action that is built through understanding and that includes different cultural behaviors, not through the imposition of one culture over another and not to the detriment of others.

The lack of consonance demands that it be corrected. Change depends, however, on full understanding of which set of cultural beliefs and values is preventing people from creating meaning in a genuine process of knowledge construction. One factor often mentioned as an obstacle to consonance and, consequently, a cause of school failure, is the social class difference between teacher and students. A major category of analysis such as social class involves a number of different possible behaviors that need to be identified so that they can be modified in order to develop consonance.

In *Projeto Inajá* consonance had to be built upon some special ground because the socially accepted ways of accessing formal knowledge were being questioned within the very framework of the institutional structure. *Projeto Inajá* represented an unusual approach to teaching and learning that, unlike other experiences of popular education, did not happen outside the official educational system. The project was official, it had government approval, and its legitimacy was recognized.

Diversity and Teaching:
The Dialectic of Teaching and Learning

From its inception the project refused to fit within the traditional school culture and proposed a new possibility: that of the community of students/teachers constructing a particular set of behaviors that would favor a dynamic relationship with knowledge itself. When students are simultaneously teachers, exchanging roles continuously, the very perception of themselves as students is greatly affected by the experience of shifting places, holding power, and letting it go, depending upon which roles are enacted as teachers or students.

As I expected, the students/teachers in the project were accustomed to expressing themselves. In order to perform the task of teaching, I needed to acknowledge them. However, the ways they expressed themselves were unfamiliar to me.

It was clear that the first thing one must face in such a situation is not the students and their culture but one's own culture. Without reflecting on one's own culturally constructed behaviors, it is unlikely that meaningful interactions with students who have other cultural experiences can be built. In order to accomplish this, I had to find a strategy that would allow me to become aware of the specificities of my own cultural behavior. The strategy I then developed operated in two complementary senses: (1) I continuously examined my own performance in the classroom; and (2) I was attentive to the students. This strategy implied a constant and successive chain of action: taking actions; observing the actions taken as if I were outside the interaction; listening to my own feelings and my perception of the situation; evaluating the formal knowledge taught and learned; recognizing the clues expressed by the students in regard to my teaching action; and putting all the information I gathered together to define subsequent actions.

This strategy created a demanding situation in which the acting teacher had dual interrelated roles: that of teaching and that of observing the action and interaction of teaching in order to evaluate its adequacy and efficiency in the very moment it was occurring as expressed by behavior and emotional experience. At the same time it required the teacher to be attentive to the students, to the messages sent, to the signs shown in order to properly relate to them, and to engage in the interactions that would contribute to knowledge appropriation. Fieldnotes and moments of privacy between classes were needed to organize perceptions, emotions, and the dynamics of actions–reactions. This opportunity for reflection gave feedback to the teaching–learning process in progress.

The students/teachers and I shared some of the behaviors that are characteristic of Brazilians in general: the smiling, receptive attitude toward others and the pleasure of socializing. We also shared a great deal of enthusiasm for music. These shared behaviors, which are culturally constructed, were the basis for some emotional exchanges that made it possible for us to establish the initial common ground that allowed us to engage in some interesting interactions. It was, however, through the identification and understanding of our cultural diversities that we succeeded in building a learning community. The process involved continuous negotiation and open discussion of our cultural diversities.

The differences I perceived in expressed behaviors between the students/teachers and myself could be classified into three categories. The most evident category of differences included singing, temporality, and the use of space. A less evident category of differences included regulation of behavior through silence and the uses of nonverbal language in interactional processes. The least evident category of differences was the use of language and the concept of narrative.

Singing

In Brazil singing and dancing are interwoven in everyday life. The fact that my students/teachers sang was nothing new, but they used music in ways totally unfamiliar to me. Spontaneous singing in the classroom erupted at different times and had different meanings. For example, singing was used both to reprimand me for being late to class and to express appreciation for my teaching.

Recognizing that singing was a strong statement, I incorporated it immediately into our course content by adding a four-hour seminar on music.[6] I also accepted singing in the classroom as part of a dynamic, which in fact allowed me to gradually understand the meanings conveyed through the students' singing. When they sang, I would listen and enjoy. They sang beautiful melodies. Listening closely to the lyrics, I noticed that some were folk songs, others were known melodies with different lyrics they had created themselves. In their own lyrics I recognized their voices as citizens of *sertão*, claiming education and health care as their right, as students of *Projeto Inajá*, as critics of social injustices, and as human beings in close relationship to nature. Their sense of strength came from this shared feeling of belonging to a social group of which they were proud. All of this was expressed and reinforced by their music.

Time and Space

Time and space in school are controlled by the institution itself. Distribution of time into segments and assignment of tasks and activities to each segment is a prerogative of school bureaucracy as is the demarcation of the sites where these activities should occur. *Projeto Inajá* was innovative in its distribution of time in school in the sense that the arrangement of the school year fit the working schedule of students/teachers. The school days, however, were traditionally set in periods of eight hours a day, with a fixed lunch break. Time limits were taken very seriously by the students/teachers. The use of time was a serious matter. Their access to formal knowledge was restricted, and they tried to get the most from this special opportunity. In the everyday life of the classroom this was translated into a commitment to the learning activities and to the use of every minute of classroom time for learning. It was a new experience for me to teach a group of students who would not shorten the length of time of each lesson. They would stay longer but would not leave earlier.

The use of time in each of the two four-hour periods was regulated by the activities themselves and the students' involvement in these activities, rather than by the time I allocated to each of them. That meant that when the distribution of my time was inadequate, they would go over the limits undisturbed. They were very comfortable with changing the use of time in the classroom, but they respected the overall schedule of the project.

In *Projeto Inajá* we also dealt with an "unstructured schooling space." In Santa Terezinha we did not have a formal classroom, and classes were held in a chapel by the river. The interior of the small chapel was, however, reorganized as a traditional classroom with chairs and a small stage for the teacher. My assumption was that due to the reality of their working conditions and their own experience at *Projeto Inajá*, the students/teachers would be quite flexible in using space and would not be restricted to the traditional codes of using and distributing space that regulate the behavior of most students. Based on this assumption, I planned my classes using the open spaces around the chapel for group activities.

Contrary to my expectations, the use of the surrounding space did not always make the class more pleasant. The use of space was well accepted during non-traditional school activities in which I used drama, role playing, performances, and activities prioritizing forms of representation other than written language, such as drawings and graphics. However, during formal learning situations it created apprehension. Students/teachers clearly expressed their preference for the standard use of the chapel space as a traditional classroom for the activities involving reading and writing.

The students/teachers always arranged themselves within the parameters of "classical" classrooms. They exerted behavioral control upon each other to ensure that the group would stand as a traditional classroom. Though they accepted and practiced nontraditional methods with their own students, they resisted these arrangements when they took the role of students. The message the students/teachers sent to me was that the special configuration of our interactions and our actions as teachers and students should fit into pre-established norms of a school setting.

Silence

Verbal and nonverbal languages are usually mediators of interactions in school settings. Silence is expected during certain assignments, lectures, and tests, for example, while in other situations it is interpreted as a sign of a lack of motivation, interest, or engagement in learning. Thus silence already has a constructed meaning in school culture.

For this reason it was very difficult for me to relate to the silent behavior of the students/teachers at *Projeto Inajá* when silence was presented, sometimes even during an ongoing dialogue. Whether working in small groups or on an activity involving the whole class, students kept silent for long periods of time. It did not mean withdrawal from the classroom or refusal to engage in learning activities. Silence was a normal part of their behavior. My understanding of this behavior came from observations of the community outside the school. I learned that periods of silence were part of the conversation among friends and neighbors in different situations such as socializing at the side of the river, in their homes, or on the sidewalk in front of their houses. While silence was very uncomfortable for me in the beginning, reminding myself of its cultural meaning helped me to deal with it every time.

Language

Portuguese was everyone's first language except for the three Tapirapé Indian teachers who were also fluent speakers of Portuguese. There were no significant structural and vocabulary distinctions in the Portuguese we used except for a few regionalisms easily understood with a simple explanation. I started focusing on narrative as a result of my earlier observation of the importance students/teachers gave to each other's discourses. My experience with teacher training programs led me to expect students who were willing to speak and be listened to by the teacher/speaker. In *Projeto Inajá* I found a group deeply interested in each other's voices. They would listen as carefully to any expressed opinion as they also expected to be listened to by everyone. However, they had a reverent attitude toward the teacher/speaker, which I came to understand not as directed at me personally but at what I represented—the possibility of giving them access to formal knowledge. Our words were important, knowledge was valued, and the group had a clear and straightforward idea about it. They valued the time they spent in learning activities and expected the same seriousness from the teacher.

The way I used storytelling to compose and illustrate my subject matter did not work well with the project students/teachers because there was a clear difference in our definitions of the function of storytelling. They understood teaching as "real content work" with the concepts clearly formulated. The use of examples to explain meaning were understood as "not teaching."

As time went on it became clear that we had many different experiences in language use. I brought the problem up and we reflected together about the functions of language in everyday life and its use in our teaching profession. This discussion led to the subject of culture and different cultural experiences. Through reflecting on language and culture, we were able to set new grounds for interaction.

This event demonstrates that, while the outline of my course remained the same, the performance of my teaching role was reconstructed through continuous interaction with the students/teachers of the project. I kept those strategies from my previous teaching plans that proved useful. The video recording of local children used as the object of analysis for children's behavior was extremely important because teachers could relate to them. They observed the children involved in an organized activity and I suggested that they discuss it with them. This was also videotaped. We watched the videos afterward in the classroom for the excellent discussions of adult–child interaction, the concept of childhood, and the learning child.

Recollecting the students/teachers' experiences at *Projeto Inajá* was also a very adequate theme for reflection. It proved to be a good opportunity to explore the learning potential of storytelling. Through their narratives they described the profound impact that formal education had on their lives and the ways they had changed through *Projeto Inajá*. They felt genuinely empowered by the knowledge they had gained during the three years of the project, and they considered sharing their knowledge with others a very serious social responsibility that would promote learning among their students.

Action in a Culturally Diverse Milieu
My experience with the students/teachers at *Projeto Inajá* showed that the only way a teacher is able to perform adequately the task of transmitting knowledge of psychology to her group of students is to become a very attentive listener and to assume the position of learner. To be willing to listen to the students' voices was only one step. To learn to recognize these voices was a much harder task since individuals expressed themselves in so many different and unfamiliar ways, including singing and using silence—the most difficult areas for me to understand and integrate into everyday pedagogical practice.

The students/teachers displayed two behaviors that I had to comprehend and quickly integrate into the classroom dynamics. I call them "silent subversion" and "questioning of meaning." "Silent subversion" refers to the many situations in which the students/teachers literally subverted my instructions without any explicit statement. It happened as if they all agreed that the structure of a given lesson was not adequate and had to be changed, and when they felt that somehow I was preventing them from expressing themselves in the way they considered they had the right to do. They did not discuss the change but acted so that the change would occur instead. There was a tacit understanding among participants based upon culturally shared meaningful behaviors.

"Questioning of meaning" is exemplified by the questions students/teachers would pose to me, directly or indirectly, about what I was teaching. I interpreted the questioning as being directed toward my intentions rather than the content of what I was teaching. They wanted to know whether it was clear to me why I chose a given topic, and they also wanted to be sure the topic was relevant to them. When they could not relate the topic to their everyday life, they would not agree to spend time on it unless I convinced them that it was necessary.

To be able to interact with this group I had to develop new skills and create new categories of seeing and evaluating reality. I went through several processes that I recognized later on: I had to develop additional perceptual skills to comprehend another form of storytelling in order to be comfortable in inserting "silent" moments into our interactional processes, and I had to reevaluate my concepts of time and intensity.

I realized that, as teachers, we prepare for teaching based on a series of assumptions. Teaching practices are supported by cultural behaviors constructed from previous experiences as students and teachers as well as members of a social group. Teachers modify their behavioral patterns in response to their students when they need to address specific needs or when they comply with the changes taking place in educational and curriculum reform. In such situations teachers are directly or indirectly challenged to change their behavior, often through the imposition of external factors. Sometimes these changes are not the ones teachers consider they need to make.

Behavior modification requires more than the willingness to do so. It depends upon the internalization of new paradigms, a process that fundamentally requires the teachers' awareness of their own personal behaviors. This process of adaptation and personal change is particularly evident when sensitivity to other cultures is raised as a crucial factor in working with marginalized working-class, minority, and immigrant groups.

An important component of the teaching–learning process is that of the teacher as a cultural actor. The role of the teacher, from a cultural-historical perspective, may assume specific postures depending on the context. A teacher is regarded as a source of formal knowledge by students and families. The teacher's function here is perceived as the socializer of this knowledge. On the other hand, from the institutional point of view a teacher is in the position of an employee who needs to comply with institutional bureaucratic demands. She/he is no longer a source of knowledge but rather one who has to improve his/her knowledge of content and teaching practice.[7] Teachers are then simultaneously considered as the source of knowledge and as subjects who need to acquire or improve their knowledge. This situation creates tension and frequently results in teachers' resistance to outsiders and increased isolation within the classroom.

The issue of changing teacher behavior is not a simple one and may not happen as immediately as administrators and policy makers might think it should happen. Based on what is believed to be necessary for children to learn, bureaucrats, technocrats, researchers, and policy makers make assumptions about what teachers should do. These assumptions may be generated by and may simultaneously generate representations about teachers that are easily generalized and end up obscuring particular aspects of teaching situations.

The literature on education from various fields of knowledge stresses the need to develop new ways of looking into students' lives and learning processes. I argue for the same approach to be taken in the study of teachers. Much more information is needed about teachers' personal and professional transformation leading to the development of an attitude in the classroom that will not contribute to further marginalization of minority/ underserved populations. Going beyond the discourse of culture has many implications, and attitude change is a complex process.

Os meninos aprenderam coisas novas
ate ja dizem que as estrelas sao do povo
os meninos
deste continente novo
hao de saber fazer historia
e ensinar.

The children are learning new things,
They even say the stars belong to the people,
The children
of this new continent
will know how to make history
and spread the word.
(Lyrics by the students)

Conclusion

The presentation of this teaching experience in an unfamiliar cultural environment exemplifies the complexity of human behavior aimed at the appropriation of formal knowledge. Culturally constructed behaviors are neither obvious nor easily modifiable. The implications for education are significant as people from diverse cultural backgrounds will increasingly need to share common ground where interactions will foster rather than impede learning.

The experience in itself reveals the importance of a research-based framework in educational interventions. Projects such as *Inajá* in Brazil demonstrate that innovative educational experiences are the result of a broader approach. This approach embodies the aims of qualitative research, that is, inquiry that is not restricted to the usual purpose of developing academic careers. Other interests are at stake—those of a community having access to formal knowledge, the development of links between education and work, and the promotion of professional development unhampered by institutional bureaucracy.

Such projects teach us how crucial it is for poor, working-class, and underserved groups to be formally educated while still maintaining their cultural experiences. Through education and cultural maintenance these groups are assured the possibility of expressing the many voices of their history while having access to the knowledge that will enable each to participate democratically in society.

Moreover, through experiences in such projects we are able to acknowledge that we are only now at the beginning of our understanding of the process of socialization of formal knowledge, and that many segments of society are excluded from access to the benefits of such education. To understand and to solve these problems, we have to depend upon research that illuminates the mechanisms of exclusion as well as the ways in which socialization of curriculum knowledge and pedagogical practices occurs. Given the current state of knowledge about these issues, qualitative research offers an invaluable tool to educators. Ethnography is particularly important since it may accurately reveal the various components constituting the sociocultural milieu, thus making our understanding of the human process of learning and of transforming oneself through the acquisition of knowledge possible. My experiences as a researcher have definitively contributed to my development as a teacher. Through the act of observing and making sense of other people's actions, the formulation of new categories of pedagogical thought is made possible.

Notes

1. In Brazil popular education refers to the many informal educational programs that are not part of the federal and state systems. The contexts in which popular education takes place include community centers, neighborhood clubs, and churches, many of which are Catholic. Popular education represents the most significant effort at the national level to eradicate adult illiteracy in Brazil, but there are also many other programs aimed at illiterate adults, children, and adolescent dropouts.

2. Among the various programs for both popular culture and popular education are the Movimento de Cultura Popular de Recife (Recife's Movement for Popular Culture); the literacy campaign *De pe no chao tambem se aprende a ler* (Barefoot people can also learn to read), in Natal Rio Grande do Norte; the Movimento de Educacao de Base (Basic Education Movement) supported by the Catholic Church; and the Centro Popular de Cultura (Popular Cultural Center) created by Uniao Nacional de Estudantes (Students' National Union).

3. The project was named after *Inajá*, which is a type of palm tree that grows in the Brazilian *sertão*. The *Inajá* has the particularity of surviving fire, deforestation, and flooding. Hence It is an important symbol of resistance for the people who live in this part of the country. *Sertão* is the name given to this geographical area of Brazil.

4. The state examination consists of a quantitative evaluation of subject matter knowledge and pedagogical knowledge (teaching theory and practice).

5. Both scholars discussed the cultural development of human beings. Wallon developed a dialectical approach to human development through his work that emphasizes the role of emotions in the human species. The concept of milieu, elaborated by Wallon, presents the theoretical framework in which culture is seen as constitutive of human development and learning processes. For him, the concept of milieu has two levels that integrate/create each other but still maintain their particularities: the material environment and the environment of "ideas."

6. This seminar was conducted at night and was entitled "The Importance of Music in Child Development." I explored the importance of rhythm, melody, and cadence for human beings in general and for babies and small children in particular. I discussed the fact that music has always been present as an important factor in the life of different communities, across cultures and historical periods. I also included as part of the course the notion of pleasure, emotional togetherness, and the psychological effects of singing and making music.

7. Many administrators or officials assume they have more knowledge about the act of teaching than the teachers themselves.

References

Bakhtin, M. (1986). *Marxismo e filosofia da Linguagem.* São Paulo: HUCITEC.

Brandao, C.R. (1982). *A questao politica da educacao popular.* São Paulo: Brasiliense.

Brandao, C.R. (1984). *Pesquisa Participante.* São Paulo: Brasiliense.

Buarque de Hollanda, S. (1974). *Historia da Civilizacao Brasileira.* São Paulo: Difel.

Davidov, V. (1988). *La enseñanza escolar y el desarollo psiquico: Investigación teórica y experimental.* Madrid: Editorial Progresso.

Elkonin, D. (1978). *Psicologia del juego.* Madrid: Visor.

Fernandes, F. (1966). *Educacao e Sociedade no Brasil.* São Paulo: Dominus and Editora da Universidade de São Paulo.

Fernandes, F. (1989). *O desafio educacional.* São Paulo: Cortez, Autores Associados.

Freire, P. (1967). *Educacao como pratica da liberdade.* Rio de Janeiro: Paz e Terra.

Furtado, C. (1964). *Dialetica do Desenvolvimento.* Rio de Janeiro: Paz e Terra.

Gazetta, M. (1989). *A modelagem como estrategia de aprendizagem de matematica em cursos de aperfeicoamento de professores.* São Paulo: UNESP.

Leontiev, A. (1972). *Le developpement du psychisme problemes.* Paris: Editions Sociales.

Minayo, M.C. (1992). *O desafio do conhecimento: Pesquisa qualitativa em saude.* São Paulo: HUCITEC.

Pereira, L. (1960). *A escola numa area metropolitana.* São Paulo: FFCL/USP.

Pereira, L. and Foracchi, M. (1969). *Educacao e Sociedade.* São Paulo: Editora Nacional.

Prado Junior, C. (1953). *Evolucao Politica do Brasil.* São Paulo: Brasiliense.

Ribeiro, D. (1975). *A Universidade Necessaria.* Rio de Janeiro: Paz e Terra.

Romanelli, O. (1991). *Historia da Educacao no Brasil.* Petropolis, Brazil: Vozes.

Souza Lima, E.S. and Gazzetta, M. (1994). From lay teachers to university students: The path for empowerment through culturally based pedagogical action. *Anthropology and Education Quarterly,* 25(3), 236–249.

Vygotsky, L. (1929). The problem of the cultural development of the child. *Journal of Genetic Psychology,* 36, 414–434.

Vygotsky, L. (1934/1992). *Pensiero e linguaggio, a cura di Luciano Mecacci.* Rome: Editori Laterza.

Vygotsky, L. (1984). *A formacao social da mente.* São Paulo: Martins Fontes.

Vygotsky, L. (1987). *Pensamento e linguagem.* São Paulo: Martins Fontes.

Wallon, H. (1941). *L'evolution psychologique de l'enfant.* Paris: Collin.

Wallon, H. (1942). *De l'acte a la pensee.* Paris: Flammarion.

Chapter Eight
Participatory Action Research in Teacher Education
A Method for Studying the Everyday Reality of Teaching in Latin America

Anita Barabtarlo y Zedansky and Margarita Theesz Poschner

Adult education in Latin America has generated alternatives in the ongoing search for new research methodologies better suited to the reality of marginalized adults who have been unable to acquire a formal education. A fundamental principle promoted by UNESCO is recognizing that all adults, by virtue of their lived experience, are bearers of a culture that allows them simultaneously to be educated and to educate others in the educational process in which they participate. In this way UNESCO recognizes an adult's potential for taking responsibility for his or her own educational process through self-education and co-learning. This framework for adult education acknowledges the need for participatory educational research, in contrast to the framework of the traditional social sciences.[1]

Within the traditional social science paradigm, the study of a given population is undertaken by "outsiders" who take data away from the population and use it in a variety of institutional contexts that serve their own interests and needs. We understand participatory research in education as an intentioned, ongoing educational process based upon a dialectical framework that emerges from the needs and problems of practice.

In this chapter we provide a description of a unique approach to using participatory research as an approach to the professional development of teachers. We begin by describing the emergence of non-formal adult education and the rise of a participatory research paradigm in Latin America. The main characteristics of this paradigm are then described along with the type of explanations of reality it offers. Different manifestations of action research that are included in this paradigm will then be discussed, followed by a discussion of the ways action research is currently being used in formal education, i.e., schools and universities. We will then describe our own experience using action research in teacher education and professional development and discuss the potential of action research for creating new knowledge in the field of education, thus representing a challenge to traditional research done by "experts." This is followed by a description of a pedagogical model that the authors have developed for educating teachers using action research methodology. The final section deals with individual, group, and institutional problems that arise when teachers critically analyze their institutions, and how action research might contribute to their transformation.

The Origins of Participatory Research in Latin America in the Context of Adult Education

Participatory research is closely related to liberatory education, influenced by Paulo Freire's (1970b) experiences in Brazil and Chile during the 1960s and 1970s, and his emphasis on conscientization. Fundamental to Freire's philosophy is the notion that teacher and learner continually educate each other as part of the same process in which both parties become learners. The popular education movements that began to appear during this period adhered closely to this notion, grounding themselves in the popular sector's reality. In this way popular education, as understood within adult education, becomes an ongoing, intentioned, and participatory process derived from a dialectical framework grounded in practice. In such a process the adult can no longer continue being an object but, rather, becomes a subject committed to his or her educational practice with a goal of conscientization.

The Participatory Research Paradigm and Action Research Methodology

According to Tedesco (1985), the predominant paradigms in Latin American education have been the economic paradigm (human capital, human resources) and the paradigm of social reproduction. The first defines the most valuable knowledge as that which the market rewards, viewing education as a cost-benefit problem. The second paradigm, social reproduction, sees education as a problem of ideological reproduction based upon the notion of cultural hegemony (Gramsci, 1976), an approach that tends to obscure education's other functions such as its potential conscientizing role. Both paradigms have tended to undervalue the teacher's place in the educational process by failing to acknowledge how educational processes are constructed within a complex interplay of human agency and social forces that act to determine the outcomes of pedagogical practices. According to Tedesco (1985), the failure of educational research to produce changes in pedagogical practices and its lack of connection to the real needs of teachers and students have led to an attempt to resolve these contradictions through a participatory research strategy.

Within the participatory paradigm, social practice is the starting point for a theory of knowledge that is wed to a theory of conscience formation. As part of its method the paradigm requires educational processes to be structured in a way that promotes participation in the joint search for solutions to problems as well as the collective construction of knowledge.[2]

Characteristics of Participatory Research

Participatory research captures and documents the dynamics involved in the process of taking part in decisions. It is based upon the collective production of knowledge, which values the role of the learning subject as a social being. As such, this process makes it possible for viewpoints to be offered, for experiences to be evoked and shared, and for the conditions of social and work life to be analyzed, thereby conscientizing people to the possibility of changing their realities.

Four basic categories characterize the participatory paradigm: (1) The sociohistorical nature of individual action; (2) the role of the individual; (3) the nature of education; and (4) the role of action in relation to theory. In reference to these categories, we pose the following premises:

The Sociohistorical Nature of Individual Action

1. The paradigm postulates understanding and explaining social processes from an historical perspective, and poses itself as a response to deep-felt, specific needs of social actors.
2. It offers active participation in the production of knowledge, grounded in the subjects' ways of life.
3. Through dialogue and consensus, everyone in the group becomes involved in all phases of the research, from the posing of the problem through its resolution and the proposal of an alternative.
4. The essence of participatory research is its conscientizing function, grounded in the group's and the community's needs, interests, and aspirations.

The Role of the Individual

5. Every individual possesses valid experience acquired through his or her own actions taken over the course of his or her lifetime.
6. In order to take responsibility for her/himself, the individual must be the subject of the educational process and, as such, the subject of action and critical reflection.

The Nature of Education

7. Education must acknowledge the individual's experiences using them as a basis for its practice and content.
8. As part of the educational process, conditions must be created that facilitate making explicit and complementing these subjects' experiences. These conditions require horizontality (i.e., equality among the participating individuals) and full participation (everybody has the same opportunity to be receiver, transmitter, and generator of knowledge).
9. In the educational process, every individual—in his or her condition as transmitter—has the right to imprint the intentionality that results from his or her conception of the world, society, politics, and culture.

The Relationship of Action to Theory

10. Productive social action directed toward transforming reality is required.
11 Without action and critical reflection on reality, there can be no possibility of such transformation.

Participatory Research As a Product of Diverse Traditions

In the Latin American context, participatory research has emerged in a variety of contexts. For this reason participatory research does not hold to a single, doctrinaire model. As a result several models exist, including action research (Fals Borda, 1978); activist research (Huizer, 1978); self-diagnosis (Schmelkes and Sotelo, 1979); participatory research (Le Boterf, 1980); militant research (Acosta, 1978; de Oliveira, 1981); the experimental workshop (Bosco Pinto, 1976); and thematic research (Freire, 1970a).

In 1982, in Pátzcuaro, Michoacán, México, the Centro Regional de Educación de Adultos y Alfabetización Funcional para América Latina (CREFAL) held the Second Latin American Participatory Research Seminar. It had among its main objectives the exchange, analysis, systemization, and dissemination of the experiences and theoretical advances of participatory research in Latin America. The goal of the conference and those that followed was to contribute at a regional level to an ongoing discussion of the theory and practice of participatory research, especially with regard to adult education.

Issues that have been debated include the need for precision in theory, epistemology, and methodology, or, in other words, the need to delimit what is and is not participatory research. Because of the interdisciplinary nature of participatory research, it is helpful to unravel the various traditions from which different researchers work. Although there is not space for such a discussion in this chapter, de Schutter and Yopo (1982) and Gajardo (1985) have provided useful overviews of these traditions.

De Schutter (1986) defines action research as "the production of knowledge and action toward the intentional modification of a given reality" (p. 173). A basic espistemological principle is that the subject doing the research is his or her own object of research and transformation; that is, no dichotomy exists between the researching subject and the researched object.

The Link between Teaching and Research:
Action Research in Teacher Education

In the area of formal education, curricular and school structures that work against the promotion of teacher professionalism continue to be maintained in Latin America. The continued use of traditional teaching methods has contributed to reproducing a framework that encourages the accumulation and transmission of knowledge, to the detriment of the creativity necessary to solve the problems presented by a changing reality.

The type of teaching most prevalent in our teacher education programs, most of which were conceived as institutions for the transfer of knowledge from those who know to those who do not know, foregrounds a passive teacher–student relationship in a context which Freire (1970b) has labeled "banking education." This emphasis on banking education has led us to rethink the link between teaching and research in the professional development of teachers. In the following section we develop a model of participatory action research as teacher education, which requires us first to reconceive of: (1) the teacher as an organic intellectual; (2) teaching as a political problem; and (3) the teacher as researcher.

The teacher as an organic intellectual. The decades of the 1970s and 1980s were characterized in Latin America by an increase in institutions for educating teachers and a search for new theoretical-methodological models that attempted to describe, interpret, and propose alternative teaching practices. These models, which feature a variety of approaches, have attempted to construct a model closer to both the teacher's daily practice and the institutional reality of teaching. All these models refer us back to the role of teachers and teaching and invite us to reconceptualize the teacher and his or her fundamental activity by using the category "organic intellectual" coined by Gramsci (1976).

For Gramsci, the notion of "intellectual" extends into civil society, i.e., church, labor unions, schools, etc. In these organizations the job of the "organic intellectual" is to help the population sketch out the objective for the development and organization of a consensual system. In the area of education, teachers as organic intellectuals "can no longer be Narcissus floating through the halls of free thought" (Gramsci, 1976, p. 22). Their function becomes helping new generations to develop their own historical and cultural identity.

Teaching as a political problem. From Gramsci's notion of the organic intellectual we can infer that educators play a basic role in building a democratic society. All of this requires a mature civil society that has broken with what Freire (1970b) calls magical or ingenuous forms of consciousness. This movement away from magical forms of consciousness paves the way to the creation of more mature forms of citizenship based on critical consciousness (Barabtarlo, 1989). Following Freire, we believe that "critical consciousness" allows us to recognize our identity as historical–social subjects and, as a result, to act maturely.

In this sense teachers' roles should be oriented toward achieving a possible consciousness (Goldman, 1977). Goldman describes "possible consciousness" as a consciousness that allows the population in question to acquire a collective vision for undertaking actions that need to be carried out. Thus possible consciousness is the result of the sum of individual critical consciousnesses.

The teacher as researcher. In one sense, reconceiving of teachers as researchers has to do with teachers taking responsibility for their professional development and cultivating a researching attitude. On the other hand, it has to do with a questioning of education's conformist perspective, which has been sustained by a hegemonic tendency that separates educational theory from practice.

A Model of Participatory Action Research for Teacher Education

Authors like Carr and Kemmis (1988), Stenhouse (1987), Elliott (1988), and McTaggart (1987) have worked from the critical perspective we have described. In working with teachers since 1981 we have developed our own particular model for educating teachers in the Centro de

Investigaciones y Servicios Educativos (Educational Research and Services Center [CISE] of the Universidad Nacional Autónoma de México [UNAM]). We have promoted teacher research in order to qualitatively improve teachers' educational processes by adhering to the idea that, fundamentally, teaching is allowing learning and that learning means being able to think and receive knowledge in accordance with our personal mechanisms for understanding, manipulating, and disseminating knowledge.

Our theoretical model begins with two basic premises. First, we believe that if teachers are to improve the quality of the teaching–learning process in their classrooms and institutions, they must become observers and planners of their own practice. For this to occur, teachers must be able to critically evaluate the worth of the methods, content, and structures that they use and to document how their own educational practice should proceed.

Second, teacher education supposes the inclusion of research projects closely related to educational practice. The action research method, as a process for producing knowledge through action, allows for testing research results in reality. For this reason we consider it an ideal method for educating a "teacher researcher."

Our theoretical model adheres to an approach to education developed by Giovanni Bertin (1981). For Bertin education is a process that stimulates the student's potential for learning, his openness to others who are different, and his commitment to social betterment. Following Bertin, our model holds that the teacher's most basic function can no longer involve the mere transmission and reproduction of knowledge. Instead the teacher is a generator of knowledge who also facilitates the generation of values.

The participatory research paradigm views science as a part of daily life. In seeing teaching practice itself as an educational space, the paradigm's logic sees teaching as an area of research. Thus, in our proposal, we understand educational research—from, within, and for teaching practice—to be essentially educational (Barabtarlo and Theesz, 1983). This educational process reconfigures the teacher's role by reconceptualizing teaching, so that teachers now attempt to understand themselves and their role in the world based upon praxis in which they accept themselves and their reality and at the same time become mature beings capable of problematizing their reality (Barabtarlo, 1989).

We understood our model as part of a larger emancipatory, conscientizing, and participatory approach (Freire, 1970b). The construction of this approach is ongoing, never finished, with reality and the model offering each other feedback based upon practice (workshops given by teachers), and with the model continually enriching itself with each synthesis in the process (as practice–theory–practice are calibrated). The process is sustained by the learning–research relationship, in which the construction of knowledge takes on a collective character.

In the educational process, learning, inasmuch as it is an appropriation of reality that takes itself as its own subject, becomes oriented toward deconstructing and reconstructing ways of thinking, valuing, and acting. Learning also becomes oriented toward educating for critical thinking and a new consciousness about how knowledge is produced, accompanied by a search for generating mechanisms that produce this knowledge. In the following section we contrast the traditional educational model with our own proposal.

The Traditional and the Action Research Models Compared

The model of the traditional teaching–learning cycle is the following:

$$T— L— T—L \dots$$

In this process teaching (T) and learning (L) are linear, repetitive, and mechanical. They turn the accumulation of knowledge into an exogenous variable, basically oriented toward reproducing the values of dominant social groups. Our proposed model, which corresponds to the action research cycle in the teaching process, is the following:

$$L—T—R—L'—T'—R'—L''—T''$$
(Learning–Teaching–Research–Learning'–Teaching'. . . etc.)

In any time or place an original act of learning (L) is produced, made up of knowledge, skills, and values, which in general seek to be reproduced through an act of teaching (T), which generally, though not necessarily, takes place in the classroom. If a situation occurs which involves research (R), then a new cycle of learning and teaching (L' and T') is in turn produced, which opens up the cycle to a larger process, which does not merely reproduce the first bit of learning but also allows for new research (R') to grow out of the same process, facilitating a new act of learning (L'') which leads to a new act of teaching (T'').

These various stages of enhanced learning and teaching compose action research, which replaces the linear process that only deposits and stores up information, banking-style, as Freire (1970b) has shown. The action research proposal is not linear, not only because it makes increments in knowledge possible but also because it is supported by various, alternate learning and teaching processes that make up the very research of educational practice. This way of teaching normally ends in multiple conclusions, which become the starting point for a new cycle in this teaching–learning process, with characteristics similar to those described above, with learning, teaching, and research moments enriched as they develop and progress dialectically (Barabtarlo and Theesz, 1982).

Research, which is present throughout the knowledge creation process, shows that the accumulation of knowledge immediately reinvests itself into the process, thus acting as an endogenous variable which, when applied, has a wide-ranging social character. The cycle continues simultaneously opening itself up at moments which, while not strictly differentiated, translate learning into teaching and research, and research into teaching and learning.

Drawing on the concept of group learning (Bauleo, 1974), we understand the teaching–learning process to be a situation that generates specific links between its participants (teachers and students) and that has as its goal "learning to learn." The concept of group learning, which is integral to the model, leads to learning and the generation of democratic relationships in order to reach a consensus that makes possible the group's collective production of knowledge.

This proposal posits a close link between group learning and the action research method. The relationship between the two characterizes the teaching–learning process in the following way: knowledge (learning) is produced simultaneously with the modification of reality, and it becomes known basically through dialogic argumentation about specific actions (understanding reality and identifying social forces and relationships that are latent in all human experience) (Barabtarlo and Theesz, 1982).

By making an active teaching–learning process possible, the participatory process implies bringing into play a multiplicity of factors whose interaction produces significant learning in the sense that it generates new knowledge and attitudes as well as new convictions. Teachers and students become protagonists in this teaching–learning process, in which both of them learn. In other words, following Freire (1970b), both the educated and the educator educate each other in the very same process.

Within this model the teacher becomes a coordinator. As a conscientizing, training, and organizing agent, he or she promotes the critical spirit and the active participation of the educated. In this sense the teacher learns as a result of feedback from the group on how to improve the quality of his or her coordination. As part of this dialogic process the teacher learns a pedagogy of reciprocal teaching and learning: a group-work methodology, and an action research methodology.

In all our experiences to date (approximately twenty workshops), we have facilitated teacher professional development adhering to the premises of participatory action research and group learning. As part of the workshops, we take into consideration the subjects' experiences and individual and social biographies. We have applied group learning techniques, that is, actions that aim toward consensus and a common language in order to understand the reality in which one is acting.

As a result of using participatory action research in the professional development of teachers, we have been able to bring daily life back into teaching practice, combining thought and action, toward the achievement of educational praxis (research tied to the transformation of the subject who is at once both subject and object).

The Action Research Workshops
Escuela Normal Superior de México

A workshop at the Escuela Normal Superior de México, a national institution of teacher education, took place over five sessions totaling twenty-five hours of group work. It was requested by some of the Escuela's academic personnel and was taught with an eye to the participants' specific educational needs in educational research methodology. The workshop attempted to introduce teachers to participatory action research.

The program was composed of two units. The first dealt with the problem of methodology in education and the social sciences. Epistemological issues were dealt with, such as: (1) the subject–object relationship in the process of creating knowledge; (2) theoretical-methodological issues within different research traditions, e.g., positivism, structural-functionalism, and historical materialism; (3) different criteria for truth claims in scientific practice; (4) origins and characteristics of participatory research and action research; (5) comparison to traditional methods; (6) how to problematize and select the topic to be researched; and (7) characteristics of the method.

Fifty-two teachers were enrolled in the workshop, so we divided into two groups with two coordinators. In the first session we introduced the workshop, dispelled doubts, and assessed the needs of the participants. In this first meeting the participants spoke about their own educational research experiences as well as their expectations of a workshop that focused on participatory research. The teachers had a wide range of experiences. Some had undertaken small research projects in their workplaces, while others had barely done any research at all.

Throughout all the sessions we worked with different group-dynamic and action research techniques, designing workshop content in the light of the teachers' personal, practical experiences. Although the participants were used to individual, mechanical, non-critical learning, little by little they started becoming conscious of the difference between individual and group learning, and the obstacles that their individual work and study habits created for them in this context. Intellectually they were not used to relating educational theory to issues that had come up in their own teaching practice.

The problem of communication and responsibility required by group work emerged when it became clear that some had not fulfilled the commitment to read the texts, thus setting back the groups' work. When this problem was specifically posed by the participants themselves and those involved became conscious of it, positive results were obtained in the work that followed. In the final session two activities (one per group) were carried out: a sociodrama and a historical-biographical reflection.

The sociodrama. Participants role-played they were an assembly discussing academic reforms within their own institution. The group divided into three types of roles: (1) assembly leaders (one teacher and one student); (2) assembly participants (teachers and students); and (3) representatives from official authorities (administration). A fourth group was in charge of observing and recording the process. The following issues were discussed: (a) the assembly's characteristics and obstacles to its organization; (b) leadership; (c) institutional power relations; (d) participation of the community; (e) dissidence; (f) representative versus participatory approaches to democracy.

The group concluded that the sociodrama technique helps to make class information more relevant and facilitates group integration, while also helping the participants to begin reflecting on and analyzing the problems that they wanted to research. Likewise it facilitated making people conscious of the essential problems that lie in the obvious. They began to see that carrying out academic reform in the Escuela Normal Superior was primarily a political problem.

Historical-biographical reflection. This group discussed the Escuela Normal Superior's origins, the reasons for its creation, who created it, and its development and current situation. The group noted that it was the teachers with the greatest seniority who were able to contribute the most information, since these teachers had for the most part themselves lived the situations described. Through the biographical history and its analysis, the participants gradually came to understand more clearly the changes and conflictive situations present in the institution. Through this reflection each one was able to contribute what he or she knew as they continued "discovering" origins and causes of events that had taken place in the Escuela Normal Superior. The group concluded that historical-biographical reflection aided in the research of historical events lived by the researching subjects and led to greater understanding of the events' origins and causes.

With reference to the institution (the Escuela Normal Superior de México), the group observed that: (1) it was necessary to include reflection in the Escuela's teacher education curriculum; (2) the role of education as agent of "social transformation" needed to be more extensively explored; (3) a disassociation between political practice and academic practice existed among the faculty; this disassociation had negative repercussions when it came to the possibility of seeing the institution more clearly; and (4) the theme that permeated all the events throughout the Escuela's history was the struggle for power.

When the two groups got together at the end of these activities and presented their conclusions, the participants observed that their conclusions coincided. In this way, by analyzing the institution, each group separately and with two different techniques came to similar conclusions. The groups saw this as very positive, and it motivated them to continue educating themselves by researching their teaching and its institutional context. They coincided in concluding that the differences between traditional research and participatory research had become clear, and began to ask themselves if traditional research could be considered obsolete, concluding that it was not. They agreed, however, that participatory research went further, since its framework completed the subject–object interaction, in which the subject becomes his or her own object of research in a process of collective reflection and transformation.

They further concluded that, when it comes to choosing the problem to be researched, it must emerge from the needs of the group. Finally, they concluded that sociodrama and historical-biographical reflection both allowed for the detection of latent forms of interaction that were getting in the way of the very process of academic reform.

Action Research Workshop for Teachers of Preparatory Schools in the Universidad Autónoma de Sinaloa

This workshop grew out of the democratic principles held by its organizers, academic personnel of the Division of Preparatory Schools of the Universidad Autónoma de Sinaloa, México It was guided by philosophical principles of liberty and democracy. The organizers believe that group learning becomes more beneficial when it allows the participants to confront ideas, construct their own logic, and enrich individual and group models. According to Sylvia Valdez, one of the workshop organizers: "The individual is not just a thinking subject, but one who has specific problems and an emotional life which influences his or her fulfillment of duties and relationships with others, because, above all, the subject is social" (S. Valdez, personal communication, April, 14, 1991).

Thirty teachers participated in this workshop, which lasted fifty-two hours. The coordinator started by exploring the group's expectations through a group dynamic exercise, which helped dissolve inhibitions and created an atmosphere of individual and collective participation as well as a climate of confidence. Next the tentative program was handed out. It was read by participants, discussed, and appropriate changes were made, with the purpose of building commitment. This was the first step toward opening up the possibility of group work. This phase established the framework (rules of the game, clarification of roles, forms of evaluation, work methodology, learning content). The framework represented a novel situation for the teachers and, at the same time, reduced anxieties and initial fears relating to the new methodology.

The workshop process takes teaching as its object of study, which in turn becomes part of the research. That is, one creates a pedagogy based upon research, and one researches in a pedagogical way. The workshop readings are chosen using the participants' teaching practice as a reference point.

Participants learn about two issues that emerge simultaneously: the program's explicit task or objectives (content); and the implicit task—that is, the values and attitudes associated with the explicit task. Changing values and attitudes imply new types of relationships. To foster collaborative group relationships, techniques for group learning were used, such as peer advisement, observation groups/learning groups, sociodramas, and debates. It should be made clear that all these techniques favored consensus, dialogue, collaboration, belonging, and solidarity. Competition also flourished, but with an eye toward complementing each other's work.

The working norms were established by the group itself. The group decided that, in order for individual and group responsibility to be assumed around punctuality, every day upon arriving each person would go to the blackboard and note his or her name and time of arrival. Other collaboratively established rules, which helped in the ongoing evaluation of changes in attitudes and commitments, were the following: (1) an attendance record; (2) an evaluation of quality of participation; and (3) record keeping of daily responsibilities the participants assumed, such as keeping a field journal, support materials, coffee, etc. All the members of the group rotated in participating in these activities. At the end of the workshop a summary report was presented in which all the participants could see themselves, thus making possible an individual and group reading of the subject's and the group's actual development profile.

The field journal. The field journal allows for the observation of daily activities. It is a tool for analysis of and reflection on classroom work, and it involves describing, valuing, interpreting, and explaining the levels of meaning in the educational process.

Because of the basic action research principle that the researching subject is both subject and object, daily journaling made possible a critical analysis with a view toward a conscious change in values and attitudes. The field journal was kept on a rotating basis by all the participants. At the beginning of each work session its observations were read, commented upon, and problematized with the goal of reaching consensus through dialogue. The field journal as a qualitative document makes possible ongoing group and self-evaluation, which also constitute a form of learning.

The educational process in the workshop managed to awake in the teachers a concern for explaining classroom and school life in a scientific and theoretical way. This was aided by the fact that, as an accreditation prerequisite, they had to undertake a research project that problematized teaching practices—a project that had as its goal the gradual modification of their practices. In content and teaching methodology the workshop offered elements that could be used in the teachers' daily duties.

After a school semester, in which the teachers put into practice what they had learned in the workshop, they returned for a collective follow-up experience in which they talked about the initiatives they had put into practice, the obstacles they had encountered, and the progress they had made. In this way the spiral opens for the teachers onto a new phase of the educational process.

Obstacles to Action Research
Doing action research within the medium of formal education in general and teacher education in particular supposes that problems will necessarily arise as projects are implemented in schools. From our own experience we find that the obstacles that arise relate to three major areas: (1) the process of self-transformation; (2) problems associated with constructing knowledge in groups; and (3) institutional barriers to implementing action research.

The Process of Self-Transformation
The construction of a methodological model for educating the teacher researcher within a participatory framework requires the subject's participation in the construction of the model itself, which is undertaken based on the teacher's need to investigate his or her own teaching process. Transformation involves the need to take on new roles and forge new networks, as well as the progressive abandonment of former roles and stereotypical attitudes that get in the way of realizing the tasks and goals individuals pose in their groups.

One obstacle is the need to go beyond the stereotypical image of the teachers and their relationship to students. This becomes problematic because of the internalization of an image of teacher as the expert "who only teaches" and the student "who only learns." It is hard to get beyond a notion of teachers transmitting "objective" knowledge to a point where one can see the socially constructed and relative nature of knowledge.

Additionally, internalized relationships of dependency resulting in such dynamics as authoritarianism, submission, resistance, and passivity come into conflict with the assumption that knowledge is based upon the participant's responsible involvement in his or her own process of constructing reality and of self-transformation. The problem for the coordinator becomes how to coordinate this process without reproducing relationships of dependency within the workshop itself.

Another issue for consideration is the resistance to change evident both in the teachers who participate in the workshops and in the application of action research to educational practice in schools. The construction of a mechanism for recording the research process—in our case the field journal, for the observation and formulation of hypotheses—is another element that is difficult to get participants to accept. They are often reluctant to engage in reflexivity through which they become conscious of the social dimension (values, ideology, and knowledge) they bring with them into their work with students and each other. Journaling is a task that participants accept only gradually, as reflexivity and methodical observation become daily practice and, ultimately, a permanent attitude.

Problems Associated with Constructing Knowledge in Groups

We have observed that there is a preponderance of competitive relationships among participants, which becomes an obstacle to the collective production of knowledge. It presents itself in the form of divisions in some of the groups, with members reproducing relationships of dominance and dependency. The group's and the individual participant's formation and growth are inscribed in a redistribution of power based upon one's relationship to knowledge (power/knowing).

For the participating teachers to get to the point of group learning requires a lengthy process in which they become conscious of the social and educational reality of the situation in which they are immersed. This process poses the most serious problems, in the sense that it does not "automatically" present itself but rather must continually be collectively constructed. In the first phase of the learning process the concept of knowledge that each one of the participants brings with him or her is generally "something to be acquired but not constructed," which in turn clearly conditions the group dynamic. The participants act by expecting things of the coordinator and of others, but they do not contribute the knowledge each one of them has so as to continue constructing things as a group. In the beginning confusion can result with respect to the objectives of teacher education, as participants cling to a notion of participation centered in the individual perspective and make constant references to other groups and far too few to the one that is in the process of being constructed. As the group works together to generate democratic relationships, seeking consensus directed toward group production of knowledge, the subjects gradually become aware of the nature of group learning. This process is aided by the close relationship between group learning and action research.

Institutional Barriers

We have encountered resistance on the part of authorities in the educational institutions where teachers apply action research methods. This resistance stems above all from those in traditional systems who have understood the changes they may need to make if teachers engage in this innovative, non-traditional method of investigation. For this reason it is necessary to educate administrators, teachers, students, and parents about action research. For action research to be carried out effectively, an awareness must exist on the part of the educational institution of what it wants to achieve. There must be an incentive for and sensitivity toward the action to be undertaken, with the goal of making possible an institutional environment that allows action research to be undertaken.

Another reason for educational authorities' lukewarm support for action research projects has to do with the fact that such projects are generally undertaken collaboratively by a group, generally by teachers, students, and/or members of the parent community. Often the institution feels threatened or pressured by these collaborative efforts. These concerns might be laid to rest as more and better information about action research projects, their objectives, goals, and methodology, is made available.

Action research undertaken in teacher professional development promises to have an impact on instruction and curriculum. Courses in action research are increasingly appearing in teacher education programs in Latin America. Recently participatory research and action research have appeared in the National Education Plans for preschool, primary, and special education. Another area for application that continues to be developed involves the construction of inter-institutional networks undertaking common action research projects. Building these networks has made possible continued interactions among a variety of educational actors: administrators, teachers, students, and communities.

Conclusion

Detecting and analyzing problematic institutional issues in order to generate positive changes based upon projects with collective participation means trying to understand the real way the institution functions and the type of social relations that exist among the various groups participating within an institution.

The analysis of problems in any educational institution must come from the teachers themselves, from the analysis of their daily pedagogical practice, from their knowledge, and from their use of theories that allow them to interpret these practices and create possibilities for change. Through research teachers attempt to create a different daily institutional reality, through an ongoing educational process in which the teachers are analysts and protagonists of change. This process starts within and against daily reality and ends up within and in support of daily reality.

In the classroom action research serves to demystify power and knowledge relationships. The action research method, as a form of critical pedagogy, challenges the existence of student–teacher relationships based on domination. The teacher, through an ongoing educational process, describes and interprets the contradictions that arise with regard to: attitudes toward teaching and research (resolving the dichotomy between teaching as transmission and teaching as construction); forms of individual and group relationships (authoritarian vs. democratic); and institutional relationships.

Finally, we should mention that, through years of working with this method, we have seen in Mexico a progressive tendency toward working with participatory action research in many institutions in a variety of regions, disciplinary fields, and educational levels, which has in turn progressively helped to strengthen and improve the quality of teaching. We have observed a greater interest and concern on the part of the educational community in searching for solutions to problems and recognizing the obstacles they face.

Lastly, we hope that the work we are undertaking motivates teachers on all educational levels to attempt to transform, in a qualitative way, their educational practice, and to understand this practice as a process of appropriating and constructing knowledge—a process that takes place every day in the classroom and that ultimately becomes an educational commitment between teachers and students. Teaching practice is inscribed in this very process.

Notes

1. A document from the Regional Center for Adult and Functional Literacy Education for Latin America (Centro Regional de Educación de Adultos y Alfabetización Funcional para América Latina) (CREFAL, 1977) notes that participatory education seeks "to achieve the participation of adults, groups and communities in decision-making at all levels of the educational process, in particular, determining needs, developing study programs, implementing and evaluating these programs, and determining educational activities aimed at the transformation of the adults' working environment and lives" (p. 24).

2. Budd Hall (1983), following Bodemann (1978) and Sanguineti (1980), in his analysis of the origins of the early experiences that helped form the foundations of participatory research, talks about the structured interview of Marx's "working-class inquiry" with French industrial workers.

    In anthropology, a structuralist like Claude Levi Strauss, in his work on *The Savage Mind*, offers ideas on popular knowledge. Margaret Mead's work on popular culture and informal education is also important.

    In sociology, see Latin Americans Orlando Fals Borda, Juan Bosco Pinto, and Antonio García Barraclough. From the Frankfurt School, see Jurgens Habermas, Theodor Adorno, and Herbert Marcuse on grass-roots movements and social organization. Other important sociologists for the theoretical foundation of participatory research are Pierre Bourdieu, Alain Touraine, and C. Wright Mills.

As far as the field of psychology is concerned, Theodor Adorno has made important contributions on fascism; Eric Fromm on authoritarianism and democracy; Carl Rogers and George Herbert Mead on socialization; and Kurt Lewin on field theory.

In philosophy, see Bachelard's structuralism, Jean Piaget's contributions to epistemology, Noam Chomsky in linguistics, and Paul Ricoeur on the relevance of experience and hermeneutics.

In political science, see the work of Antonio Gramsci and his concept of the "organic intellectual."

References

Acosta, M. (1978). Una línea política revolucionaria: La investigación militante. In *Crítica y política en cincias sociales: El simposio mundial de Cartagena* (pp. 361–378). Bogotá, Colombia: Editorial Punta de Lanza.

Barabtarlo, A. (1989). *Propuesta didáctica para la formación de profesores en investigación educativa: Método de la investigación-acción*. México, D.F.: CISE-UNAM.

Barabtarlo, A. and Theesz M. (1982). Propuesta metodológica para la formación de profesores-investigadores en América Latina: Ruptura con un modelo dependiente. *Revista de la Educación Superior, 34,* 57–75.

Barabtarlo, A. and Theesz, M. (1983). Algunas consideraciones sobre la investigación-acción y su aplicación en un país capitalista dependiente: La formación de profesores en México. *Foro Universitario, 33,* 46–55.

Bauleo, A. (1974). Aprendizaje Grupal. In *Ideología, Grupo y Familia* (pp. 13–94). Buenos Aires: Editorial Kargieman.

Bertin, G. (1981). *Educación y Alienación*. México, D.F.: Nueva Imagen.

Bodemann, M. (1978). El caso a través de la praxis: La encuesta obrera de Marx. In *Crítica y política en cincias sociales: El simposio mundial de Cartagena* (pp. 96–115). Bogotá, Colombia: Editorial Punta de Lanza.

Bosco Pinto, J. (1976). *Educación liberadora: Dimensión, teoría, y metodología*. Buenos Aires: Ediciones Búsqueda.

Carr, W. and Kemmis, S. (1988). *Teoría crítica de la enseñanza y la investigación-acción en la formación del profesorado*. Barcelona: Martínez Roca.

CREFAL (1977). *Recomendación relativa al desarrollo de la educación de adultos*. Pátzcuaro, Michoacán, México: CREFAL.

de Oliveira, D. (1981). A oservacao militante: Una alternativa sociológica. In C.R. Brandao (Ed.), *Pesquisa participante* (pp. 24–44). São Paulo, Brazil: Brasiliense

De Schutter, A. (1986). Método y proceso de la investigación participativa en la capacitación rural. *Cuadernos del CREFAL, 19,* 1–23.

De Schutter, A. and Yopo, B. (1982). Desarrollo y perspectiva de la investigación participativa. In G. Vejarano (Ed.), *La investigación participativa en América Latina* (pp. 56–87). Pátzcuaro, Michoacán, México: CREFAL.

Elliott, J. (1988). Teachers as researchers. In *Educational research, methodology and measurement: An international handbook* (pp. 78–81). London: Pergamon Press.

Fals Borda, O. (1978). Por la praxis: El problema de cómo investigar la realidad para transformarla. In *Crítica y política en cincias sociales: El simposio mundial de Cartagena* (pp. 209–249). Bogotá, Colombia: Editorial Punta de Lanza.

Freire, P. (1970a). Investigación y metodología de la investigación del tema generador. In *Sobre la acción cultural* (pp. 12–38). Santiago, Chile: ICIRA.

Freire, P. (1970b) *La pedagogía del oprimido*. Montevideo: Tierra Nueva.

Gajardo, M. (Ed.). (1985). *Teoria y práctica de la educación popular*. Pátzcuaro, Michoacán, México: CREFAL.

Goldman, L. (1977). Importancia del concepto de conciencia posible para la comunicación. In *El concepto de información en la ciencia contemporánea*. México, D.F.: Editorial Siglo XXI.

Gramsci, A. (1976). *La alternativa pedagógica*. Madrid: Nova Terra.

Hall, B. (1983). Investigación participativa, conocimiento popular y poder: Una reflección personal. In G. Vejarano (Ed.), *La investigación participativa en América Latina* (pp. 31–54). Pátzcuaro, Michoacán, México: CREFAL.

Huizer, G. (1978). Investigación activa y resistencia campesina: Algunas experiencias en el tercer mundo. In *Crítica y política en ciencias sociales: El simposio mundial de Cartagena* (pp. 197–236). Bogotá, Colombia: Editorial Punta de Lanza.

Le Boterf, G. (1980). *Investigación participativa como un proceso educativa critica: Lineamientos metodológicos*. Paper presented at the 2nd Technical Regional Meeting of Rural Coordinators (PEDRI), CREFAL, Pátzcuaro, Michoacán, México.

McTaggart, R. (1987). *Como planificar la investigación-acción*. Barcelona: Laertes.

Sanguineti, Y. (1980). *Factores esenciales de la metodología de la investigación participativa en América Latina*. México, D.F.: CENAPRO/AMEDA.

Schmelkes, S. and Sotelo, J. (1979). *Guía de investigación campesina: Autodiagnóstico*. México, D.F.: CEMPAE/CEDEPAS.

Stenhouse, L. (1987). *La investigación como base de la enseñanza*. Madrid: Morata.

Tedesco, J.C. (1985). Calidad y democracia en la enseñanza superior: Un objetivo posible y necesario. *Revista de Educación Superior, 18*, 21–49.

Chapter Nine
The Development of a Longitudinal Model for Teacher Training
Applied Ethnographic Research in Urban,
Low-Income Elementary Schools in Costa Rica

Margarita Brenes, Natalia Campos, Nidia García,
Marta Rojas, and Emilia Campos

Background

Costa Rica stands out as a unique country in Latin America in that its educational system has provided free and compulsory schooling at the elementary level since 1848. Costa Rica views the education of all of its citizens as one of the highest resources and benefits of the country. School completion rates at the elementary school for all Costa Rican students are 93 percent, and they are 41 percent at the high school level (Segunda Vice Presidencia de la República de Costa Rica, 1994).

Costa Rica is also one of the oldest ongoing democracies in Latin America, having eradicated its army in 1948. This has earned Costa Rica the reputation of being "the Switzerland of the Americas," a country where peace is greatly valued and where "there are more teachers than soldiers." Such recognition was exemplified by former president Oscar Arias, who received the Nobel Peace Price in 1987.

Its population of 3,333,223 is relatively homogeneous, with about 97 percent being made up of whites of European descent, 2 percent blacks of West Indian ancestry, and 1 percent Indians from different tribes.[1] Like most Latin America countries the majority of its population is concentrated in urban areas, particularly San José, the capital. Due to the economic crisis of the 1980s, which affected all of Latin America, rural farmers and workers were forced to emigrate to the city in search of economic betterment. Concurrently, an unprecedented number of immigrants from war-torn Nicaragua, El Salvador, and Honduras began to arrive in Costa Rica, where asylum and refugee status were readily granted. The national currency, which had until then maintained itself at 8.60 *colones* per dollar, rose to 200 colones per dollar, setting off an inflation that the country has still to recover from. The once traditional middle class of Costa Rica, which had not been openly aware of poverty in its midst, experienced drastic economic and social changes. The once poor areas of the city, which had gone unnoticed because they had become stable over time, were now overrun with shantytowns that sprung up all around San José. Since the 1980s poverty in Costa Rica has continued to grow steadily.[2] Today it is well known that it is better to be poor in rural than in urban areas in Costa Rica. In the rural areas there is 75 percent access to health care for the poor in comparison to 53 percent access in urban areas; unemployment for the poor is 8 percent in rural areas versus 17.4 percent in urban areas; and 31.3 percent of the poor are without housing in rural areas compared to 50.2 percent in urban areas (Segunda Vice Presidencia de la República de Costa Rica, 1994). Thus poverty in Costa Rica is no longer an unnoticed phenomenon, but a central issue in meeting educational needs.

One of the ways that Costa Rica has responded to understanding its educational issues in a changing environment has been to study the outputs of its students and schools. El Instituto de Investigación para el Mejoramiento de la Educación Costarricense, the Institute for the Betterment of Costa Rican Education (IIMEC) at the University of Costa Rica, which was created during 1979, undertook the first national survey of the status of Costa Rican education in mathematics, social studies, language arts, and science, which was commissioned by the Ministry of Education between 1981 and 1983.[3] The purpose of such study was to identify the actual academic achievement levels of students in mathematics, science, social studies, and language arts throughout Costa Rican schools. Criterion reference tests were applied to a 20 percent sample of Costa Rican public and private schools in grades 4, 6, 7, 10 and 11. The findings of the tests and results were published between 1983 and 1986, and, in each subject area, identified different levels of achievement between public and private schools as well as gender differences in relation to subject areas (Esquivel and Brenes, 1988). The findings indicated that private schools had statistically significant gains in all subject areas in comparison to the results of public schools. Moreover, marginal-urban schools[4] as well as the schools in outlying provinces such as Guanacaste and Limon, showed poor academic achievement in contrast to the schools in the central plateau (Rojas et al., 1985).[5] The analysis of quantitative data indicated that glaring differences existed between and within schools. However, what accounted for such differences remained unknown, since there was no other available information on the actual classroom learning situation nor the role that teachers played in helping students achieve. Several of the researchers at IIMEC questioned what other data might provide answers for explaining the interactions of classrooms and how the relationship of teachers to students functioned to engage/disengage students. These questions remained unanswered and lingered for a year, until the opportunity for understanding qualitative methods presented itself in the summer of 1984.

Martha Montero-Sieburth, who had been visiting researcher from the Harvard Graduate School of Education during 1983, under an Organization of American States Fellowship, was invited to teach an introductory course in qualitative research at the University of Costa Rica in the summer of 1984. The authors, along with forty other students, took the course and began to realize how the use of ethnographic research could help define and illuminate the questions they had raised about classrooms. Having gained the skills for conducting ethnographic research, the authors conducted an extensive literature review of the field of sociolinguists, literacy, classroom discourse, and ethnographic studies, and in December 1984 submitted a proposal to the University of Costa Rica for funding. Because this was the first qualitative study of its kind to be undertaken by the university, and the university had no other basis on which to value ethnographic research, the process for securing funding was met with great resistance. In early 1986 the project was finally funded, after a protracted negotiation process had taken place.

During the summer of 1986 Montero-Sieburth gave a follow-up course, "The Use of Qualitative Research in Curriculum Design," in which several of the authors participated. Armed with additional knowledge and guiding questions, the first study herein described was designed and conducted between March 1986 and December 1989.

The study was a response to finding alternative explanations for the quantitative analysis that had been made of poor and outlying areas in previous years, and it was also a response to the growing concerns several university researchers shared about teaching and learning in underserved communities, particularly marginal-urban elementary schools. This first study focused on discovering the patterns of classroom interactions in one school. It set the stage for the second study, which took place between 1990 and 1992 in four schools in the same marginal-urban area. The second study expanded upon the results of the first, in terms of the development of taxonomic codes and the patterns of classroom behavior.

The two ethnographic studies from Costa Rica are presented in this chapter, with the first study being reviewed briefly and the second emphasized in greater detail. The overall intent of the combined studies was threefold: (1) to find out what was going on in these marginal-urban classrooms; (2) to develop an understanding of how teachers are trained and

what types of curriculum support their work; and (3) to intervene in changing those training and curricular processes that the team of researchers and
teachers identified as not being conducive to learning. The completion of
the two studies, over an eight-year period, gave rise to the development of
an intervention model for teacher training, parts of which are presented
herein.

The sections that follow outline the development of qualitative educational research in Costa Rica. The description of the first study is followed by the elaboration of the second study; we show the development of
modules for in-service training with printed examples in specific areas,
and we discuss the implications of such studies for teacher training.

Qualitative Educational Research in Costa Rica

The introduction of qualitative research in Costa Rica is influenced by
three main developments that took place during the 1970s and 1980s:
(1) the Organization of American States's creation of El Centro
Multinacional de Investigación Educativa (CEMIE) to support the Ministries of Education throughout Central America in educational research;
(2) the development of a regionalization or descentralization plan for Costa
Rican education, particularly curriculum reform; and (3) the collaboration of Costa Rican educators and universities in learning about qualitative research firsthand from diverse sources.

During the 1970s the Organization of American States created an
educational center known as CEMIE to conduct research studies throughout Central America in support of the educational policies of the different
Ministries of Education. Since most of the research conducted was mainly
quantitative in nature, attempts at using qualitative research were meth-
odologically made throughout the educational system through several studies of achievement gains and student outcomes. While such research was
purported to be qualitative, CEMIE was, in fact, generating outcome-
based research. Given that the researchers were trained primarily in quantitative methodologies, their transition to qualitative research was still dominated in large part by a quantitative format. In addition, the research was
targeted to the development of specific methodologies that would allow
schools to adopt administrative systems to facilitate the attainment of institutional goals. Given such ideological rationales, several studies were
undertaken, but these did not have any measurable impact. CEMIE was
thought by other researchers in Costa Rica to be oriented toward presenting theoretical elaborations and not implementation of research. By 1983

CEMIE did not continue conducting research on achievement gains but instead redirected its efforts toward maintaining a network of scholarly publications Red de Documentación en Educación (REDUC) in Costa Rica, and developing a series of qualitative research seminars and workshops between 1985 and 1986. These seminars and workshops were sporadically offered by CEMIE and included in their initial phase much of the work that was being conducted in Chile in participatory action research. Among those involved in these efforts were Abraham Magendzo from the Programa Interdisciplinario de Investigaciones en Educación (PIIE), (Interdisciplinary Program for Research in Education), and Rolando Pinto, who settled in Costa Rica and later became a researcher at IIMEC. Magendzo (1986) had been influenced by the notion of cultural analysis derived from the work of Denis Lawton in Great Britain, and he discussed the theory of qualitative research in terms of cultural knowledge, power, and control. Pinto, on the other hand, used participatory research and participatory action research as synonymous with qualitative research. Influenced by Fals Borda (1979), Silviera (1985), De Shutter (1983), and Darcy de Olveira (1975), Pinto (1986) emphasized the epistemological dimensions of participatory research. At these seminars and workshops, readings and instructional materials were circulated, in some cases translated from English versions, and an understanding of qualitative research as participatory action research grew.[6]

Between 1978 and 1982 the process of regionalization or decentralization of the curriculum was developed in Costa Rica under the leadership of Maria Eugenia Dengo, who was then Minister of Education (Costa Rica, Plan de Regionalización). It was her belief that the content of the centralized curriculum of the urban centers was not relevant to the experiences of students in the regional rural areas. In fact rural students were being exposed to ideas that were not contextualized. For instance, rural students might study the importance of traffic lights without ever having seen one in their context, hence the curriculum content was often saturated with useless or decontextualized information that made little sense to students and their families. Under regionalization, several projects were undertaken that adapted the centralized curriculum to the regional areas and made the curriculum used for multigrades more user-friendly. Such attempts to regionalize the curriculum emphasized the role of context in understanding how learning takes place, and it also created greater sensitivities toward appreciating the cultural variations that were apparent from region to region. The curriculum developed in the area of Limon, where there is a high concentration of black and Indian populations, highlighted the linguistic variations between Spanish, the patois of the black people, and the Bribri language of indigenous groups.

This steady emphasis on taking the educational content from the center (Central Plateau) to the periphery (outlying areas) allowed for the creation of curricular space and knowledge that progressively became more qualitative over time. During the ministry of Eugenio Rodríguez (1982–1986), PRONAFOCO, the National Program for Curriculum Development and Training, which was based on a qualitative orientation, became institutionalized. Also during that same period (1981–1983), the first student-produced oral histories of the indigenous peoples of Talamanca were recorded and developed into resource magazines by students from one of the agricultural high schools, who worked closely with Paula Palmer. Their work, similar to that of Foxfire in Georgia, was supported for national distribution and training of administrators (Montero-Sieburth, 1997).

At the same time that the Ministry of Education was moving toward a qualitative orientation in its curriculum, the Institute for the Improvement of Costa Rican Education (IIMEC), which had been established in 1979 as the first research institute of the University of Costa Rica, had begun to develop criterion-referenced testing to evaluate the state of the art of primary and secondary education in mathematics, science, language arts, and social studies. Although the IIMEC was mainly oriented toward quantitative research, it began to explore qualitative research as a way to find explanations that extended the results of the diagnostic survey and presented research alternatives. Under the directorship of Juan Manuel Esquivel, IIMEC at the University of Costa Rica, along with the National University of Heredia and the National Council of Scientific Research, offered the first introductory course on qualitative research to forty graduate students taught by Martha Montero-Sieburth in 1984 (Montero-Sieburth, 1984). As part of the course students were exposed to the theory and methodology presented by the North American tradition of qualitative research and by the British school's approach to ethnographic research. The rationale behind their selection was the fact that both orientations were precursors to qualitative research in industrialized countries, and their theory and methods were unknown in Costa Rica. The students who attended the course went on to conduct their own ethnographic research over the year and attended the follow-up course, also taught by Montero-Sieburth, on the use of qualitative methods in the development of curriculum offered during the summer of 1986.[7] These courses, plus their own experiences, led several of the researchers, including the authors of this chapter, to later formulate their own approach derived from several eclectic theories. In the case of the IIMEC group the emphasis was toward sociolinguistic and cultural analysis since these were newly discovered arenas.

The University of Costa Rica, along with the University of Heredia and the Technological Institute, began to include qualitative research as part of the Costa Rican conferences in educational research. At the First Central American Forum and Fourth National Conference of Researchers in Education in 1987, which took place in Alajuela, Costa Rica, several Central American and Mexican ethnographers presented their work. Among some of the presenters was Anita Barabtarlo y Zedansky from Mexico, who discussed teacher training using participatory action research. Among the invited discussants were Martha Montero-Sieburth from Harvard University, who had worked with the IIMEC team, and Flora Rodriguez-Brown from the University of Illinois at Chicago, who provided feedback on the sociolinguistic aspects of IIMEC's team research. It was clear that ethnographic research had begun to take hold in Costa Rica, and researchers were trying to experiment with diverse theoretical and methodological positions.

Researchers at IIMEC began to consider the use of qualitative research as an additional tool that could complement the analysis of the quantitative studies that had previously been conducted. Moreover, they wanted to uncover other reasons than those projected by the achievement rankings of schools and what the tests indicated for students. After reviewing the literature in sociolinguistics, literacy, language discourse, and ethnography, four researchers at IIMEC decided to develop a team project in which they could assess classroom language interactions. The team consisted of Nidia García, an educator who teaches reading and language arts to students studying elementary education at the University of Costa Rica; Marta Rojas, a linguist who specializes in philology; Natalia Campos, a curriculum specialist who had a Ph.D. from the United States; and Margarita Brenes, a psychologist who specializes in developmental psychology and women's studies. Influenced by the theories of Dell Hymes (1985), Courtney Cazden et al. (1986), Michael Stubbs (1984), Muriel Saville-Troike (1982), Frederick Erickson (1973), and the work of Jeannie Assaél (1983) and Gabriela López (1984) from Chile, the team decided to focus on the study of verbal interaction and cultural norms in a marginal-urban school. Their purpose was not to compare or contrast middle-class schools with marginal-urban schools, but rather to begin to identify classroom interaction factors that might illuminate why students in marginal-urban schools usually fared poorly in the tests, while others fared well in more middle-class schools. By December 1985 the University of Costa Rica funded the proposal made by this interdisciplinary IIMEC team, and the study officially began in March 1986.[8]

A caveat in this process is the fact that qualitative research in Costa Rica assumed a pedagogical thrust that was commensurate with the interest of universities struggling to find new paradigms for explaining educational issues. In fact, because there was not a popular education base for promoting qualitative research in Costa Rica, it was up to the universities to generate such interest without presenting a given political posture. In that regard IIMEC responded with enthusiasm in beginning its first study of this type without emphasizing a political, but rather a pedagogical agenda, unlike the development of qualitative research in other parts of Latin America such as Chile, Brazil, and Mexico, where qualitative research was closely linked to leftist political positions.

The First Study: Verbal Interaction in the Classroom, Micro-Ethnographic Research in a Marginal-Urban School
Marginal-Urban Context

In Costa Rica the school year begins in March and ends the last day of November; hence the summer months are December, January, and February. Students have a two-week break in July and during Easter. Attendance in school varies according to whether the school is public or private. In public schools students attend a total of five hours per day. In private schools students attend between six and eight hours a day. To accommodate the growing numbers of students, most public schools schedule two shifts, one from 7 A.M. to 12 P.M. and the other from 12:30 to 5:30 P.M. All schools, public or private, require students to wear uniforms.[9]

Schools in Costa Rica are classified by the Ministry of Education according to the number of students who attend, the number of teachers, and the location of schools within a community. Such classification ranges from urban, rural, private, and public schools to single-teacher and multigrade classes within a school. Urban schools are markedly different from rural schools, both in terms of socioeconomic base and also in terms of delivery of educational programs.

The level of poverty in each community determines the types of resources available to each school. Traditionally, public schools have been financed by the government. Until the 1980s such financing was 30 percent of the GNP; however, after the economic crisis of 1982 there was a steady decline of funding given to education, dipping at one point to 14 percent of GNP and now believed to be about 18 percent of GNP. The reduction in funding from the government from 1980 to 1987 has only left monies to pay salaries, which account for 98 to 99 percent of the total allotted educational budget, in contrast to 92.9 percent toward salaries for all of Latin America and 79.6 percent toward salaries for all industrialized countries (Sanguinetty, 1992, citing UNESCO Yearbook 1981). Such reduction in funds has made the financing of schools part of the responsibility of the communities in which they are found. Thus schools are partly sustained with the help of the *Patronato Escolar* (parent groups, which are like the Parent–Teacher Associations) and the *Juntas de Educación* (in which a representative of the Ministry of Education develops policies with community resource people to raise funds). For example, the *Patronato,* or parent groups, may help with supplying food for the end of the year celebration, or by buying basic school supplies—cardboards, paper, markers—while the *Juntas de Educación* may set policies for the school as well as help raise funds through school fairs and bingo games.

Given the lack of available resources in schools and the limited economic base, it is not surprising to see that marginal-urban communities blossom rapidly in cities as people become displaced from rural areas. In their attempt to seek better jobs and pay than that afforded by agricultural work in the rural area, many families migrate to the city. Starting anew in cities like San José where employment opportunities can be found, these families experience newfound poverty because many of the skills rural people bring to the city do not fit the demands of the more industrialized environment of the city.

Over half of the Costa Rican population considered to be poor is found today in urban areas. Many of these so-called marginal-urban areas are found south of San José, where the combination of low-income housing and slums makes it possible for migrants to settle. Over 86.25 percent of the inhabitants in the south of San José come from rural areas and are poor by Costa Rican standards. Close to 136,000 families in 1993 were considered to be poor, and of those 12 percent were indigent, without any likely resources. Sixty percent of the heads of households of these families did not have any permanent jobs, and they worked within what is called the "informal economy" (Segunda Vice Presidencia de la República de Costa Rica, 1994). In this informal economy there are no salaried positions and no health benefits. Work is temporary and occasional and consists of receiving pay for watching cars from being stolen, cutting grass, doing handyman jobs, street vending, and house cleaning.

Selection of Marginal-Urban School/Classrooms/Teachers

It is in this context of the marginal-urban area that the IIMEC team negotiated entry into three school sites and selected one for their study. With some trepidation and a great deal of excitement, the team of IIMEC researchers ventured into the marginal-urban areas of San José, which were unknown to them. This was the first time that a qualitative educational study of this type had been designed by researchers from the University of Costa Rica, and the team realized that before they went into the school they had to overcome their own fears and biases. To prepare themselves the IIMEC team underwent a consciousness-raising process in which their biases and stereotypes as well as their fears and expectations were openly discussed. They analyzed their middle-class perspectives by attempting to understand what it meant to be poor. They also openly discussed how they would react to the students and the teachers, particularly when their differences impacted them. After much self-reflection and open criticism of each other's values, even about their dress codes, their own reactions to poverty, and how they wanted to present themselves, the team felt open to learning about the marginal-urban school context.

After visiting several schools, one was selected based on the willingness of the principal and teachers to participate even though no stipend or funding was made available to them. The negotiations hinged on both teachers and researchers developing a process for understanding classrooms and gaining knowledge about such contexts.

While the initial focus of the study was primarily on verbal interactions in the classroom, once in the school the team decided to identify the sociolinguistic and cultural norms of two elementary first-grade classrooms. Such a decision came about from interviewing teachers and observing in the school. The team decided that capturing the use of language in classrooms and the types of relationships that ensued for socializing students in schools through systematic participatory observation was the crux of their study. Two teachers independently volunteered to have their classes observed. Of these two teachers, one had a twenty-five-year teaching record without a university degree; the other teacher was a university graduate with eleven years of teaching experience, two years in a public urban-marginal school and nine years at a private school.

Methodology

Classes were observed twice a week by two of the IIMEC researchers during a three-hour period for more than two years. The two classes had a total of 58 students, 28 in one and 30 in the other. Using participatory research, the team focused on four focal students at each observation session, so that at the end of seven sessions all students were observed.[10] This continued throughout two years and each student was observed at least fifteen times over the span of the research. Approximately six videotapes and a few audiotapes of each class were made. The pattern that emerged for each of the observation sessions was as follows: after each session, the two researchers individually analyzed their fieldnotes and then met with each other to compare notes, from which questions and analysis arose. The questions raised were used to guide the next set of observation sessions. Each month the IIMEC team shared their analysis with the teachers involved in the research, and they used the feedback to clarify discrepancies and to generate other research questions. Both researchers and teachers learned about each other's style of discourse and ways in which their social relationships evolved. As a consequence of learning about each other's perspective in each other's homes, at the university, and through outings with the team, a warm and friendly rapport between teachers and researchers was established.

As data and observations continued into the second year, taxonomies of the language of the teacher, student–teacher interactions, and student–student interactions were created as a means to systematically decode the interactions of the classroom. The taxonomies derived from the work of James Spradley and David McCurdy (1972), and the learning that took place from the courses in qualitative research served to describe the field observations and frame the categories that emerged from the data collected. As new data were collected at each session, these categories were continuously modified. In the student-to-student interactions, there were three consistent categories found: (a) the academic, referring to the language associated with content; (b) the personal–social, associated with language about the life of the teacher or that of the students; and (c) control, here used to establish discipline. Within each of these categories there were also subcategories. For instance, the language used for content, emphasizing the exchange of instructional materials that occurred between students and indicating the degree of cooperation in lending materials; or the explanations used to clarify or resolve doubts; or the comments made by students to add information. Students accused each other in order to sustain the discipline of the classroom in using control among themselves. They blamed each other and tattled on each other to the teacher. They also made snide remarks to each other as a means to enforce the discipline of the classroom (Rojas, García, Campos, and Brenes, 1992).

Findings

Close to five thousand verbal interactions were analyzed. However, in this chapter only the salient summary of findings is presented derived from the analysis of taxonomies and associated behaviors and interactions. For the complete analysis of this study see the publications by Rojas, García, Campos, and Brenes (1991, 1992).

Of these verbal interactions, the general categories identified were analyzed as being used for giving directives, defining procedures, using guiding statements, presenting content, and demonstrating social behaviors. Close to 65 percent of the interactions were initiated by teachers, 25 percent were interactions initiated by students to teachers, and 9 percent were interactions between students. Of the interactions initiated by the teacher, 37 percent accounted for the use of language to guide students, 27 percent for the use of language to control behaviors, 1 percent for personal and social issues. Only 31 percent of the language use of teachers dealt directly with the academic content of the class. The fact that only 1 percent of the language use was allocated to personal and social issues by teachers suggests that teachers socialized students in their classes though hierarchical relationships without allowing much space for social and personal communication. Such emphasis on teacher control and guidance appears to nurture a classroom environment where dependency is strongly stressed, confirming similar findings of qualitative studies on control issues made in the United States. A case in point are the following statements commonly used to guide students:

Teacher: *Sit down, open your book to page 27, and start answering the questions.*

These commands were often repeated up to three and four times before students acted. The point here is that such pervasive use of guidance cues from the teachers did not elicit the expected behavior. Instead it appears that the teachers used such guiding statements more for rhetorical than academic purposes, often frustrating their ability to gain control over the students.

The use of endearment by teachers was also evident in the control of students. At times teachers sugar-coated their expectations when addressing students, a pattern that is culturally common in Costa Rica, where direct and confrontative behavior is not generally socially accepted nor promoted. Some examples of this type of control with endearment are the following statements:

Teacher: *My dear love, sit down right now, or else you will be punished!*
Teacher: (scolding a male student for hitting a girl) *When a man hits a woman, what is he called?*
Students: (in choral response) *A coward!*

Whether such interactions served to hide the teacher's biases toward poor children was not apparent, since the teachers were kissed each day before and after class and often publicly praised students.

An example of the use of academic language initiated by the teachers, to which students responded orally and in chorus, is the following:

Teacher: *Milk comes from_____?*
Students: (In choral response) *From Borden milk.* (Borden refers to one brand of milk that is distributed in cardboard boxes throughout Costa Rica.)
Teacher: *No, no, I told you it comes from cows.*

It is clear that in this example the teacher has only one answer in mind and expects only that answer. She does not search for other alternative answers the students might have. Instead she insists on having a memoristic response.

Student-initiated interactions appeared to imitate those of the teachers in that 31 percent of the language used by students was either requests for guidance, demands for attention, or complaints about other students' behaviors. Close to 32 percent of the language between students was used primarily for personal and social concerns. For example:

Student: *Niña* [girl, the word used in Costa Rica to address teachers, who were traditionally unmarried women], *that boy pulled my hair while you were not looking!*
Student: *Niña, would you please check over my work? Do you like my drawing?*
Student: *What else shall I do?* (Waiting for the next task, which had previously been explained.)

Student: *Niña, that student got up and went to the wastepaper basket without asking for your permission!*

To summarize, this study surfaced several issues that were new in the Costa Rican context: (1) There are styles of teaching and learning for students and teachers in marginal-urban schools where guidance and control are stressed over social and academic interactions. Teachers basically learn to control because they are not able to guide their students effectively. They tend to revert to control when all else fails. (2) The authority of the teacher over students and the submission of students to authority indicate that teachers transmit conformity-driven social norms to students. Students likewise respond by demanding attention and requesting guidance from teachers in an over-dependent manner. (3) Individual deskwork rather than group work is stressed in these classes. (4) The learning of academic content is repetitious without being elaborated or expanded. Students tend to readily forget what they learn.

The findings of this micro-ethnographic study revealed that the complexities of engaging students in academic learning, while at the same time fulfilling their social and interpersonal needs, went unmet because much of the time was not spent on teaching and learning but rather on guiding and controlling students.

The Evolution of the Second Study:
Teacher Training Model Development
Purpose

The second study evolved from the findings of the initial study, which characterized teachers as not being sufficiently engaged in teaching but rather focused on guiding and controlling students. The IIMEC team wanted to further understand how teachers like those of their previous study might be able to change their practice and engage students in learning. Thus the team decided that the focus of this second study would be to utilize the findings of a larger number of schools and teachers to identify ways in which teacher training might be improved.[11] Such findings could be readily translated into the development of instructional modules to be used in in-service training and teacher education programs at different Costa Rican universities (see Appendix, p. 216, for a diagram on the development of each stage of research).

Influenced by the work of Walter Doyle (1986) in classroom management, Jere Brophy (1987) in teacher behavior, Barak Rosenshine (1979) in terms of direct instruction, content, and time, Beatrice Avalos (1985) in teacher training, Donald Schön (1983) in relation to reflective practitioners, and Martha Montero-Sieburth et al. (1989), who stressed the role of teachers as managers and curriculum-makers, the team reviewed major studies in this field and saw the relevance of their work fit similar theories. Unlike the qualitative research introduced by the CEMIE and OAS in Costa Rica, influenced primarily by participatory action research in communities, the IIMEC team considered the work of North American ethnographers and Latinos doing ethnographic work in the United States such as Montero-Sieburth and Rodríguez-Brown in classroom interactions and sociolinguistics to be closer to their needs. Their research in bilingual classrooms and on language issues resonated with the work they had begun in the previous study. By expanding their literature review to include classroom management and reflective teaching, the team attempted to understand the processes by which teachers could reflect on their practice and identify activities that could be used to formulate a teacher training model with instructional materials. Hence the study, which began by being focused on discovering ways in which teachers' practice could be better understood in order to create change in their classrooms, gravitated toward Doyle's (1986) four dimensions of positive classroom management, namely: the interrelationship of content, behavior, time, and space. These dimensions became significant classifiers in the collection of data and in the analysis. The initial team of researchers from the IIMEC expanded to include one of the teachers who had participated in the initial study as a coinvestigator.

Selection of Sites

Several urban-marginal schools were visited by the research team with the purpose of selecting three fourth grades. However, because there were four teachers who enthusiastically wanted to participate, two fourth-grade classes at one of the schools were included along with one fourth-grade class at each additional school for a total of four classes in three schools. The three schools were located in the school district of Hatillo, where the neighborhoods have names like *Aguanta Filo*,[12] (Withstanding Hunger), *Sagrada Familia* (Holy Family), and *15 de Septiembre* (Independence Day of Costa Rica). The selected schools shared the same demographic characteristics of the school in the first study in that the surrounding neighborhoods were made up of rural people and people from other slums in San José and represented working to lower-middle-class communities.

The population of the three schools ranged from 400 to 1,500 students, had limited resources, lacked teacher training, and had high teacher and student turnover. In one of the schools 50 percent of the students were transfers from other schools at the fourth and fifth grade level, and over 25 percent of the students in all three schools were repeaters. Forty-four percent of the students came from single-parent families, most of them headed by females.

In these poor communities, safety as well as security maintenance were expected concerns. In one of the schools, the principal took the telephone and the only typewriter home each night in order to safeguard them from being stolen. The principal could request that the Ministry of Education provide him with a security guard for the school; however, the fear that the guard might be killed by robbers prevented him from doing so.

The three female and one male teachers in this project were self-selected. All of the females had university degrees, and the one male, who did not have a teaching certificate, was currently completing coursework in a teacher-training institution. The male teacher was a newcomer at his school, but the females had anywhere from ten to fifteen years of experience at their schools. The reasons given by the most veteran teacher to join the project were motivated out of her own need to explore her creativity, whereas the two other female teachers and the male teacher felt their teaching could be improved by their joining the research team.

Methodology

The IIMEC research team for this study included Nidia García, Marta Rojas, Natalia Campos, and Margarita Brenes plus Emilia Campos, the newly added teacher who had been observed in the first study and wanted to participate fully in this second study. Data were collected using participant observation by pairs of researchers at each of the three schools. The reason pairs were used was not only for obtaining inter-rater reliability but also to gain multiple perspectives on the classrooms. Each pair of researchers rotated between the schools, observing three times a week in each of the four classrooms during the first six months. Specific attention was given to the four focal students who were identified in each 80-minute class session, and since each class had an average of twenty-nine students, four focal students were observed at each session until all students had been observed at least four times.

In each of the classes maps of the classrooms were created to identify spatial and temporal relationships of teacher and students. Mobility charts of the teachers' and students' movements were also made. The maps enabled the research team members to focus and follow the focal students from week to week, and they also helped to detect patterns of interactions that emerged. In addition to the observation and mapping processes, informal interviews with principals, teachers, and students were continuously made as part of the data collection. Students were queried during recess and as they mingled with each other between classes. Formal interviews were conducted after each observation with the teachers of the study. These interviews offered insights into the ways that teachers thought they had taught versus what the researchers had recorded.

Data Analysis

Data Reduction and Analysis. During the first six months of the research project, classroom observations were conducted, recorded, and transcribed. At each of the monthly meetings the cumulative data were then analyzed by the IIMEC team and all of the participating teachers. These meetings became a collaborative effort in which each person contributed to the identification of categories within the four dimensions, where each classroom observed was characterized. The characteristics elaborated were contrasted with the profiles developed by the IIMEC research team during the following six months. From this analysis made at these meetings and the elaboration of classroom characteristics and profiles, the training program for teachers began to emerge and take shape during the first year.

The extensive data collected were analyzed through the triangulation of data sets during each of the full-day monthly meetings between the teachers and IIMEC research members. Data were coded according to each of the dimensions—the use of space, time, academic content, and behaviors for all of the four classes. Relationships between the descriptions and each of the dimensions were made by the research team and were listed so as to identify similarities as well as differences from one class to another. Next came the development of what the team labeled as "profiles"—these were dense characterizations of each of the classrooms in terms of the use of time, space, content, and behaviors. Each profile consisted of a variety of descriptive statements, sometimes as many as twenty-five statements, which the IIMEC team members developed to substantiate all of the factors observed in each of the dimensions for each of the observed classrooms. For example, the use of space in a teacher's classroom might be characterized by the following statements:

Class No. Three: (1) Arrangement of desks appears to be unrelated to educational activities; (2) Arrangement of desks tends to be rigid, set in straight lines; 3) Arrangement of desks favors differential treatment in the classroom, with some children receiving varying degrees of attention, from none, to some, to most attention; (4) The teacher's zone of action, that is, the teacher's mobility, tends to be concentrated at the front of the classroom; (5) Teacher's mobility is unrelated to evaluating students, reviewing homework, or engaging in teacher-to-student interactions; (6) Children's mobility is strongly controlled by the teacher; (7) There are no areas for independent work in the classroom; (8) Teachers do not incorporate spatial aspects in their planning; (9) The classrooms do not have many decorations or cultural material (García, Rojas, Campos, Brenes, and Campos, 1994).

Afterward each of the four classroom teachers was independently provided with the statements developed by the IIMEC team in each of the four dimensions (time, space, behaviors, and content). Teachers sorted through these statements, acknowledging some and rejecting others, and thereafter developed their own profiles using those statements that aptly described their classes. The purpose was to have the teachers self-assess their understanding of space, time, treatment of academic content, and student behaviors and whether they concurred with the statements of the IIMEC research team. Comparisons and contrasts between the profiles developed by the researchers and those elaborated by teachers were made, and students were also asked to contribute to the development of the profiles. Where discrepancies appeared, the team and teachers used the raw or cooked and expanded data to select the closest approximation to the classroom.

Such sorting and use of heuristic processes had several results. First, the teachers and IIMEC researchers were able to validate the profiles as close representations of the classrooms and at the same time, through agreement and disagreement with each other as they analyzed the classroom profiles, reflect on their own practices with each other and with themselves. Second, the openness created by such processes allowed both teachers and researchers not only to raise critical questions about teaching and learning within the parameters provided by the four dimensions but also to question each other. A case in point was provided when teachers were provided with a variety of statements from the researchers about the use of objectives in their classroom for the beginning of a lesson. The teacher would indicate through sorting which of these statements directly applied to his/her practice. Thereafter, the researchers would provide the teacher with raw or cooked classroom data that would confirm or challenge the statements selected by the teachers. In such an encounter the teacher would reflect by thinking back on what he/she was actually attempting to do in class and what he/she finally did, uncovering in the process what changes he/she would need to make. By analyzing what teachers said they did with what they actually enacted in the classroom, the team of teachers and researchers was able to formulate relevant topics and themes for the development of teacher training. It is noteworthy that while this process of working through reflection may closely resemble Donald Schön's notion of the reflective practitioner, the IIMEC team and teachers designed this process from the input and discussions they had throughout the research.

The assessment and characterization made by the IIMEC team and the three teachers were in agreement and were uniform in all but one case. The one discrepant case was due to the way that the fourth teacher characterized the behavior of her students as being negative. Whereas "students provoked her," the IIMEC research team observed that this teacher lost control of her classroom and had difficulty maintaining general control.

The Emergent Design of Teacher Training Program. During the last two months of the project's first year, teachers and researchers identified emergent themes from which topics were to be developed for teacher training based on the compilation of the classroom profiles on the use of time, space, behaviors, and content. The topics developed around the use of space for example, were:

1. awareness of teacher's use of space;
2. space and communication;
3. organization of space in relation to content of lesson;
4. organization of space as related to conditions of urban-marginal schools; and
5. mobility of teachers and students within the classroom space.

This same process was applied to every dimension so that each had a series of topics and, in some cases, subtopics. Questions related to the topic, procedures to be followed, time allotted, available resources, and trainer needed for teaching and developing the lesson activities were identified. More than thirty topics were identified and elaborated by teachers and researchers during a two-month period, and within a month's time lessons were developed for implementation.

Implementation of Teacher Training

During February 1990, twenty-four teachers, including the four teachers of the study, three research assistants, and fifteen new teachers from elementary schools gave up part of their summer vacation and family time to attend a three-week intensive training program. Normally the Ministry of Education would provide credits or the University of Costa Rica would pay a stipend to teachers using their vacation, but because there were no funds available for such stipends teachers willingly and voluntarily participated in the training. The fifteen teachers were recruited by the four teacher/researchers from the study through word of mouth. The faculty for the training consisted of the IIMEC research team and fourteen additional consultants, all selected because of their familiarity with qualitative research and given expertise in specific subjects. Throughout the training, none of the teachers, mostly women and mothers, dropped out.

The IIMEC researchers taught in the program, facilitated the consultants' teaching, and served as sharpshooters in identifying concerns and providing support to the teachers for the development of lesson activities. The consultants also worked collaboratively with one or two members of the IIMEC team to design the workshops, set the goals and objectives to be achieved, and evaluate the outcomes of their teaching. Among some of the topics selected from many others were: discipline in the classroom, working in urban-marginal communities, teaching the working student, and identifying sexual abuse in children. When the actual workshops and training sessions took place, the IIMEC researchers were also present. This was done to support and create bridges between the knowledge transfer of the consultants and the needs of the teachers.

The focus of the training, which attempted to integrate theory with practice, was interdisciplinary, participative, reflective, and critical. For instance, in training teachers about how to understand the marginal-urban context of their students, one of the IIMEC trainers presented a videotape of a child who works from one of the marginal-urban communities; the teachers debriefed the video and discussed the teachers' ideas. This was followed by an activity in which participants had to guess what the social and economic statistics were for urban areas. From all of their guesses an average was made of the numbers and these were displayed. Then the actual statistics of the social and economic conditions of the area were provided. The purpose of this activity was to demonstrate the discrepancies between the assumed data teachers had in their heads and the actual statistics. The assumptions of teachers vis-à-vis their students' reality gained from their experiences in working in marginal-urban areas was challenged by the presentation of actual figures. In this instance not one of the teachers was able to accurately guess the number of unemployed parents who lived in the marginal-urban area. Confronted with social, economic, and educational indicators, the teachers then had the responsibility of developing lesson plans that accurately reflected the social and economic conditions of their students. As part of the workshop the teachers read William Ryan's *Blaming the Victim* and Jonathan Kozol's *Death at an Early Age* in order to show contrasts in contexts and bring the reality of children in marginal-urban areas home.

The training also strongly stressed the development of teachers' self-evaluation and collaborative group process. One example of this type of evaluation was witnessed when the consultant for teaching science developed a checklist with teachers to verify whether students had understood the stated science objectives and whether the activities of the lesson actually fit the indicated objectives. The teachers taught using the criteria developed by the checklist of the objectives and later interviewed students about what they understood about the lesson and how they came to understand the objectives' relationship to the content and the activities they performed. To further help these teachers, the consultant suggested that the teachers be observed by colleagues who knew what the intended lesson was. Their role was to check whether the objectives of the lesson were fully met by the teacher. Once teachers received the feedback from their students and colleagues, they could begin to focus on the areas they would want to change. Thus, in this example, the opportunity to gain feedback from multiple perspectives allowed the teachers to reflect on whether they had or had not accomplished their teaching objectives.

At the end of each training session teachers developed a set of action plans for implementation in their classrooms. These plans defined the ways they would change their pedagogical practice while working with a group of participating teachers. Such action plans included peer observation, feedback from students and peers, as well as evaluation of teaching objectives. As an offshoot of working together, knowledge exchanges about instructional resources and innovative teaching ideas became commonplace. At the conclusion of the training, the individual action plans were integrated into a comprehensive year-long plan to be put into action by each teacher.

Post-Training: Implementation of Changes in the Classroom

The research continued into its second year (from March 1990 to November 1991) with the implementation of changes that the four teachers of the study defined in their year-long action plans. To do this, teachers requested the continuation of observation in their respective classrooms. During year two, classroom data and teacher changes of their practices continued to be observed, and additional training workshops were provided to support these changes throughout the year.

Renewed Classroom Observation. The four teachers who participated in the research study were observed in their classrooms by the IIMEC research team for sixteen weeks after the training, using the same methodological sequence of group observation and analysis previously used. The goal of this observational sequence was to identify the types of post-training changes that may have occurred in each teacher's practice, after teachers had had the opportunity to put into practice their plans of action and the changes they had proposed. Thus the impact of the training program in the observed teachers' practice, assessing any apparent changes in the teachers' pedagogical styles, could be evaluated. The IIMEC team and participating four teachers met monthly to analyze the data collected. At the same time they continued to receive feedback from the IIMEC researchers about each of their classes. The same methodological procedures for triangulation of data sets, comparison and contrast, as well as coding and thematic development were used.

Findings. While specific changes in the teachers' pedagogical style were readily identified in the use of time, space, content, and behaviors (i.e., setting up reading areas and space for individual student work, making the learning objectives of a lesson explicit, or integrating male and females students in activities), teachers were nevertheless concerned about the less noticeable situations where change was implicit. They wanted to understand the underlying basis of their own resistance to change their pedagogical style. The questions that appeared to concern them were: How could the control patterns of their teaching change to more participatory and student-centered teaching? How were the changes they were trying to effect in their classroom influenced by the organizational structure of the school?

For example, in one case, the idea of conducting a field trip with students was met with resistance by the administration because the administration believed that letting students out of the building disrupted the natural flow of the school day. In another case, a teacher's desire to have students experience safety by viewing traffic lights was limited by an administrator who believed students could learn about safety issues directly from books without leaving the building. Teachers, in such cases, had to deal with their own resistance to change as well as the restrictions imposed by a formal educational system, and they looked to each other and to the IIMEC team for answers. At the same time the IIMEC researchers also recognized the deep-seated entrenchment of the institutional structure upon change.

The limitations encountered by these teachers resulted in their requesting additional ongoing training each month as part of the research program. The research team responded by offering nine additional training sessions that addressed the teachers' needs, provided follow-up to the previous training, and identified new areas for future training.

At the end of this study it was clear that the results extended beyond expected outcomes. For example, of the four teachers who participated, three improved their status within their schools and gained leadership positions, which ranged from being curriculum planners to resource specialists and evaluation specialists. For these teachers, these newly acquired leadership roles confirmed them as professionals and recognized their newly gained knowledge to assess their pedagogical strengths and weaknesses. For the principals, the fact that these teachers, after undergoing the research and training, could in turn help their schools justified them as leaders and their being appointed to positions of power within the schools.[13]

Instructional Model Development:
Teacher Training/Self-Evaluation Modules

The Development of Instructional Materials. Another major result of the research study and training was the development of an instructional model to be used for teacher training as well as self-evaluation. From the analysis of data sets and the evaluation of explicit and implicit changes in classroom practice, the teachers and IIMEC researchers decided to develop the processes and content of the research into instructional materials that went beyond their own experiences. They believed that these materials, which included case studies, could be used to serve teachers' in-service training, and at the same time could be used to guide and evaluate one's teaching and progress in each of the specific dimensions.

From March 1992 to November 1993 the IIMEC and four teachers developed instructional materials into modules for teacher training to be used to guide and evaluate teachers' progress in the use of time, space, content, and student behaviors. The teachers contributed cases of their own, developed other cases with the IIMEC team, and gave feedback on questions, issues, content, and concerns that arose. They even participated in pilot testing some of the materials to be sure other teachers would be able to use them. Thus the modules became a collaborative process that produced case studies, review of relevant research, self-reflective questions, and strategies for change, as well as self-evaluations of what was learned from each module. The end product was a set of modules, produced as individual workbooks, to help teachers appropriately use space, time, content, and behaviors in the classroom. A teacher manual to be used for trainers was also developed.

As a result of the notoriety the project received at different paper and conference presentations, the Minister of Education provided stipends for teachers to work with the research team in writing and testing the instructional modules at the early stage of model development.

Between 1993 and 1994, three of the four teacher training modules with the following subtitles were published as a series of workbooks under the title *Conocimiento, Participación y Cambio* (Knowledge, Participation and Change): (1) *Espacio en el Aula* (Space in the Classroom); (2) *Tiempo en el Aula* (Time in the Classroom); and (3) *Comportamiento en el Aula* (Behavior in the Classroom). The fourth module/workbook, *Contenido en el Aula* (Content in the Classroom) and the trainer's manual, entitled *Manual de Capacitación* (Training Manual), are in press.

Each workbook analyzes how well teachers understand and manage concepts and activities using time, space, student/teacher behaviors, and content issues, and each uses illustrative cases, both in and out of the classroom, to represent the issues under discussion. The workbooks also emphasize best practices drawn from the research literature and offer suggestions for teachers to conduct their own research in classrooms.

The modules were produced following the general structure of the research design. Thus they present the reality of the use of time, space, behaviors, and content by making these experiences concrete examples that could be described in and out of classrooms. For example, the workbook *The Use of Time* (1992) shows through a case study how a teacher normally uses each day for specific activities. Questions are then asked about how time is used and in what areas. With regard to the use of time outside the classroom, the following questions were used: "Does Adele have a clear objective on the use of time for exercising that does not conflict with her personal family time? How would you evaluate Adele's behavior in relation to establishing limits with her family so that her time is respected?" This is followed by an analysis of the questions being asked and serves to highlight the main points of the case study. For example: "In defining the objectives for the use of time, it is important to define limits for the use of time as well. Once limits have been set, it is important to maintain those limits with oneself and with others" (1992, pp. 7–16).

Another example can be found in Unit 4 of the workbook entitled *Space in the Classroom* (1992). In this unit the results from the research on the use of space are explained through comparisons of two teachers' classrooms observed during the first and second year of the study. Because the teachers taught first grade and then second grade, contrasts in the maps of their classrooms are presented to indicate their differences. To provide the flavor of how the workbook units flow from concrete to reflective practice, and how the workbook is presented to teachers, the following descriptions are directly paraphrased from the workbook on *Space in the Classroom*:

In the case of teacher 1, the use of space in terms of seating arrangements is determined by three straight rows in which males are seated next to females. The teacher indicates this is a way she can control their behavior, and it also implies that students of different sexes will have less interaction than students of the same sex. 71 percent of the maps which were made of this classrom indicate that is the case. Children who are repeaters, have to take a grade over again, tend to be placed at the back of the room, isolated from interacting with the teacher and other children, as well as from the blackboard and teacher's desk. The teacher uses the desk as the mainstay of her control and students who do not have access to her desk do not receive feedback. This suggests that repeaters are in a sort of "spatial marginalization." And it is clear that participative interaction is affected by the use of space in the classroom. The only time the physical distribution of space in the class changes is when there are exams, hence the class space tends to be static and non-dynamic in terms of content learning and activities. Time is inefficiently used and children loiter without any direct learning objective, they interfere with each other and obstruct the activities which are underway. In some of the observations, of the 28 children present, 9 or 11 are usually standing without being directed to any learning tasks. The wastebasket is the point of convergence for many of these children. The teachers' desk is the evaluation center in which students take turns to have their notebooks checked. The teacher rarely moves beyond the front of the class and does not walk through the rows of seats (García, Campos, Campos, and Rojas, 1992, pp. 65–68).

The workbook proceeds to provide the reader with the opportunity to think through the same questions in his/her situation. Because each workbook consists of case studies derived directly from the research, teachers can self-evaluate as they answer the questions posed to them and as they reflect on the issues presented. Lastly, the workbooks attempt to help teachers develop a full understanding and efficient use of time, space, content, and behaviors by presenting problem-solving strategies they can use. The case of teacher 2 is characterized as follows:

The use of space in teacher 2's classroom appears to be more dynamic due to the flexibility which the teacher demonstrates in arranging groups. Children are formally seated in rows, by pairs, of different sexes, but this teacher uses a variety of seat arrangements for discussion, reading, seatwork, and whole-group discussion. Even her desk is used as a resource area from which reading lessons are conducted. The teacher frequently uses working centers and an area designated for free time, so that she can spend more time with the students needing attention and less with those working independently. The teacher in this class evaluates student work by moving between the rows of the different arrangements. While the two teachers' use of space is different, the fact that both use space similarly with regard to arranging straight rows, indicates that the second teacher appears to be more willing to experiment with the use of space for different tasks and activities. The classroom appears to constitute a context in which individuals move and live diverse experiences. Thus the use of space in relation to learning activities, requires planning for space to be used appropriately. Understanding how teachers can research the use of space in the classroom becomes a very valuable tool (García, Campos, Campos, and Rojas, 1992, pp. 69–73).

Once teachers read about these two teachers in unit 4, they are asked to consider some tasks in unit 5 in which they can observe their own classrooms, draw a map of their class, identify how they use space and materials, identify the mobility of their students as well as their own, and then answer a series of questions regarding the use of space. For example, "What criteria did you use to organize your students' seating arrangements? Does the distribution of the desks change in your class? In the planning of lessons? Do you become annoyed when the students stand and move from their seats? Always, sometimes, when?" (1992, p. 77). This is then followed by a series of tasks, which suggest that teachers use their observation notes, maps, and interviews of other teachers, determine the flexibility or rigidity in the use of space in their own classrooms, and draw conclusions about what can be done to change the space.

To help them think through these issues, in unit 6, teachers are asked to go through a checklist describing the use of space for their classrooms and are asked to use a guide to obtain student's input into how they think space in their classroom is being used. For example, the checklist includes the following statements:

- I don't move the students' desks around;
- I change my desk frequently;
- I organize the space in my classroom around groupwork;
- I use specific and defined spaces in order to control discipline;
- I use the blackboard for my lessons and I tend to place children at the front of the class;
- I seat them in the back of the class or I take them out of class.

Finally, in unit 7, teachers are exposed to the characteristics of efficient use of space in the classroom, which include good communication and interaction between students and teachers, greater participation, appropriate seating for different tasks, timeliness in didactic presentations, etc. Teachers are provided with different maps of the relationship of seating arrangements to teaching: circle, semi-circle, reading corners and working areas, block seating, and frontal seating. In addition, this unit provides a series of ideas and suggestions on developing learning centers and how they operate. The unit ends by raising the question: "How will I put into practice my newly acquired knowledge regarding the use of space? The answer will need to be constructed by you and your students." Unit 8 is an evaluation which teachers can use to assess what they have learned from the module on space. Teachers are provided with open-ended questions as guides to indicate the results of positive and negative outcomes for changing their space. Teachers are also asked to comment on statements regarding space and classroom climate, and are asked to qualify questions such as: "Why is it not fair to judge the movements of students within the classroom as only interferences in the teaching–learning process? What other purposes could these movements have? What types of learning are favored by group work? What are some of the criteria for organizing work in groups?"

Dissemination of Teacher Training Model. The Ministry of Education financed approximately ten training workshops, each with twenty to twenty-five teachers of marginal-urban schools, taught by the IIMEC team using the training modules, with the expectation that teachers could on their own focus on space, time, content, and behaviors while also researching their classrooms. In 1994 the three modules were further disseminated by the Ministry of Education when funding from UNESCO made possible an intervention at the institutional level. In this study all grades were to be impacted at one of the local schools using the research gained from this model. The IIMEC team of researchers chose a marginal-urban school where the findings and application of this research and development project could be studied in terms of institutional change. An entire school, from grades one through six, has been participating in a research program that will teach teachers how to be researchers and collaborators as well as how to become involved in teacher training and self-evaluation. This project has been under way for the past two years and the preliminary findings indicate that even with a national teachers' strike in 1995, twenty-five teachers at this school have successfully completed the research. Currently their work is being produced into a report for dissemination. Thus what began as a study of two teachers has now become a ten-year study of the development of reflective and action-oriented teachers.

Educational Implications of the Eight-Year Research and Development of a Teacher Training Model

From what was learned from the first and second research studies as well as the development of the teacher training model, the development of instructional materials, and the teacher training modules and workbooks, several implications useful to other ethnographers, trainers, and educators can be made:

1. The use of collaborative research. Collaborative research, which involves the participation of in-service teachers and researchers, can and does evolve into an action-research model, as has been demonstrated in these two studies. Collaborative research requires the building of trust, time, and skill development that is mutually shared and supported. This action research model entailed using the knowledge gained from participation as a group to advance the training of other teachers. It also enabled teachers to become researchers of their own knowledge and practice. More important, the research process involved re-

flection to action, that is, thinking through pedagogical practices within the context of available options, as well as reflection in action, recognizing the needed changes in pedagogical practice from peer and student feedback as well as one's own evaluation.

2. Understanding teachers' practice. Research of this type allows for a systematic analysis of how teachers think, act, reflect, and change their practices over time, and how they are able to transfer such learning to other teachers. The length of time spent in a given context such as the marginal-urban area allowed for the development of researcher sensitivities, which short-term ethnographic studies often bypass. The research suggests the need to develop research in contexts where teachers can have continuity and can actually observe their own interpretations of change. Otherwise, innovation in teaching becomes an isolated experience devoid of the critical feedback and group learning that it can stimulate.

3. Pedagogical investment over monetary gains. The engagement of teachers for pedagogical ends in this case superseded monetary gains. Although long-term research requires funding and resources for its initial development, it can also use human resources efficiently. Once teachers become involved in the process of doing their own research and reflection, they appear to be willing to participate actively in their own learning irrespective of funding or other incentives since it helps them gain useful knowledge for their practice. Thus the notion of more physical and plant resources may not necessarily be applicable when addressing teacher training needs. What seems to be more important is engaging teachers in their own process of learning and reflection, and this may be a process of "less is more, rather than more is less."

4. Teacher change and institutional change. This research also highlights the difficulty in implementing change at the school level independent of the influences of the institutional structure. This longitudinal development of a teacher training model shows the complexities of understanding change as an organic and reflective process that needs to be continuously revisited by teachers. Change in teachers' pedagogy requires change in the institutional structure, from hierachical and authoritative leadership to more open, horizontal team building, and from passive memoristic teaching to active teaching and learning. It is relationships of power and control that need to be fundamentally studied in depth, in order to uncover the ways in which research can help mobilize teachers, students, and parents to action.

5.   Impact on personal and professional perspectives. Collaborations of the type engendered by this research help teachers change their personal and professional perspectives. Through one of the videotapes produced at the end of the teachers' experiences in 1991, it was evident that teachers assessed as their personal and professional changes, having gained a sense of self-confidence in conducting research and knowing they had the ability to change their teaching.

6.   Local development of qualitative research. Long-term intervention research like the study presented herein generates interest in ethnographic research from a global perspective, since international literature on ethnographic research is applied to the context of Costa Rican life. From the initial introduction of qualitative research through foreign sources, educators from abroad, and trainers, the researchers in this study have been able to develop their own local process for conducting ethnographic research and for developing teacher training that speaks to the specific needs of Costa Rican reality. The need for cross-fertilization of innovative ethnographic theories and methods is evident from the outcomes of the eight-year research studies.

7.   Consciousness-raising: learning to teach. Finally, such research leads to pedagogocial consciousness-raising and what still needs to be learned. Some of the teachers in this study have only begun to uncover the power of teaching. And in the case of one of the teachers, who was interviewed and visited after training, her thirst to learn about how to be the best teacher possible was still not quenched. Teaching is not only a continuous but an arduous process that requires a great deal of observation, peer observation, self-reflection, critique, and development of knowledge base and action. The need to support such learning is in the best interest of students and families.

Conclusion

The first research study began with the simple notion of finding out why students in marginal-urban areas fared as poorly as they did on the national survey studies the IIMEC had conducted. The need to understand what went on in marginal-urban classrooms that would explain such situations revealed that not only is there a culture of the classroom in which language is used by teachers for control and teaching, but there is also the language of learning of students, which requires understanding the pedagogical styles of teachers and the issues they face in negotiating space, time, content, and student behaviors. These needs led to the development of the second study. From these two studies covering eight years, an intervention model for teacher training emerged, which has been expanded and developed into practical teacher training modules with workbooks. The fact that these teacher modules are now being implemented in a school at an institutional level, from grades one to six, speaks to the benefits arising from collaborative research. Ethnographic research has proven to be a useful tool in uncovering the concrete experiences in the interactions of marginal-urban students and their teachers, but, more significantly, it has also contributed to a process that has taken on a life of its own in advancing the knowledge of teachers and their pedagogical practice (García, Rojas, Campos, Campos, and Brenes, 1993). In this regard the eight years that have transpired in understanding marginal-urban classrooms have affected not only the schools, students, and teachers but the researchers as well. Ethnographic research has come of age in Costa Rica and it is being used to create needed change.[14]

Notes

The teachers who participated in this study, both as researchers and as trained teachers, are thanked for their willing collaboration and quest for knowledge. The authors of this study worked with the editorial assistance and guidance of Dr. Martha Montero-Sieburth, who initiated the first qualitative research courses in Costa Rica, trained many of the members of the IIMEC in ethnographic research and curriculum design, provided feedback and research literature support, and worked closely with the IIMEC research group during the evolution of this project.

1. The Census Bureau in Costa Rica does not use race as a characteristic to describe the Costa Rican population. Blacks are simply identified as Costa Rican nationals and Indians are identified only in terms of the numbers who live on reservations. Hence the U.S. typology using racial identifiers does not apply.

2. The standards of poverty applied here are based on limited indicators of basic necessities and constitute 30 to 38 percent of the total families. However, if calculated by poverty level indicators, such poverty is between 27 and 25 percent. If both indicators are combined, then the level of poverty for all families in Costa Rica is 38 percent (Segunda Vice-Presidencia de la Republica de Costa Rica, 1994).

3. The Institute for the Improvement of Costa Rican Education, or IIMEC, was created under the auspices of the University of Costa Rica in 1979 as the country's premier research institute to conduct educational research. Since then other universities in Costa Rica have developed their own research centers.

4. The term marginal-urban is used as a category by the Ministry of Health to distinguish among diverse communities based on their socioeconomic status. It includes factors such as housing, access to health services, occupation of dwellers, and income levels.

5. As a consequence of the dire results in these studies, a national program of achievement tests was enacted under the presidency of Oscar Arias in 1987.

6. Among one of the first introductory seminars in qualitative research, action research, and participative research to be offered was the Curso de Capacitación en Investigación Cualitativa (Training in Qualitative Research), sponsored by the Organization of American States, the Regional Program on Educational Development, the Multinational Center in Educational Research (now defunct), and the Ministry of Education, January 14–18, 1985. Using local faculty, which included José Antonio Camacho, Yolanda Rojas, and

Rolando Pinto, the participants had lectures, discussions, and group work on the following topics: the epistemological notions underlying qualitative research; action research; qualitative research methods; application of qualitative research to education; analysis of qualitative research design; and comparisons between qualitative and quantitative research. Much of the instructional mimeographed materials consisted of translated works by North American ethnographers such as Ray Rist, Perti Pelto, and Charles Osgood, and publications of Latin American action researchers such as Silvia Manfredi, Carlos Rodrigues Brandao, Joao Bosco Pinto, and Ernesto Cohen.

7. Montero-Sieburth, Martha. Visiting Professor. "Qualitative Research: Theory and Methods," course offered by the IIMEC at the University of Costa Rica, sponsored by the University of Costa Rica, the University of Heredia, and the Costa Rican Science and Technology Council, Summer 1984; "The Use of Qualitative Research in Curriculum Design," course offered at the University of Costa Rica, sponsored by the National University in Heredia and the University of Costa Rica, 1986.

8. The first micro-ethnographic study was financed by a grant from the Office of the Vice-President for Research at the University of Costa Rica from 1985 to 1989.

9. Costa Rica has 3,300,000 inhabitants, of which one million are under the age of 15. Half a million are in preschool and elementary school; 150,000 are at the high school level.

10. The term *focal* is applied in anthropology and education to specific informants who are participants in a study and who meet a series of criteria that the researchers have previously identified.

11. The second research project was supported by a grant from the International Development Research Centre, Canada, and the Office of the Vice President for Research at the University of Costa Rica from 1990 to 1993.

12. *Filo* refers to "being hungry" in the colloquial Spanish of Costa Rica.

13. In 1991 a Seminar on Qualitative Research in Latin-American Education, under the auspices of the Centre for International Research and Development from Ottawa, Ontario, Canada, the Vice Chancellor's Office of Research at the University of Costa Rica and the Vice Chancellor's Office for Social Action at the University of Costa Rica, as well as the IIMEC, took place in San José, Costa Rica, on October 18–20; the proceedings were later published as a memoir. Such work indicates the growth and expansion of qualitative research in Costa Rica and throughout Central America.

14. There is a great deal of experimentation occurring in qualitative research in Costa Rica. Currently there are several theoretical and methodological influences evident in Costa Rican qualitative research. For example, the work of the East Anglia University group in CARE is being used by some researchers at the Centro de Investigación y Desarrollo Educativo (Center for Research and Educational Development) at the National University in Heredia. The IIMEC research team is recognized for its impact on the development of teacher training and its sociolinguistic focus. Other researchers are using the work of Kenneth Tobin on constructivism at the National University in Heredia. Yet some individual researchers prefer to combine different approaches while purporting to maintain a "nationalistic" brand of qualitative research.

References

Assaél, J. et al. (1983). *La cultura del fracaso escolar.* Chile: Red Latinoamericana de Investigaciones Cualitativas de la Realidad Escolar.

Avalos, B. (1985). Training for better teaching in the word: Lesson from research. *Teaching and Teacher Education,* 1(4), 289–299.

Brenes, M., Campos, N., García, N., and Rojas, M. (1987). Interacción verbal en el aula: Análisis microetnográfico de una escuela de una comunidad urbano-marginal en Costa Rica. Trabajo presentado en el Cuarto Encuentro Nacional y Primero Centroamericano de Investigadores de Educación, C.I.P.E.T. Alajuela, Costa Rica.

Brenes, M., Campos, N., García, N., and Rojas, M. (1988). Interacción verbal en el aula: Análisis microetnográfico de una escuela de una comunidad urbana marginal en Costa Rica.

Informe Final. IIMEC. Vicerrectoría de Investigación, San José, Costa Rica: Universidad de Costa Rica.

Brenes, M., García, N., Rojas, M., and Campos, N. (1991). Memoria del Seminario: La Investigación Cualitativa en la Educacion Latinoamericana. San José, Costa Rica: Universidad de Costa Rica, Facultad de Educación. Instituto de Investigación para el Mejoramiento de la Educación Costarricense.

Brophy, J.E. (1987). Teacher behavior and its effects. *Journal of Educational Psychology,* 71, 733–750.

Campos, N. (1991a). Estilos de enseñanza-aprendizaje en aulas de escuelas ubicadas en zonas urbano-marginales. *Revista Educación,* 15(2), 32–45.

Campos, N. (1991b). Training teachers in urban-marginal city schools: An ethnographic study in Costa Rica. *Journal of Global Education,* 4(2), 19–28.

Campos, N. (1993). Un Modelo para Capacitación de Maestros, In *Conocimiento, Participación y Cambio.* San José: Editorial Universidad de Costa Rica.

Campos, N.(1995). Caracterización de los procesos de enseñanza-aprendizaje, a partir del análisis de la interacción verbal en el aula costarricense. *Revista de Filología,* 10, 1–26.

Campos, N. and Rojas, M. (1993). Caracterización microetnográfico del aula escolar al diseño de un plan de capacitación. *Revista Educación,* 17(2), 111–118.

Cazden, C. et al. (1986). Classroom discourse. In M. Wittrock (Ed.), *Handbook of research on teaching* (pp. 432–463). New York: Macmillan.

Costa Rica, Ministerio de Economía, Industria y Comercio. (1995). *Costa Rica cálculo de población por provincia, cantón y distrito.* San José, Costa Rica: Dirección General de Estadística y Censos.

Costa Rica, Plan de Regionalización del Sistema Educativo en la Educación (1993). *Revista Interamericana de Desarrollo Educativo,* 88, 24–39.

Darcy de Oliveira, R. and Darcy de Oliveira, M. (1982). The militant observer: A sociological alternative. In *Creating knowledge: A monopology?* Toronto, Ontario, Canada: International Council for Adult Education.

De Shutter, A. (1983). *Investigación Participativa: Una Opción Metodológica para la Educación de Adultos.* Pátzcuaro, Michoacán, México: CREFAL.

Doyle, W. (1986). Classroom organization and management. In M. Wittrock (Ed.), *Handbook of research on teaching* (pp. 392–431). New York: Macmillan.

Erickson, F. (1973). What makes school ethnography "ethnographic"? *Anthropology and Educational Quarterly,* 4(2), 10–19.

Esquivel, J.M. (1986). Situación de la educación pre-universitaria en Costa Rica. Working Document. San José: Universidad de Costa Rica, IIMEC.

Esquivel, J.M. and Brenes, M. (1988). Gender differences in achievement in Costa Rican students: Science, mathematics and Spanish. Paper presented at the Annual Meeting of the National Association for Research in Science Teaching, Lake of the Ozarks, Missouri, April 10–13.

Esquivel, J.M., Delgado, V., and Peralta, T. (1983). Diagnóstico Evaluativo de la enseñanza de las matemáticas en la educación general básica y educación diversificada. Working Document. Instituto Investigación para el Mejoramiento de la Educación Costarricense (IIMEC). San José: Universidad de Costa Rica.

Esquivel, J.M. and Quesada, L. (1984). Diagnóstico evaluativo de la enseñanza de las ciencias generales en la educación general básica, rendimiento académico y procesos científicos. San José: Universidad de Costa Rica, IIMEC.

Fals Borda, O. (1979). Por la praxis: El problema de cómo investigarla realidad para transformarla. Bogotá, Colombia: Ediciones Tercer Mundo.

García, N. and Brenes, M. (1992a). Hacia la construcción de un concepto del uso eficiente del espacio. Paper presented at the VI Encuentro de Investigadores en Educación, San José, Costa Rica.

García, N. and Brenes, M. (1992b). El cambio en educación: Análisis cualtiativo de una experiencia de intervención en el aula. San José: Editorial de la Universidad de Costa Rica.

García, N., Campos, N., Campos, E., and Rojas, M. (1992). *Conocimientos, participación y cambio: Espacio en el aula.* IIMEC, Editorial de la Universidad de Costa Rica, San José.

García, N. and Rojas, M. (1993). La capacitación del maestro desde la perspectiva etnográfica. *Revista Educación.* San José: Universidad de Costa Rica.

García, N., Rojas, M., and Campos, N. (1989). La eficiencia del proceso de enseñanza-aprendizaje: aportes para la capacitación de maestros de escuelas urbano-marginales. Proyecto IIMEC, San José: Universidad de Costa Rica.

García, N., Rojas, M., Campos, N., and Brenes, M. (1991). La eficiencia del proceso enseñanza-aprendizaje: Generando currículum a partir de del dato microetnográfico. In *Memoria del Seminario La Investigación Cualitativa en la Educación Latinoamericana.* pp. 193–204. San José: Universidad de Costa Rica.

García, N., Rojas, M., Campos, N., Campos, E. and Brenes, M. (1993) *Conocimiento, participacion y cambio: Capacitación de docentes a partir de la Investigación en el aula.* IIMEC. Editorial de la Universidad de Costa Rica, San José.

García, N., Rojas, M., Campos, N., Brenes, M., and Campos, E. (1994). *Conocimiento, participacion y cambio: Comportamientos en el aula.* IIMEC, Editorial de la Universidad de Costa Rica, San José.

Hymes, Dell. (1985). *La Sociolingüística.* Barcelona: Editorial Amagrama.

Instituto Mixto de Ayuda Social. (1994). Presidencia Ejecutiva. Programa de Reformulación Institucional, San José, Costa Rica.

López, G. et al. (1984). *La Cultura Escolar Responsable del Fracaso?* Chile: Programa Interdisciplinario de Investigaciones en Educación.

Magendzo, A. (1986). *Currículum y Cultura en América Latina.* Chile: Programa Interdisciplinario de Investigaciones en Educación.

Montero-Sieburth, M. (1984). La investigación cualitativa en el campo educativo de Latinoamérica. *Boletín,* 20 (August), 117–129. Centro de Documentación del Centro Multinacional de Investigación Educativa (CEMIE), Proyecto del Programa Regional de Desarrollo Educativo de la Organización de los Estados Americanos y el Ministerio de Educación Pública, San José, Costa Rica.

Montero-Sieburth, M. et al. (1989). *Classroom management: Instructional strategies and the allocation of learning resources.* Harvard Institute for International Development, Harvard Graduate School of Education and Office of Education, Bureau for Science and Technology, United States Agency for International Development. April, No. 4, pp. 1–31.

Montero-Sieburth, M. (1992). Enfoque y Reflexión en la Investigación Cualitativa. En Memoria del Seminario, "La Investigación Cualitativa en la Educación Latinoamericana" (pp. 21–46). San José: Universidad de Costa Rica.

Montero-Sieburth, M. (1997). Reclaiming indigenous cultures: Students' oral histories in Talamanca, Costa Rica. In A.E. Robertson and D. Bloome (Eds.), *Students as researchers of language and culture in their own communities.* New York: Hampden Press.

Palmer, P. and Alumnos del Colegio Técnico Profesional Agropecuario de Talamanca. *Nuestra Talamanca . . . Ayer y Hoy.* Proyecto de Investigaciones sobre la Historia Local del Cantón de Talamanca, 1981–1982. Coopetalamanca, R. L. Inter-American Foundation, and Ministerio de Educación Pública, San José, Costa Rica.

Pinto, R. (1985). Algunos problemas epistemológicos y metodológicos que surgen del actual nivel de desarrollo de la llamada Investigación Participativa en América Latina. En *Revista Educación,* IX(1&2), 7–21.

Pinto, R. (1986). *La Investigación Participativa en la Educación entre Adultos.* Centro Multinacional de Investigación Educativa, CEMIE-PROCAMIE, Organización de Estados Americanos, Ministerio de Educación Pública, No. 130, San José, Costa Rica.

Rojas, M., Garcia, N., and Brenes, M. (1992) Conocimiento, participación y cambio: Tiempo en en el aula. IIMEC, Editorial de la Universidad de Costa Rica, San José.

Rojas, M., García, N., Campos, N., and Brenes, M. (1991). Interacción verbal en el aula: Análisis mircoetnográfico de una escuela de comunidad urbano-marginal de Costa Rica. In *Memoria del Seminario La Investigación Cualitativa en la Educación Latinoamericana* (pp. 125–140). San José, Costa Rica: Editorial Universidad de Costa Rica.

Rojas, M., García, N., Campos, N., and Brenes, M. (1992). Funciones del lenguaje en el aula. *Revista Educación,* 16(1), 45–56. San José: Editorial Universidad de Costa Rica.

Rojas, M., García, N. and Fajardo, D. (1985). Diagnóstico evaluativo de la enseñanza del Español en la educación general básica y la educación diversificada: Rendimiento académico. Working Document. Institute de Investigación para el Mejoramiento de la Educación Costarricense (IIEMC), Universidad de Costa Rica, San José.

Rosenshine, B.V. (1979). Content, time and direct instruction. In P.L. Peterson and H. J. Walberg (Eds.), *Research on teaching: Concepts, findings and applications.* Berkeley, CA: McCutcham.

Sanguinetty, J. (1992). *La Crísis de la Educación en América Latina: La Restricción Financieray el Dilema de la Calidad versus la Cobertura.* Washington, D.C.: U.S. Agency for International Development.

Saville-Troike, M. (1982). *La etnografía de la communicación: Una introducción.* Baltimore: Basil Blackwell.

Schön, Donald A. (1983). *The reflective practitioner. How professionals think in action.* New York: Basic Books.

Segunda Vice Presidencia de la República de Costa Rica. (1994). Consejo Social: Plan Nacional de Combate a la Pobreza: Hacia una Costa Rica Integrada por las Oportunidades. San José, Costa Rica.

Silviera, V.E. (1985). La investigación participativa: algunas consideraciones sobre su aplicación a nivel local. Documento de Trabajo No. 3. Pátzcuaro, Michoacán, México: CREFAL.

Spradley, J. and McCurdy, D. (1972). *The cultural experience.* Chicago: Science Research Associates.

Stubbs, M. (1984). *Lenguaje y escuela: Análisis Sociolingüístico de la Enseñanza.* Madrid: Editorial Cincel-Kapeluz.

Appendix

Stages of Development of Research

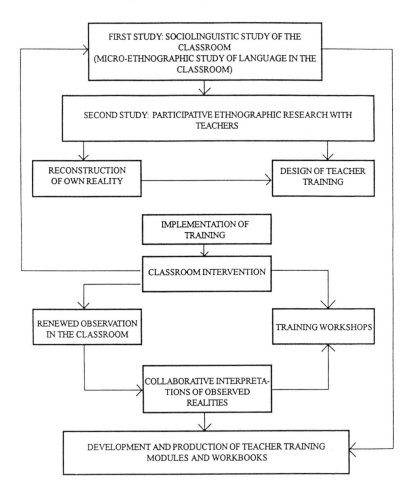

Conclusion
The Emerging Latin American
Paradigm in Qualitative Research

Martha Montero-Sieburth and Gary L. Anderson

From the chapters included in this volume, it is clear that a new paradigm for qualitative research is emerging throughout Latin America, a paradigm that includes many of the ideological and epistemological struggles experienced by North American ethnographers who rejected positivism, but that is nonetheless firmly grounded in the historical and educational contexts of Latin America, the persistent dominance of positivist research, and the social and cultural conditions of class, influence, and power.

As has been echoed throughout this volume, during the past thirty years qualitative research in Latin America emerges through different sources—traditional anthropology; sociolinguistics; sociology; the influence of international agencies; and contractual arrangements demanding greater community participation; community development projects such as the *comunidades de base* (communities undergoing changes through the influence of liberation theology); activists in women's and parents' groups; and political groups seeking approaches that best represent their positions.

The emergence of qualitative research in education is closely associated with the historical and political development of research in Latin American countries. The research of Souza Lima in Brazil, and Zorrilla, Bertely, and Corenstein in Mexico demonstrates the degree of acceptance qualitative research has received in the research arena and shows how it corresponds to the historical and social/cultural evolution of education in each country. Souza Lima's contribution to qualitative research stems from her understanding of Brazil's historical and political backdrop of the 1960s to the present and her presentation of students/teachers' understandings of the social construction of knowledge and meaning. Zorrilla, on the other hand, applies Durkheim's concept of anomie to describe the conditions that resulted from politically motivated reforms at the high school level. Bertely and Corenstein's description of qualitative research, and spe-

cifically ethnography in Mexico, provides a panoramic view of its development as well as the concrete realities that indigenous groups face as they
confront the dilemmas of assimilation, accomodation, and resistance to
the dominant groups in Mexican society. Such groundings of ethno-
historical accounts, combined with theoretical and social constructions of
knowledge, are indicative of the experimentation and applications of qualitative research currently taking place in Latin America.

The acceptance of qualitative research in Latin American educational
and academic terrains, however, is not without opposition and struggle.
Qualitative research emerges in the midst of the pervasive science-driven
quantitative research dominating Latin America. In the minds of many it
has become closely associated with academic and community leftist positions, making its legitimation even more difficult. At the same time it has
been taken up by diverse research institutes and programs as the newest
innovation in research.

Its emergence and development in academic circles, particularly research institutes and centers, is most likely due to a unified anti-positivist,
anti-hierarchical, and anti-authoritarian response by educators and researchers alike, who are seeking to find answers to intractable social and educational questions that quantitative research has not been able to address. Its
development in some research centers has been made possible through the
efforts of small groups of committed researchers who have sought funding
to stabilize the introduction and evolution of qualitative research in their
milieu. In some instances it has been the work of ethnographers with teachers that has had widespread appeal (Achilli, 1996), and in other instances
it has been the transfer of such knowledge to understanding the workplace
conditions of teachers and administrators that has galvanized and raised
awareness of the field over time. This has certainly been the case for the
DIE as documented in Elsie Rockwell's chapter.

Traditional educational ethnography continues to develop in interesting directions. A second generation of educational ethnographers has
apprenticed with veteran DIE ethnographers such as Elsie Rockwell, Ruth
Paradise, Ruth Mercado, Eduardo Remedi, Antonia Candela, and others.
For example, Maria Bertely, who worked with Ruth Paradise on research
with the Mazahua, is extending theories of the role of schools in cultural
adaptation and challenging findings of North American researchers such
as Margaret Gibson, John Ogbu, and Jim Cummins (Bertely, 1992).
Antonia Candela and others are using discourse analysis and micro-
ethnography (Candela, 1994). Ruth Mercado has recently applied the work

of Mikhail Bakhtin to a study of teacher knowledge. The work of Clifford Geertz, Agnes Heller, and Antonio Gramsci continues to influence this group of ethnographers.

Qualitative research has also explored the possibilities of postmodern and feminist theory. Jacobo (1994), drawing on the postmodern writings of Lyotard, Lacan, and the Mexican Carlos Fuentes, calls for qualitative researchers to

> . . . *opt for pluralism: the heterogeneous, the ever changing, the uncertain, the explosive, the discontinuous, and to proclaim the RIGHT TO DIFFERENCE. After all, if we find this condition in the social, economic and political world around us; in the mobilization of social movements by marginalized groups who are different and excluded by a normalizing society (gays, sweatshop workers, retired persons, people living with AIDS, etc.), then there is no reason to believe that it shouldn't also exist in our own house—in the construction of knowledge, in educational research. . . . We are confronted with a wave of diverse studies in the field of education. Let's welcome them in the spirit of the right to be different (Jacobo, 1994, p. 87).*

More surprising to Jacobo than the external critics of methodological diversity are the internal criticisms coming from within qualitative research. Why, she asks, do qualitative researchers dedicate so much energy to justifying their methods from the validity criteria of scientific discourses?

> *The contribution of Lyotard helps to problematize the issue of validity. For Lyotard, it is more relevant to see such issues as representing different language games with different rules. That is, the production of scientific knowledge is just one of many different discourses or language games that one might play (Jacobo, 1994, p. 89).*

This new diversity has encouraged qualitative researchers, most of whom are women, to explore issues of gender in education. Besides the focus on women of the chapters by Schmukler and Stromquist in this volume, Delgado Ballesteros (1994) describes an incipient but vibrant ethnographic research program on women in education (Cortina, 1984; Sandoval, 1992; Delgado Ballesteros, 1993). Latin American researchers are documenting the ways women are discriminated against in classrooms and society (Delgado Ballesteros, 1993) and also the ways they are proactive in schools (Medina, 1993) and professional organizations (Sandoval, 1992).

Unlike many of their North American counterparts, Latin American feminists and critical theorists tend to view schools as relatively progressive environments for students when compared to the cultural messages that Latin American girls and working-class youth get through other social institutions, such as the church and the home.

While in North America studies of social production have now challenged the notion that students are passively reproduced in schools, the reconceptualization of schools as possibly progressive spaces from which to launch social projects that depend on "critical rationality" is intriguing. This return to a more social reconstructivist notion of schools would be helpful in meeting the challenges of the environment, increased social class and racial polarization, and other crises facing North America. Even for those less optimistic that the nature of schooling would allow such activism, it is becoming increasingly clear that, given current tendencies toward privatization, educators may have to defend the very public spaces that schooling provides while simultaneously critiquing its worst excesses (Berliner and Biddle, 1995; Meier, 1995).

Latin American qualitative research that focuses on public schools is taking up many of the same issues as North American research, in part because the blurring of public and private sectors is a product of neoliberal policies that seek ultimately to open up public schools to market forces. In the age of the North American Free Trade Agreement (NAFTA), North and Latin American researchers will increasingly need to dialogue with each other to help sort out these complex issues.

This dialogue is currently occurring on the U.S.–Mexican border. Led by Beatriz Calvo at the University of Ciudad Juarez and the Institute of Border Studies in Caléxico, California, groups of qualitative researchers from both sides of the border are meeting regularly to discuss their research. Calvo (1994; in press), Gómez Montero (1994), and others are providing ethnographic accounts of education in the border area.

The acceptance of qualitative research is also a departure from the more traditional imposition of research models from industrialized countries through international agencies, researchers, and contracts, which dominated much of Latin American educational development prior to the 1970s. Qualitative research in education in Latin America becomes accepted pragmatically as an innovative process that can attempt to answer questions about education that quantitative research cannot answer. Concerns about what goes on in schools, how children fail, how teaching and learning occur in classrooms, and how teachers understand their students are issues that drove early ethnographic studies in Latin America.

Yet another way that qualitative research becomes appropriated throughout Latin America is by becoming its own amalgamation of theory, method, and practice. Even when European and North American influences can be identified in the theories and methods used to inform the research, qualitative research in education in diverse Latin American contexts is thought of as a local and/or national asset. A case in point is Paulo Freire's work in literacy which, although highly influenced by Feuerbach, Marx, and Gramsci from Europe, emerged from Latin American traditions such as liberation theology and grass-roots literacy campaigns to ultimately become a Latin American model worthy of consideration in other countries (McLaren and Lankshear, 1994; Escobar et al., 1994) This blending of theory, method, and practice in Latin American qualitative research in education converges to create qualitative research prototypes, which, in order to justify their use, take on a national or local identity. Hence the theory of teachers' constructivism from North American researchers such as Kenneth Tobin or critical pedagogy from North American theorists such as Henry Giroux and Peter McLaren (themselves heavily endebted to Freire's work) or British ethnographers such as Sara Delamont or Paul Atkinson are appropriated and modified in local application to assume a national or local character in Latin American qualitative research.

Contributions of the Field

Today qualitative research in education in Latin America is recognized for its eclecticism of theories and methods, its adaptability and widespread application in diverse contexts, and in some cases its syncretism with quantitative research. The current information exchange via computer networks and programs has further enhanced its opportunities for impact in the academic and research communities throughout Latin America. As in North America and Europe, qualitative research in education in Latin America has gained a strong following that continues to grow in academic and community circles. Whether the field is now beyond criticisms of the faddism of "blitzkrieg" ethnography in which everyone is doing qualitative research but may not be as concerned with its inherent theoretical and methodological traditions, or whether the field has now moved to a stage where the epistemological basis of qualitative research has greater appeal beyond academic researchers to include teachers and community members as researchers is hard to define. What is evident is that qualitative research is fast becoming a research alternative in the traditional domains of research in Latin America. Its variety and growing eclecticism is fast becoming the norm, and even though it may be difficult to identify the many approaches and experiments that go under the term *qualitative research*, it has nevertheless captured the attention of educators, community people, academicians, bureaucrats, and policy makers as a bona fide research orientation. To what degree will qualitative research be influential in defining Latin American education? How will it help shape the educational policies and practices of the future? These are questions that will need to be closely monitored in the implementation of qualitative research over the years.

One of the purposes of this book has been to demonstrate the widespread use of qualitative research by different Latin American researchers and possibly to impact North American and European researchers. Another purpose has been to capture some of the findings that cut across subfields and present a growing body of knowledge that qualitative researchers have produced. It would seem presumptuous on our part to predict where qualitative research in education might go in the next century, especially given the changes the field is undergoing and its reinvention in different contexts. Yet despite our limited knowledge of its future directions and influences, there are some discernible trends and contributions that qualitative research in Latin America is making and that may be of interest to other qualitative researchers.

Montero-Sieburth (1992, 1993) provided overviews of the trends, influences, and contributions that British and North American traditions in qualitative research have made in the field, and identified the emerging traditions being shaped in Latin America. In reviewing the extent to which qualitative research can benefit from the cross-fertilization of ideas from North American researchers and Latin American researchers, she identified the following issues as important for future Latin American qualitative researchers:

1. The importance of context in defining qualitative research for Latin America, that is, an awareness of the social, economic, ideological, and political pressures that allow for its emergence.
2. The need to analyze the specific local context in which qualitative research is to be used, since qualitative research in Honduras may be quite different from that in Brazil, and the transfer of its theory and method will need to be adjusted to the reality in which it unfolds.

3. The need to disseminate qualitative research beyond the institutional walls of universities as tools for those who need to understand its application and formulation of action.

4. The creation of communication networks that are collaborative in nature so that qualitative research can be reinvented in appropriate contexts.

5. The need to identify qualitative research models that are relevant to the realities of Latin American countries.

6. The need to develop clear understandings of the use of theory and method in qualitative research so that the intent with which it is being conducted is appropriate to answer the research question(s) formulated.

7. An understanding of diverse methods of qualitative research in fieldwork so that its use is understood by those participating as well as those carrying out the research and so that the methods sustain the research's validity and reliability.

8. The development of collaborative research in the truest sense, involving participants in the stages of design, planning, implementation, and evaluation of the research process.

9. The recovery of research processes from oral traditions, case studies, and oral narratives of everyday life.

10. A recognition of the vulnerability of the researcher and participants in the research process and the need to openly discuss roles and responsibilities in developing the research process.

We hope to advance these contributions by including the lessons provided by the authors in this volume as well as the caveats that need to be considered. We conclude with several open-ended questions for readers to consider in furthering the dialogue that we hope has been begun by this book.

Current Issues in Latin American Qualitative Research in Education

From reading the authors in this volume, it becomes clear that Latin American qualitative research in education has raised several issues that further contribute to our understanding of the field. The following are some of the main areas that the authors have individually or collectively identified:

I. Understanding the Significance of Context.

Conducting qualitative research in Latin American education is necessarily context-specific in the sense that while patterns can be identified and shared regarding classroom culture, teachers' pedagogy, and students' behavior, the specific situation in which such interactions unfold cannot be commonly characterized across contexts. For this reason, there exists a growing phenomenon of identifying the particularities of given situations, their descriptions and interpretations. What is being learned is that to transfer qualitative research from one country or region to another requires an understanding of the contextual variables in which the research was done and, hence, the variability of description and interpretations. Results of studies of classrooms in the Andean region of South America may be quite different from those conducted in Central America or other Latin American countries, even though they may share some general linguistic and cultural characteristics. This makes the very notion of the focus of this volume—Latin American qualitative research—problematic. Thus non–Latin American researchers should assume that there is perhaps as much variability within studies in Latin America as there is between Latin America and North America. We do agree, however, with Juan Carlos Tedesco (see introduction) that there are sufficient commonalities among Latin Americans to warrant making some generalizations toward a paradigm of research more appropriate to the social and cultural realities found in Latin American education.

II. Using Qualitative Research to Focus on Underrepresented Groups within Latin America

One of the most evident contributions of Latin American qualitative research in education is the focus on underrepresented groups. From the initial qualitative research projects in education, attention has been directed to understanding the plight of marginalized and underrepresented groups. Studies of the poor, the disenfranchised, or those who were failing in schools and classrooms became commonplace. Such concern has clearly signaled both a growing interest and a need to invest in the education of those who have received insufficient attention and resources.

Qualitative research has also served to identify throughout Latin America the persistence of oppressed groups, whether the Mazahua Indians of Mexico, through the research of Ruth Paradise and Maria Berteley, or the research of Beatriz Schmukler on the role of women in the democratization of social institutions in Argentina. By recounting the experiences of migration and empowerment processes through ethnographic studies, such groups become a focus of social concern, particularly in countries where the social and political pressures from outside their spheres exert influence. Thus qualitative research has become a powerful tool for documenting the existence, survival, and resistance of oppressed groups in Latin America.

III. The Relation of Qualitative Research to Critical Consciousness Raising
From Beatriz Avalos's initial studies in classrooms during the 1980s to those currently reviewed in this volume, qualitative research in education in Latin America demonstrates a departure from the assumption that education was serving the interests of all Latin American students to a questioning of whose interests were best served by education. Moreover, case studies of poverty and disenfranchised students began to call attention to unequal class and cultural capital distribution. Such research began to support the notion that education meant more than being *instruido*, being well instructed, to being well-educated and critical knowers.

The appearance of the first qualitative studies focusing on the "culture of failure" in some schools represented a radical shift from the assumed pedagogical delivery taking place under a centralized system of education (Avalos, 1989). Rather than accepting the knowledge base, codified and distributed in schools through teachers, as a taken-for-granted situation, qualitative research began to explore the ways knowledge was constructed in specific teaching and learning interactions. Inequities in knowledge production and distribution in marginal-urban and peripheral regions began to surface through such studies as well as the contradictions identified in equitable educational delivery (Oyola, et al., 1994).

More important, what qualitative research began to show was that transfer of knowledge within schools did not need to be unidirectional and linear, from teachers to students. Identifying and documenting not only what the experiences of students were but how they were socialized through student–teacher interactions, recognizing the use of language as control and the negative as well as positive conditions for learning, promoted the search for explanations that went beyond blaming the students. Blaming teachers was also avoided through in-depth analyses of teachers' professional lives, gender relations, workplace conditions, and labor unions.

Just how widespread such understanding has become is difficult to judge, but it is clear that the lens through which the problems of teaching and learning can be viewed takes on not only different agendas but also different proportions within Latin American qualitative research in education. The focus on a variety of epistemological frameworks allows for questions to be generated that attempt not only to identify patterns within social settings but, more important, to ask why these patterns persist.

IV. Networks of Scholars, Researchers, and Community Members

With the help of computer networks and Web sites, the possibility of creating networks of scholars, researchers, and community members who have access to critical data and information about qualitative research becomes increasingly important. Obtaining updated information on the most recent research has been one of the most difficult tasks for Latin American researchers. With the advent of the REDUC networks and published Latin American journals, extant literature on qualitative research is now more readily available. This flow of information, and marketing of innovative programs such as Ethnograph, Hypertext, and Qualpro, are allowing Latin American ethnographers to have the latest technology at their disposal. It also allows ethnographers from North America and Europe to have access to the issues and questions that qualitative researchers in Latin America confront. Network communication has superseded the more traditional flow of information of graduates attending U.S.-based institutions and returning to their home countries to reinvent qualitative research in those arenas. It can be expected that the information sites will engender a different approach to qualitative research in the future and that it will be as advanced as the technology and human resources available to support it.

V. The Contributions of Qualitative Research in the Democratization of Knowledge Production and Use

Although we do not know to what degree qualitative research can be linked to the democratization of knowledge production and its use throughout Latin America, a task that would require tracking previous levels of democratic participation, it does appear that increasing importance is being given to the knowledge production and decision making of teachers, students, parents, and administrators.

The value and appreciation for how knowledge is constructed, particularly as socially constituted acts, is demonstrated through Souza Lima's case study in this book, and through the eight-year analysis of teachers' language, discourse, and reflective action in the two Costa Rican qualitative studies. These examples seem to suggest that knowledge production is organically driven in the one case, and in the case of the two Costa Rican studies, the ways teachers use language for social control have direct impact on classroom teaching and learning, which can unfold into questioning why such occurrences take place.

How qualitative research is introduced to teachers and parents and how it is used by them also appears to be acquiring new meaning, not only for the researchers but also for those participating in the research. Thus one of the impacts that qualitative research appears to be making is helping researchers learn how to collaborate. In Latin America such an impact translates into opening up new spaces for dialogue. Consequently community members, teachers, or educators who participate in qualitative research and especially in teamwork seem to be finding their voices as they describe their situations, identify the issues to be studied, and research their questions. This contrasts with the way that knowledge production along hierarchical systems has prevailed throughout Latin America. Qualitative research may be providing the forum in which knowledge from grassroots efforts can be heard and taken seriously by those in power. If such permutation continues to occur, a stronger orientation with actions toward democratization is sure to be developed.

VI. The Role of Participants at Different Stages of Research
Design, Implementation, Analysis, and Dissemination
within Latin American Qualitative Research
This issue is closely related to the previous one. The role participants assume in the research and fieldwork process is an arena of growing concern that will need to be closely examined. What is envisioned as full participation in the different stages of research design, implementation, analysis, and dissemination is still in need of being worked out in qualitative research throughout Latin America. What types of membership can be afforded participants in the field? At what stage of the research process do participants begin to have voice? What are the role shifts that are to be expected at different stages of research? These are some of the questions voiced by several of the authors of this volume. How teachers, parents, or students become incorporated into the research as co-researchers is increasingly being discussed. Some answers are being found in the longstanding tradition in Latin America of participatory action research.

Participatory action research, which grew out of an interest in popular education in Latin America, was extensively theorized during the 1980s, but relatively few studies were documented. According to Salinas (1993), the few studies that were published were difficult to access and many lacked methodological rigor. Entering the 1990s, however, the popular education movement and the participatory research methods associated with it have made inroads into attempting to define a research paradigm that responds to the Latin American reality (Latapí, 1994; Salinas, 1993; Puiggrós 1994; Torres, 1992). It is also moving beyond a concern limited to popular education and is increasingly merging with other more institutionalized forms of public education. In fact, Puiggrós (1994) has broadened the notion of popular education to include any practice that generates antihegemonic discourses and practices, inside or outside the formal educational system. Following this notion, Sirvent (1990) has elaborated a view of participatory research that links with participatory models of curricular reform in public schools in Argentina (See also Golzman and López, 1989; Solves, 1993). Thus we should expect to see some interesting adaptations of collaborative modes of qualitative research in the future.

VII. Ethical Issues of Qualitative Research:
Ownership of Communities and Transfer of
Research Processes to Individuals and Communities

As qualitative research begins to mature in Latin American education, the ethical issues of ownership, transfer, and proprietorship become increasingly significant. Just how much feedback is being provided to informants or individuals who work with ethnographers does not normally appear in print, nor is such information published in any of the reports. Thus the question of whether participants review manuscripts in which their thoughts appear before they are published is an arena that may need further exploration and examination. Also the question of who has the right to represent whom is increasingly being recognized as a sticky issue for ethnographers. Clearly the ethical dimensions of researcher-informant relations loom high in the development of Latin American qualitative research in education and it may be expected to have greater delineations in future research.[1]

Qualitative Research in Relation to Current
Social, Cultural, and Political Transformations

As Latin America undergoes social and economic changes, the role that qualitative research plays in relation to such transformation is one that should be closely watched. Whether the impact of qualitative research will serve to identify inequalities in education so as to offer alternatives has to be studied on a case by case basis, but that qualitative research has become a tool for constructively questioning the educational system is beyond doubt. Current and future research in the field will continue to document the broader social and economic transformations and their impact on education. We conclude with a few questions that have arisen from our work with the authors and their contexts.

Questions for Reflection

As qualitative research continues to grow and develop throughout Latin America, some of the questions we raise as a means to reflect on its impact and continue the dialogue are the following:

1. What has qualitative research taught in Latin America about the appreciation of the capacity of humans to reflect, learn, and change? What educational transformations are occurring?
2. How has qualitative research contributed to the commitment to effect non-violent change throughout Latin America?
3. How can we utilize the qualitative research of Latin America to diminish the alienation felt by marginalized and disenfranchised groups in ways in which the research methodologies do not represent yet another alienating rationality?
4. How are ethnographers actually responding to their own biases and reflective practice? Is the research being analyzed by those participating as well as those conducting the research?
5. Is qualitative research, like participatory research, coherent with its own purpose? Whose rationality becomes dominant? Is qualitative research an expression of what Armando Loera-Varela calls, "the rationality of intellectualized groups with emancipatory and enlightened interests, who in the name of 'giving voice' to the disempowered, in fact, impose their own rationality"? (Loera-Varela, 1986, p. 2).

Closer examination of these questions and those that continue to emerge as qualitative research becomes widespread will provide the grounding for its expansion and institutionalization throughout Latin America. Although qualitative research is currently most developed in Mexico, Brazil, Chile, Argentina, Colombia, and Costa Rica, it is beginning to seep across borders through inter-American conferences and publications. As Cuba continues to open up to academic exchanges, it is becoming apparent that there is a rich field research tradition there, drawing particularly on the work of Vygotsky and Bakhtin. This book is a humble beginning in establishing a dialogue between North and Latin America. It is up to you, the readers, to make sure the dialogue continues.

Notes

1.   Latin American collaborative research parallels a recent movement within the field of evaluation in the United States. Fetterman (1995; 1996) has described an approach that

he terms "empowerment evaluation," which fosters collaboration and self-determination among participants.

References

Achilli, E.L. (1996). *Practica docente y diversidad sociocultural: Los desafíos de la igualdad educativa frente a la desigualdad social.* Rosario, Argentina: Ediciones Homo Sapiens.

Avalos, B. (1985). Training for better teaching in the Third World: Lessons from research. *Teaching and Teacher Education,* 1(4), 289–299.

Avalos, B. (1989). Enseñando a los hijos de los pobres: Un estudio etnográfico en América Latina. Ottawa, Ontario, Canada: International Development Research Centre.

Berliner, D. and Biddle, B. (1995). *The manufactured crisis: Myths, fraud, and the attack on America's public schools.* Reading, MA: Addison-Wesley.

Bertely, M. (1992). Adaptaciones escolares en una comunidad mazahua. In M. Rueda and M.A. Campos (Eds.), *Investigación etnografía en educación* (pp. 211–234). México, D.F.: CISE-UNAM.

Calvo, B. (1994). Modernización de la educación básica en la frontera norte de México. In M. Rueda Beltrán, G. Delgado Ballesteros, and Z. Jacobo (Eds.), *La etnograía en educación: Panorama, prácticas y problemas* (pp. 329–370). México, D.F.: CISE-UNAM.

Calvo, B. (in press). The policy of modernization of Education: A challenge to democracy in Mexico. In H. Trueba and Y. Zou (Eds.), *Ethnic identity and power: Cultural contexts of political action in school and society.* London: Falmer Press.

Candela, A. (1994). La enseñanza de la ciencia y el análisis del discurso. In M. Rueda Beltrán, G. Delgado Ballesteros, and Z. Jacobo (Eds.), *La etnografía en educación: Panorama, prácticas y problemas* (pp. 149–169). México, D.F.: CISE-UNAM.

Cortina, R. (1984). La mujer y el magisterio en la ciudad de México. *Fem: Publicación Feminista,* 36(8), 37–40.

Delgado Ballesteros, G. (1993). Las influencias del género en las relaciones en el aula. In P. Bedolla, O. Busto, G. Delgado Ballesteros, B. García, and L. Parada (Eds.), *Estudios de género y feminismo* (pp. 32–51). México: UNAM Fontamara.

Delgado Ballesteros, G. (1994). La importancia de la etnografía en los estudios de género. In M. Rueda Beltrán, G. Delgado Ballesteros, and Z. Jacobo (Eds.), *La etnografía en educación: Panorama, prácticas y problemas* (pp. 83–94). México, D.F.: CISE-UNAM.

Delgado Ballesteros, G., Paradise, R., Hernandez, J., Robles, A., and Bertely, M. (1993). *La investigación educativa en los ochenta, perspectiva para los noventa: Comunicación y cultura.* Mexico, D.F.: Segundo Congreso Nacional de Investigación Educativa.

Escobar, M., Fernández, A.L., and Guevara-Niebla, G. (1994). *Paulo Freire on higher education: A dialogue at the National University of Mexico.* Albany, NY: SUNY Press.

Fals-Borda, O. (1981). The challenge of action research. *Development: Seeds of Change,* 1, 55–61.

Fetterman, D.M. (1995). Empowerment evaluation: An introduction to theory and practice. In D.M. Fetterman, S. Kaftarian, and A. Wandersman (Eds.), *Empowerment evaluation: Knowledge and tools for self-assessment and accountability.* Thousand Oaks, CA: Sage.

Fetterman, D.M. (1996). *Empowerment evaluation.* Thousand Oaks, CA: Sage.

Golzman, G. and López, D. (1989). *Atención: Maestros trabajando: Experiencias participativas en la escuela.* Buenos Aires: Coquena Grupo Editor.

Gómez Montero, S. (1994). Lectura y escritura en la frontero México-Estado Unidos. In L.E. Galván, M. Lamoneda, M.E. Vargas, and B. Calvo (Eds.), *Memorias del primer simposio de educación* (pp. 527–534). México, D.F.: CIESAS.

Jacobo, Z. (1994). Metodología cualitativa: Un ejemplo polisémico. In M. Rueda Beltrán, G. Delgado Ballesteros, and Z. Jacobo (Eds.), *La etnografía en educación: Panorama, prácticas y problemas* (pp. 83–94). México, D.F.: CISE-UNAM.

Latapí, P. (1994). *La investigación educativa en México.* México, D.F.: Fondo de Cultura Económica.

Loera-Varela, A. (1986). Can participatory research give us an emancipatory insight on popular knowledge? Unpublished manuscript for Special Reading Course with Dr. Noel McGinn, Harvard Graduate School of Education, Cambridge, MA.

McLaren, P. and Lankshear, C. (Eds.). (1994). *Politics of liberation: Paths from Freire.* New York: Routledge.

Medina, P. (1993). Ser maestra, permanecer en la escuela: Las estrategias de acción cotidiana. In M. Rueda, G. Delgado Ballesteros and Z. Jacobo (Eds.), *La etnografía en educación: Panorama, prácticas y problemas* (pp. 389–412). México, D.F.: CISE-UNAM.

Meier, D. (1995). *The power of their ideas: Lessons for America from a small school in Harlem.* Boston: Beacon Press.

Mercado, R. (1994). El diálogo de voces sociales en los saberes docentes. In M. Rueda, G. Delgado Ballesteros and Z. Jacobo (Eds.), *La etnografía en educación: Panorama, prácticas y problemas* (pp. 371–388). México, D.F.: CISE-UNAM.

Montero-Sieburth, M. (1992). Enfoque y reflexión en la investigación cualitativa. In *Memorias de la Primera Conferencia de Investigación Cualitativa en la Educación Latinoamerica* (pp. 21–46). San José, Costa Rica: Instituto de Investigación para el Mejoramiento de la Educación Costarricense.

Montero-Sieburth, M. (1993). Corrientes, enfoques e influencias de la investigación cualitativa para Latinoamerica. *La Educacion,* 116, 491–517.

Oyola, C., Barila, M., Figueroa, E., Leonardo, C., and Gennari, S. (1994). *El fracaso escolar: El éxito prohibido.* Buenos Aires: Aique.

Puiggrós, A. (1994). *Imaginación y crisis en la educación Latinoamericana.* Buenos Aires: Aique.

Salinas, B. (1993). Educación popular, comunitaria e investigación participativa. In B. Salinas and E. Safa (Eds.), *La investigación educativa en los ochenta, perspectivas para los noventa: Educacion de adultos, popular y comunitaria* (pp. 35–45). México, D.F.: Segundo Congreso Nacional de Investigación Educativa.

Sandoval, E. (1992). Condición feminina, valoración social y autovaloración del trabajo docente. *Nueva Antropología,* 42(12), 57–71.

Sirvent, M.T. (1990). *La investigación participativa aplicada a la renovación curricular.* Washington, D.C.: Programa Regional de Desarrollo Educativo/ Organización de Estados Americanos (PREDE/OEA).

Solves, H. (Ed.). (1993). *La escuela, una utopía cotidiana.* Buenos Aires: Paidós.

Torres, C.A. (1992). Participatory action research and popular education in Latin America. *Qualitative Studies in Education,* 5, 51–62.

Latin American Research Centers in Education

Many of the references cited in this book refer to working papers, conference papers, and publications in Spanish that are only available directly from research centers and institutes. Many of these centers have lists of publications, which they will send along with order forms and price lists. Some of these centers are associated with REDUC (Red de Documentación en Educación), which is the Latin American equivalent to ERIC (Educational Resources and Information Center). The center for REDUC in the United States is located at:

Office of International and Technical Cooperation (OITEC)
The University of New Mexico
1712 Sigma Chi Road N.E.
Albuquerque, New Mexico 87131

Selected Latin American educational research centers

Argentina
Centro de Investigaciones y Promoción Educativa y Social (CIPES)
Av. Pueyrredon #538, 5B
C.P. 1032, Buenos Aires, Argentina

Bolivia
Centro Boliviano de Investigación y Acción Educativa (CEBIAE)
Hnos. Manchego 2518
C.P. 1479, La Paz, Bolivia

Brazil
Fundación Carlos Chagas
Av. Prof. Fco. Morato 1566-Caixa Postal 11478
CEP 05.513, São Paulo, Brazil

Instituto Nacional de Estudos e Pesquisa Educacionais (INEP)
UnB, Asa Norte-Ala Sul
CEP 70.910, Brasilia D.F., Brazil

Colombia

Centro de Investigaciones (CIUP)
Universidad Pedagógica Nacional
Calle 127 #12 A 20
Apartado Aéreo 59530
Bogotá, Colombia

Centro Internacional de Educación y Desarrollo Humano
   (CINDE)
Carrera 33 #91–50, Barrio La Castellana
Bogotá, Colombia

Costa Rica

Instituto de Investigación para el Mejoramiento de la Educación
   Costarriicense (IIMEC)
Universidad de Costa Rica
San Pedro Montes de Oca
2066
Costa Rica
Tel. 253-5323, ext. 4105
Fax: 225-5822

Red de Documentación en Educación (REDUC)
Ministerio de Educación Pública
Antigua Embajada Americana
Avenida 3 y Calle 3
San José, Costa Rica

Chile

Centro de Investigación y Desarrollo de la Educación (CIDE)
Erasmo Escala No. 18525
C.P. 13608, Santiago, Chile

Programa Interdisciplinario de Investigaciones en Educación
   (PIIE)
Brown Sur 150 Nuñoa
Santiago, Chile

UNESCO-OREALC (Oficina Regional de Educación en América
   Latina y el Caríbe)
Enrique Delipiano 2058
C.P. 3187, Santiago, Chile

Guatemala

Centro de Investigación y Documentación de Guatemala (CINDEG)
Universidad Rafael Landivar
Campus de Vista Hermosa III, Zona 16,
C.P. 39C, Guatemala, Guatemala

Honduras

Centro de Información y Recursos Educativos (CIRE)
Universidad Pedagógica Nacional "Francisco Morazán"
Boulevard Miraflores,
C.P. 3394, Tegucigalpa, Honduras

México

Centro de Estudios Educativos (CIE)
Av. Revolución 1291, Col. San Angel
C.P. 01040, México, D.F., México

Centro de Investigaciones y Servicios Educativos
Universidad Nacional Autónoma de México (CISE-UNAM)
Circuito Exterior, Ciudad Universitaria
C.P. 04510, México, D.F., México

Centro de Investigaciones y Estudios Superiores en Antropología
    Social (CIESAS)
Juarez 87
C.P. 14000, Tlalpan, D.F., México

Centro Regional de Educación de Adultos y Alfabetización Funcional
    para América Latina (CREFAL)
Quinta Erendira s/n
C.P. 61600, Patzcuaro, Michoacán, México

Departamento de Investigaciones Educativas (DIE)
Centro de Investigación y de Estudios Avanzados del Instituto
    Politécnico Nacional (CINVESTAV-IPN)
San Borja #932
Apartado Postal 19–197
C.P. 03100, México, D.F., México

Perú

Centro de Estudios y Promoción del Desarrollo (DESCO)
León de la Fuente #110
Lima 17, Perú

Uruguay

Centro de Investigación y Experimentación Pedagógica (CIEP)
18 de Julio 465 Piso 3-Casilla de Correo 10688
C.P. 11.100, Montevideo, Uruguay

Venezuela

Centro de Reflexión y Planificación Educativa (CERPE)
Avenida Santa Teresa de Jesús
Edificio CERPE La Castellana
C.P. 62654, Caracas 1060-A, Venezuela

Contributors

Gary L. Anderson is an associate professor in the College of Education, University of New Mexico. He has given workshops and consulted throughout Latin America on educational administration and qualitative research. He currently teaches in a master's degree program at the University of New Mexico which is taught in Spanish. He has written a number of books, including *Studying Your Own School: An Educator's Guide to Qualitative Practitioner Research* (Corwin Press, 1994, with K. Herr and A.S. Nihlen); *The Micropolitics of Educational Leadership: From Control to Empowerment* (Teachers College Press, 1995, with J. Blase); and *Democratic Principals in Action: Eight Pioneers* (Corwin Press, 1995, with J. Blase, J. Blase, and S. Dungan).

Anita Barabtarlo y Zedansky is a professor and researcher at the Centro de Investigaciones y Servicios Educativos (CISE) of the National Autonomous University of Mexico (UNAM). Her areas of interest include action research, teacher development, and higher education. She is the author of *Investigación Acción: Una Didáctica para la Formación de Profesores* (Castellanos Editores, 1995).

Graciela Batallán is a professor at the University of Buenos Aires and a researcher in the Programa Interdisciplinario de Investigaciones Educativas (PIIE) in Santiago, Chile. Recent publications include "Lógicas Contradictorias en la Construcción del Trabajo Docente en Argentina: Etnografía del Cuaderno de Actuación Profesional" in *IV Congreso Nacional de Antropología* (1994) and "Autor y Actores en Antropología: Tradición y Etica en el Trabajo de Campo" in *Revista Academia*, No. 1, (1995).

María Bertely is a professor and researcher at the Centro de Investigaciones y Estudios Superiores en Antropología Social (CIESAS) and the Instituto Superior de Ciencias de la Educación del Estado de México. She has a master's degree from the Departamento de Investigaciones Educativas (DIE) of the National Polytechnic University, and is currently completing a doctorate in education at the Autonomous University of Aguascalientes. Her areas of interest include ethnographic research methods and the relationships among culture, ethnicity, and schooling. Recent publications include, "Adaptaciones docentes en una comunidad mazahua" in *Nueva Antropología*, No. 42, (1992) and "Adaptaciones escolares en una comunidad mazahua" in the book *Investigación Etnográfica en Educación*, edited by Mario Rueda and Miguel Angel Campos and published by UNAM Press (1992).

Margarita Brenes is an independent consultant and has a private practice in psychotherapy in Massachusetts. She was a researcher at the Instituto de Investigación para el Mejoramiento de la Educación Costarricense (IIMEC) (the Research Institute for the Betterment of Costa Rican Education) at the University of Costa Rica from 1982 to 1992. There she collaborated with other researchers on ethnographic studies of marginal-urban (low-income) schools. This research led to the production of a series of training modules for teachers, which she co-authored with Nidia García, Marta Rojas, Natalia Campos, and Emilia Campos, entitled *Conocimiento, Participación y Cambio*. While in Costa Rica, Ms. Brenes was also active in establishing a master's program in women's studies at the University of Costa Rica.

Emilia Campos is an elementary school teacher who has a bachelor's degree in education from the University of Costa Rica. She taught at a private school for eleven years and has been teaching for the past nine years at a marginal-urban school. After being observed in the first study, she joined the IIMEC team as one of the co-researchers for the second study. She has participated in all phases of the research from its inception to the development and production of the teacher training modules.

Natalia Campos has been a researcher at the Instituto de Investigación para el Mejoramiento de la Educación Costarricense (IIMEC) since 1980, and is an associate professor in the Teacher Training Program at the University of Costa Rica. Her expertise is in curriculum, assessment, and evaluation at the national and local levels. She coordinated PRONAFOCO, el Programa Nacional de Formación y Capacitación en Curriculum (the National Program for Curriculum Development and Training) from 1983 to 1985. For the past decade, she has conducted ethnographic research in urban-marginal schools with a team of researchers at the IIMEC. She currently coordinates the restructuring of curriculum at the College of Education at the University of Costa Rica. From 1988 to 1993, she was the director of the IIMEC. She has published widely on curriculum, ethnographic research, assessment in science, language arts, English, French, mathematics, social studies, physical education, and teaching and learning in *Revista Educación, Revista de Filología, Semanario Universidad,* and *Review of Global Education.*

Martha Corenstein is a professor in the Colegio de Pedagogía, Facultad de Filosofía y Letras, National Autonomous University of Mexico (UNAM), and Deputy Director of Educational Research at the Consejo Nacional de Fomento Educativo (CONAFE), Secretaría de Educación Pública (SEP). Her interests include qualitative research methods and education in rural communities. Recent publications include "La investigación etnográfica en educación" in *Algunos Enfoques Metodológicos de la Investigación Educativa,* edited by María Eugenia Alvarado and Rebeca Mortera (1993), and "Procesos de Enseñanza y Prácticas Escolares" (with various authors) in *La Investigación Educativa en Los Ochenta: Perspectiva para los Noventa,* Segundo congreso Nacional de Investigación Educativa (1993).

Nidia García is a researcher at the Instituto de Investigación para el Mejoramiento de la Educación Costarricense, (IIMEC) at the University of Costa Rica and is a professor in the Teacher Training Program at the University of Costa Rica where she has taught for the past seventeen years. She is a former elementary school teacher. She was one of the contributors to the National Assessment Studies, which were conducted by the IIMEC in 1981–1983 in the area of language arts. From 1989 to 1993, she was a member of the National Council of the Secretariat of Education, which develops national educational policy for Costa Rica. She has published books and articles in children's literature, language arts, education, and ethnographic research. She co-authored with Marta Rojas the language arts textbooks for first and second grades in a series entitled "Towards the 21st Century." She also coauthored the teacher training modules *Conocimiento, Participación y Cambio* with Natalia Campos, Margarita Brenes, Marta Rojas and Emilia Campos and a book entitled *Conocimiento, Participación, y Cambio: Capacitación de Docentes a Partir de la Investigación en el Aula* (Knowledge, participation and change: Teacher training from research in the classroom) currently in press with the University of Costa Rica Press. She is currently the director and editor of the journal *Educación* published by the University of Costa Rica.

Martha Montero-Sieburth is an associate professor in the Graduate College of Education at the University of Massachusetts, Boston. She was formerly the director of educational research at the Mauricio Gastón Institute for Latino Community Development and Public Policy at the University of Massachusetts, Boston. Of Mexican and Costa Rican descent, she became involved in the ethnography of schooling during the 1960s when she studied with Jules Henry at Washington University. During the 1980s she introduced qualitative research in Costa Rica through a series of courses offered through the University of Costa Rica and the National University in Heredia. Her publications have appeared in *Educación, Comparative Education Review,* and *Anthropology and Education Quarterly.* She has edited several books, including *Bilingual Education Teacher Handbook: Strategies for the Design of Multicultural Curriculum; Bilingual Education Teacher Handbook: Language Issues in Multicultural Setting* and is co-editing *Latino Adolescents: Building Upon Our Diversity* with Francisco Villarruel. Her current research attempts to analyze the integration of Latino immigrants and parents within the Boston public schools.

Elsie Rockwell helped initiate educational ethnography in Mexico as professor at the Department of Educational Research, Center for Research and Advanced Studies, National Polytechnic University. Trained in history and social anthropology, she has combined both disciplines in her study of rural schooling and literacy, has contributed to ongoing theoretical debates in Latin America, and has coordinated a rural curriculum project in Mexico. Her recent publications include the edited collection *La Escuela cotidiana* and "Schools of the Revolution" in *Everyday Forms of State Formation: Revolution and the Negotiation of Rule in Modern Mexico,* edited by G. Joseph and D. Nugent (1994).

Marta Rojas has been a researcher at the IIMEC since 1983 and is professor in the School of Linguistics and Literature at the University of Costa Rica. Her research ranges from studies of linguistics to the application of sociolinguistics in education. She has published four textbooks in a language arts series for the elementary grade levels entitled *Waking Up to Words.* In 1992, she conducted research on the context and perspective in the development of reading textbooks and instructional materials in basic education in Costa Rica under a grant from UNESCO, the University of Costa Rica, and Germany. She is one of the co-authors along with Nidia García, Natalia Campos, Margarita Brenes, Marta Rojas, and Emilia Campos of the teacher training modules *Conocimiento Participación y Cambio.* Among her numerous publications is a recent book on poetry entitled *The Smile of Penelope and Her Custom of Saying Good-Bye.*

Beatriz Schmukler is a researcher with the Instituto de Investigaciones Dr. José María Luis Mora in Mexico City. She received a Ph.D. in sociology from Yale University in 1985. Her publications include *Historias de Encuentros y Desencuentros* (GEST, 1988, with Marta Savigliano); "Women and the Microsocial Democratization of Everyday Life" in *Women and Education in Latin America,* edited by Nelly Stromquist (1992); and "The Invisibility of Mothers in the Democratic Transition of Argentina" in *Women, Children and Human Rights in Latin America,* edited by Margorie Agosín (1992).

Elvira Souza Lima is a researcher at Northwestern University. She has traveled widely in Europe and Latin America as an educational consultant. She recently co-edited an issue of *Anthropology and Education Quarterly* on Vygotsky's cultural-historical theory of development. Another recent article is "From Lay Teachers to University Students: The Path for Empowerment through Culturally Based Pedagogical Action" (with Marineusa Gazzetta) in *Anthropology and Education Quarterly.*

Nelly P. Stromquist is professor of international development education in the School of Education at the University of Southern California. She specializes in gender issues, particularly education for empowerment, adult literacy, and state policies and practices in girls' and women's education. She has edited *Women and Education in Latin America* (Lynne Reiner, 1992) and *Education in Urban Areas: Cross-National Dimensions* (Praeger, 1994). She recently authored *Gender and Basic Education in International Development Cooperation* (1994).

Margarita Theesz Poschner is a professor and researcher at the Centro de Investigaciones y Servicios Educativos (CISE) of the National Autonomous University of Mexico (UNAM). Her areas of interest include action research, teacher development, and distance education. Recent publications include "La Formación en Investigación Educativa en la Educación a Distancia" in *Revista Cubana de Educación Superior,* Vol. 14, 1994, and "La Modernización Educativa y la Formación del Docente en Investigación Educativa" in *Revista de la Asociación Méxicana de Investigadores de la Educación,* No. 1, 1994.

Juan Fidel Zorrilla is a researcher at the Centro de Estudios Sobre la Universidad (CESU) in Mexico City. His areas of interest include qualitative sociology, social theory, and secondary and higher education. He has published extensively from his research on the innovative secondary school *Colegio de Ciencias y Humanidades.*

Index

as change agents, 45
as cultural actors, 157
as organic intellectuals, 165–166
as powerful subordinates, 45
teacher subjectivities, 17
Tedesco, Juan, x, 37, 162
tranformative learning, 95

Vygotsky, Lev, 144

Willis, Paul, 6
women
  as active participants, 92

emancipatory literacy, 81, 95
empowerment of, 114
literacy and age, 95
mothering, democratic potential of, 101
workshops
  action research workshops (Mexico), 170–175
  Workshops for Democratic Education (Chile), xiii–xiv
  Workshops for Educators (Argentina), 40, 41, 43

Zapatista movement, Chiapas, Mexico, 22